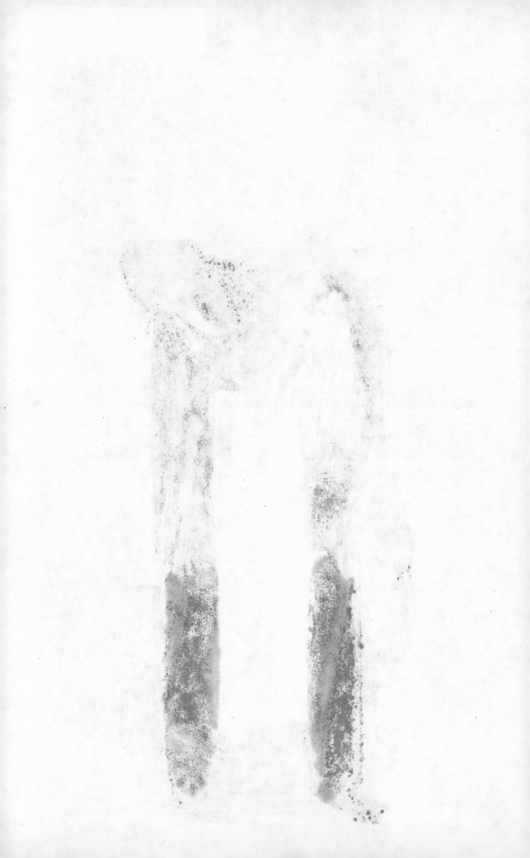

POLICE PASSAGES

POLICE PASSAGES

John G. Stratton Ph.D.

POLICE PASSAGES
Glennon Publishing Company
First Edition
July 1984

All rights reserved.

Artwork by Mahlon Coleman

Copyright ©1984 by Dr. John G. Stratton
Library of Congress Catalog Card Number: 84-80826
ISBN 0-918523-00-1

Glennon Publishing Company
636 23rd
Manhattan Beach, California 90266
Printed in the U.S.A.

TO BARBARA

Who adds Rainbows, Sunshine and a little Rain
to my life passages and our joint adventure.

During the past years in California
We've lost a lot of good cops.
They didn't make the laws,
The just tried to enforce them.
They didn't make the city,
They just tried to make it work.
Now, nobody's asking you to love cops.
But they've got a tough job,
Don't make it tougher.
It could be a matter of life and death,
Theirs & maybe yours.
What if you called a cop and nobody answered?

—Peace Officer's Wives' Clubs Affiliated of California

CONTENTS

ACKNOWLEDGMENTS

I can't adequately thank Barbara, my wife, for her contributions to this manuscript. She has provided her expertise, personal support, encouragement and time. Our children Jim, Matt and Glennon, have sacrificed time that they might have spent with their father, and now that this book is done we can be together more. My family has been wonderful.

I am also indebted to my editor, Tom Huth, whose assistance has been invaluable.

The men and women of the Los Angeles County Sheriff's Department have always been helpful, but their trust and confidence have been most rewarding. I am appreciative to former Sheriff Peter J. Pitchess who hired me providing an opportunity to work in a great organization. Without Sheriff Sherman Block, who took an active interest in my selection and in establishing my responsibilities, I never would have had the opportunity to have so many varied and rich experiences. He continually demonstrated what a great law-enforcement officer is by his professional and ethical standards and his depth of caring, compassion, and concern. Being able to work closely with Undersheriff Theodore von Minden, Assistant Sheriffs Robert Edmonds and Jerry Harper, and all of the administrative personnel has provided me with strong admiration for them and their mission.

From the beginning of this lengthy endeavor, many have been instrumental: Earl Carnes, Francis Caselaine, Melvin Cohen, Marge Francis, Evelyn Garcia, Sheldon Kardner, Maggie Myers, David Parker, Dennis Slocum, David Smith and Jack Whitehouse made special contributions in their own unique ways.

However, without the openness, honesty and courage of officers from many departments who shared their personal tragedies, struggles and successes, this book could not have been written. Individual stories have been altered

to protect the privacy of those involved and their departments. If some examples appear recognizable, it is because
as human beings, our problems and successes are not all
that dissimilar.

FOREWORD

BY JOHN A. O'LEARY, J.D., EXECUTIVE DIRECTOR
SOUTH CAROLINA CRIMINAL JUSTICE ACADEMY

Too frequently, individuals who have no immediate need for those persons in law enforcement, tend to think of them abstractly. There is a hazy notion that police enforce laws, protect property, catch criminals and help children at school crossings.

Others, who for one reason or another, come into antagonistic confrontation with police, will allude to them as "cops", "pigs", "fuzz", and too many other critical, or angry, epithets to mention.

John Stratton, whom I know as a decent and caring human being, draws from his many years of experience as a highly-dedicated psychologist working in the law enforcement area to give us a work that is incisively analytical, yet couched in humanistic approaches. The reader, professional or layman, is given fresh insight into the social and often-contradictory role of law enforcement officers in American society.

The scope of issues addressed—training, stress, marriage, promotion, minorities, traumatic incidents, retirement and widows, encompasses all phases of police life. This publication also reflects many sensitive social ills that not only affect the role of the police officer, but the relationship that exists between the law enforcement function and the community which it serves. John's use of personal case histories and social scenarios provides us with a well-rounded grasp of the incredible pressures a police officer must face in day-to-day service to his family, his department and his community.

I recommend that this book be required reading for all individuals responsible for the social well-being of our law enforcement officers and the people they serve.

FOREWORD

BY SHERMAN BLOCK
SHERIFF, LOS ANGELES COUNTY

From a historical perspective, Dr. John Stratton shows the evolution of police: Their duties, responsibilities and attitudes in a continually changing society. The police, like all society's members change within the wider social context, influenced by social events and their life experiences.

The range of police life events from application through retirement, cover many of the areas Dr. Stratton deals with on a daily basis. He provides an approach to police, learned working with them in an intimate way rather than from knowledge gained through university courses and the literature. Though no one will agree with everything he writes, his insights provide valuable food for thought to all seeking more information about the police.

John's work as Director of Psychological Services for the Los Angeles County Sheriff's Department has led to the development of many meaningful and effective programs for deputy sheriffs and their families which have been implemented by other law enforcement agencies throughout the world.

Whether it be a spouses program, a peace officers' fellowship for alcoholism, counseling groups for officers involved in shootings, seriously injured, paralyzed, or a support group for widows, these ongoing programs have been extremely beneficial. In the text, program models and approaches are presented for easy reference and adaptation where appropriate.

John's dedication and caring are obvious to those who know him. Whether you're interested in thought provoking ideas about current issues in law enforcement, knowing more about the police or establishing programs, Dr. Stratton, a pioneer in police psychology, presents a unique and interesting perspective.

Preface

After working for ten years with police administrators, detectives, line officers, their families and friends, I decided to write about their experiences and their struggles from the time they entered the profession until they left. In the process, I couldn't help but look back and take stock of my own evolution as a practicing psychologist.

Earlier in my career, I had worked with people on the other side of the fence—those who had unfavorable encounters with the police. This exposed me to the intense negative attitudes that many Americans held toward law enforcement's representatives. Consequently, when I became the first psychologist to be hired by the Los Angeles County Sheriff's Department, I held certain prejudices and was eager to right all of the wrongs within the police community. However, my work during the last decade has humbled me. It has taught me the limits of my profession and shown me that policemen need to be—not saved or reformed—but simply understood.

Most people expect policemen to be better than the rest of us. Because of the extremely sensitive nature of their jobs, they are constantly open to criticism and their mistakes are judged more harshly than those of the average citizen. Yet, as I have learned, they are only human. This is their burden and their blessing: They are no better, and certainly no worse, than you and me.

I can never repay what I have gained from those officers who have shared their most intimate concerns with me. Hopefully, their openness will contribute to a further understanding of those who choose this very important and challenging profession. In this book I might have concentrated on police officer's problems and underemphasized their joys and satisfactions. But I trust that they will forgive me, and I can only add that, as a group, police officers are dedicated, well-intentioned and hard-working as any people on the face of this earth.

The names and stories depicted in this book have been changed. They represent situations of the past which, I hope, will enlighten others in the future.

1

THE POLICE IN AN EVERCHANGING SOCIETY

The evolution of law enforcement takes place within the evolution of the society which it serves. The two cannot be separated.

We have all been raised differently, with unique parents having their own set of values and beliefs. However, we are all affected by the continually changing events of our society and world. Though we experience the same major events whether they be war, social movements, economic fluctuations or whatever—we are affected differently.

The major events that occur in our childhood through our early twenties greatly influence how we will view the world.

The people whose value development began during the 1930's and 1940's experienced some very difficult times. Their experiences included the Great Depression, World War II with the emphasis on teamwork—sticking together. The power of America and what it stands for was stressed. Being Number 1 and the best were highly valued. There was a strong belief in sacrificing one's self and giving to others for the welfare of the total society. The feeling was, "We are in this together and we'll conquer it together."

The movie newsreels that stressed the victories of our boys abroad, President Roosevelt's informative and encouraging fireside chats, and gas and food rationing, were indicative of this time. Personal inconveniences were generally accepted because it was for the good of the country. The country's needs were more important than personal needs.

One result of war and depression was a closely knit unit. The family included the immediate members and relatives who generally lived nearby. While the men went to war, the women stayed home and tried to preserve some type of normality within the family. The women continued to stress the importance of the military, manhood and bravery to their children along with the hopes of seeing their father return home safely. Tradition, authority and respect were honored in the family. There were rules to be followed, the parents were in charge and the children knew and accepted this. The family often lived in one house for their entire lives. Their home was security. Women had very structured roles to carry out.

In the 1920's through the 1950's women who participated in premarital sex were seen as somehow being evil. And at one time, it was the goal of every woman to be a mother. The only careers open to women were nursing and teaching. The main responsibility for women were home and family.

After World War II, many police officers came from the military. The armed forces were highly respected and admired, as they had saved our country. Those who had served in the military were honored and given privileges. They were a brotherhood in the service of their country. Once they had moved into law enforcement, they felt once again they were a brotherhood but this time they were serving a city. They felt they had left one highly-respected service to become part of another. They changed uniforms and continued in the service of protecting and upholding security.

People who grew up during this time would likely value America, the family, winning, being Number 1, military strength, manliness and might. Many people who are the top administrators of today's law enforcement grew up during this period. They possess many of these values, although their unique personal experiences may alter them. Therefore, the role of the cop in the 80's is influenced with values from another era.

When discussing his difficulties with today's breed, Sergeant Mike S., a twenty year veteran, said to his peers. "A lot of these officers that we have now have never, never dealt with authority themselves. They are Dr. Spock's children and once they got to the schools they entered a free environment where no punishment was allowed which really meant that the goddamn kids could do anything they pleased. Many don't have a military background and they came directly from college campuses where they raised cain about the Vietnam War and were hostile to any authority.

Well, all of a sudden they're cops, have a badge, gun and stick and are authority figures. They don't know what they're doing. They either overreact or underreact. And as a supervisor trying to guide these cops, it's next to impossible. When you try to give them direction, particularly if they don't want to follow it, they balk like a mule."

People who were in their formative years during the 1960's and early 70's experienced a much different world. Major events included the civil rights movement, the Vietnam conflict, draft dodgers, protests, demonstrations, drugs, the killing of four Kent State students by the

National Guard, Watergate and the resignation of President Nixon. This was a period of questioning and skepticism; there was questioning of one's self, one's values, the military, war, America, the president and virtually anyone who had authority. Everyone was encouraged to "be yourself" or "do your own thing" and recognize people on individual merit rather than race, sex, age or social status.

People growing up in this period likely valued such concepts as individuality and freedom. They may have some conflicting values about the family, and might be opposed to the military and war. They have questions about the usefulness of marriage and family. They lived in the same house for an average of 5 years or less. Divorce is more common, with estimates in the 80's of 1 out of every 6 children growing up in a one-parent home and 1 out of 5 having a step-parent relationship.

The majority of people who have recently entered law enforcement grew up during this period. Their values may be different from those of their supervisors and co-workers who grew up during the 30's and 40's.

People who grew up in the 1960's will view civil and individual rights differently than those who were raised earlier in the century. Regardless of whether they are black or white, their values and views about the races may be radically different. Both will have been influenced by the social, political and economic events occurring during their formative years and will have their own views about the role of a police officer. The roles of women drastically changed. Premarital sex by women became more accepted by the general culture. Women began to have more options in their lives. Not only could they be mothers, but also senators, executives, police officers and astronauts. The attitudes toward women continued to change as a new era of human rights and equality was entered.

In the 1960's and 70's, the police, like all authority,

became suspect. To question authority, to be skeptical, to presume that authority was wrong—these were common themes in a society concerned with individual rights and freedom. The police, society and our expectations of the police officer were drastically different for those entering the police department in the 1940's and 50's compared to those entering police departments in the late 60's and 70's.

It is essential for police managers and police officers to understand these differences in personal values, not only between themselves, but also within the context of society as a whole. Most people in law enforcement are well-intentioned, and yet differences arise. This is evidenced by the recent phenomena of a stronger police association, job walkouts, strikes, "Blue Flu," etc. Unfortunately, such differences seem to be accelerating making the gap between the line officer and the administration even greater, although their concerns about law enforcement are often similar.

In the middle 1970's, Officer Penn D., a man in his late twenties, began to let his hair grow longer than regulations allowed. In fact, the department's standards had been relaxed but Penn went farther than that. Finally, Lt. Doug T. ordered the officer to get his hair cut, and Penn did, but still his locks weren't short enough to suit the lieutenant. Penn was ordered to get another haircut, and he responded by showing the lieutenant a copy of the appropriate regulations. So Doug T. said, "Fine, you don't have to cut your hair, but I'm reassigning you." He put Penn on traffic patrol in a slow part of town, reminding him that he could return to criminal work as soon as his appearance shaped up. This time, Penn's response was to shave his head bald. Naturally, it angered Doug, and his response was to put Penn on an unpopular early-morning shift. But Penn's fight was taken up by some of his fellow officers, and about two dozen of them—including three sergeants— eventually shaved their heads, too. In the end, the lieutenant had to back down and let his younger charges wear their hair shaggy.

Lt. Harrison S. called Officer John G. into his office and lectured him about his slow response time to calls. But John turned the tables on his superior and delivered a little lecture of his own. He told the older man: "You've heard of the old English adage, 'I Got mine, Jack.' Well, that's just what I think of this job. I might be part of this department and I might be part of this town, but I'm only responsible to me and mine. I don't mean that I won't do my job, and I don't mean I don't like my job, but it's just the way I see it . . . I'm not responsible for what those people on the streets do to each other. My job is to pick up the pieces and gather evidence. I'm not about to go into a bar and duke it out with drunks. I'll wait until the fight is over and haul them to the tank. I'm doing this job for the wages, and the wages aren't good enough for me to risk my neck for people I don't even know—people who don't give a damn about me anyway." The lieutenant didn't make any attempt to discipline the young officer for those remarks, but that encounter was the beginning of a feud between the two. John G. stood for everything that the lieutenant detested in the new generation of police officers. Six months after the argument, when John refused to keep his hair cut to regulation length and then tried to take the issue to court, the department was able to dismiss him from the force. Lt. Harrison S. was overheard remarking on the day of John's firing: "Well, he got his all right . . . and I still got mine, Jack."

Let's not forget the in-between generation, those who experienced their formative years during the late 40's and 50's. These were the people who got a little of everything. They were the children of war veterans who had promised, "My children are never going to have it as bad as I did." They had more cars, more money, more everything than anyone had before.

The in-between generation knew something about war and sacrifice from the stories of their parents, and also enjoyed some of the wealth, education and comforts of the 60's. They are the ones who, if they are sensitive, understand the values of both the earlier and later generations. Many of these people are in their mid-careers and are likely the ones who can bridge the gap between the older and younger officer.

Police live in a world of violence. They see, hear or read about it every day. And at times, they are asked to take violent, even deadly action for the good of society. The gun, a weapon of violence, is carried by all police in our society. And sometimes when we read the headlines, whether they be proclaiming a terrorist act or a gruesome murder, we become even more aware of the need for police to have weapons.

Violence has been a constant theme since the beginning of recorded history. Early in the Bible, it is reported that Cain killed his brother Abel, and continuing throughout are repeated references to war, slavery and man attempting to exert dominance over his fellow man.

America began with violence and it has continued in one form or another into the present day. The native Indian tribes were often war-like. A great number of American settlers were deported from England for criminal activity and independence was assured by violent revolution. The early economic policies of the country were based on a system of indentured servants and slavery. We have a history of devastating warfare between the states. Settlement of the Far West in particular was accomplished through the use of violence and war.

In the international arena, countries attempt to demonstrate their immense power by the number of missiles, planes and tanks they produce along with the soldier under arms.

Violence or aggressive behavior brings out ambivalent feelings. It is viewed as exciting but also frightening. We glorify aggression by praising and rewarding initiative, courage, winning and coming out on top. We discourage aggression by criticizing or degrading brashness and arrogance.

These mixed feelings also come up when we think about the police—our most dominant authority over individuals. When there is violence in the community we want the police there. When a serious crime is committed, we want the suspect caught and most people want him in jail. When police in pursuit of a suspect are shot at, we allow them to shoot back.

But if they make a mistake whether it be because of fear, poor perception or accident, we are outraged.

If violence is used to stop a hostage-taker or capture a murderer, we approve. If a mistake is made causing the death of an innocent citizen, we disapprove, criticize and blame.

Sgt. Frank M. was one of the most popular officers in the department and had earned respect from his colleagues for two incidents in which he had shot armed suspects. Then one day he shot and killed a 15-year-old burglar who had been armed with, not a shotgun, as Frank had thought, but merely a crowbar. Frank was suspended for three days pending the outcome of a review board investigation, and during that time he was found shot to death in his car a few blocks from his home. A coroner's inquest ruled that the sergeant had killed himself, but many fellow officer refused to believe it. One friend of Frank's who did accept the ruling remarked to another cop as they were leaving the cemetery on the day of the funeral: "Everybody made a hero out of Frank because of the other shootings—and now they were getting ready to hang him for his last one. I guess Frank just couldn't accept the demotion."

The 1980's began with an increase in violent crimes. Cities had an increase in stranger-to-stranger murders of

82%. More people were purchasing and carrying weapons (52% of American households have guns) which adds to the increase of violence and apprehension on the part of the police.

Television has had a large impact on our view of violence. Research indicates that on-the-scene criminal reporting, dramatic presentations and others which portray violence, produces more aggression in children.

Throughout the school years, children spend 50% more time watching television than they do in school. A child between the ages of 5 and 15 will see the destruction of over 13,400 fictional people. This is exclusive of murders and other violent behavior shown daily on news programs.

Through highly dramatized presentations, the public is presented with violent images of police work. It is made to appear that violence, shots fired and people getting killed are everyday events for almost every officer on patrol, despite the fact that about 50% of officers never fire their weapons on duty. The media presentations of police activity can even shape the police officer's self-image. He comes to feel that he should be as invincible or tough as any fictionalized T.V. or movie cop.

Even though these characters and their behavior may be as foreign to police work as Bugs Bunny is to a rabbit, the distorted image between fantasy and reality of police work can cause a misperception either by the citizen reacting to the television image or the officer believing he really is the fantasy. Having guns and violence removed from television may help. Having them removed from the streets would be better. But, like many effective methods to deal with violent crime, it is difficult, if not impossible to accomplish.

There is no one reason for violence. A lack of concern for human life, harder economic conditions and frustrations from interacting socio-economic variables contribute. When these pressures build, the individual feels less in control, less powerful, causing him to become agressive.

We've all read in the newspapers about acts of violence committed by citizens who had been frustrated beyond the breaking point by a system that didn't work for them. I think of the Cincinnati mortgage-company executive who was strung up in a noose by a man who was denied a loan; the New Yorker who shot several people to death at the moving company where he'd been fired; the Los Angeleno, Tyrone Mitchell, who opened fire on an elementary-school playground.

The changing American family may also contribute to our increase in violence. What we think of as the average American family, (father working, mother home raising children, etc,) actually exists in fewer than 15% of today's homes. With both parents working with step-parents and one-parent households, close personal ties are lost between parents and children. This, combined with television's influence on reducing further human contact and relating with fictional characters, rather than family, can cause people to be less sensitive to others. They may even imitate those seen on television, expecting their reaction to be no different than when watching their television heroes. Crime statistics show that since 1900 over 800,000 people have been killed by guns in America; 20,000 are killed yearly, and approximately 200,000 citizens are injured or maimed. Casualties from civilian gunfire exceed the military casualties of all our wars. However, with our limited expertise, there is no way to accurately predict violence.

Everyone agrees that something must be done. But the solutions—from vigilante force to intense educational efforts—have been so diverse they have prohibited people from making a concerted effort. Violence is a problem no society has solved and the police are in the middle.

For cops who see a great deal of violence, the era in which they grew up may not be as important as their day-to-day experiences. These give them a view of society and the world which may at times become distorted and affect their personal lives. The impact of man's destruction to man can effect every aspect of an officer's life.

> Officer Sheldon K. worked homicide. When asked, "How are you doing?," he responded, "I'm waiting for another dead body."
> Officer Mel C. is so concerned about violence on the streets that he won't allow his wife to leave the house without calling him. She also calls him upon reaching her destination.

Police officers' values and attitudes about people, minorities, women, violence, and the role of police affect how they do their job.

One way to examine our values is to pay attention to how we behave rather than what we say. The two are often quite different. I'm talking about the man who espouses the equality of women and yet refuses to let his wife work; the officer who talks about the importance of family and yet is never home; the cop who in certain circles talks about the equality of man but who on the street refers to racial minorities in derogatory terms.

Our personal experiences will continue to change as will our attitudes, values and the way we treat others. Our values are always being tested—and through this we change.

> Gerry B. was a training officer at the police academy. After nine years on the force he had an outstanding service record and a seemingly solid marriage—qualities that were essential for training officers. However, other cops who knew Gerry well were amused to hear him lecturing recruits about the importance of not having prejudices, because in private he always called black people "niggers," women "bitches" and poor people "trash." Then one day he got tripped up: He was riding back from lunch with another officer, and the car radio's microphone was inadvertently stuck in the "transmit" position, and so the rest of the department was treated to a

20-minute diatribe against all blacks in general and against one city councilman in particular. For that, Gerry earned a 30-day suspension and a return to patrol duty. Then, about a year later, his wife caught him in yet another lie. She did his packing for him when he went on his annual bird-hunting trip with his buddies, and when he returned Gerry bragged that he had shot down eight birds but complained that his wife hadn't packed any socks. The wife promptly unzipped Gerry's shotgun case, and out tumbled the four pairs of socks that she had packed there. This is how she confirmed her suspicions that the birds Gerry had been hunting were double breasted mattress thrashers, and she thereupon divorced him.

Our concept of each other as human beings along with our values and attitudes affects how we treat one another. Often in our society we do not consider the whole person. We look at each other in one dimensional or isolated ways. Today many of our institutions are established to address only certain facets of a person. A physical injury is treated at a doctor's office or hospital. For man's intellect, there are schools and institutions of higher learning. Social aspects may be handled by various social groups and membership in particular organizations. The emotional components may be handled by self-help groups, psychological counseling and mental-health clinics. For one's spirituality there are temples, churches and synagogues.

These institutions, as established, may not involve the entire person, and so people might come to feel compartmentalized.

Holistic medicine is a recent phenomenon. Rather than conceptualize people as parts, the holistic approach attempts to deal with all aspects of a person. Holistic centers have been developed on the belief that all parts of a person are interrelated. To treat the physical man while not dealing with how he feels spiritually, emotionally, socially and intellectually is seen as inappropriate. It is considered impossible to treat a man who is depressed without questioning his overall physical, social, intellectual and spiritual health. The holistic center attempts to provide all services in one location.

In holistic thinking, each of a person's facets is related to the others so that if one is affected, the others will be. Here is an example:

> Highway Patrol Officer Bob W., was injured in an on-duty automobile accident. He experienced severe injury to his lower back and kidneys. Bob's physical injury affected his body and his whole person. Emotionally he had reactions of anger, depression and frustration. Socially, his life was limited to his family. The time spent with them was not totally fulfilling because he felt less himself. And he was isolated from work and the camaraderie of his officers. Intellectually, his stimulation was reduced except for TV and an occasional book. His usual political discussions came to a halt. Spiritually, he lost his positive attitude and fell into a "why me?" response. His injury affected all aspects of his being. If his injury is all that is treated, other aspects which would lead to a fast and healthy recovery are neglected.

This interdependence of our being is a meaningful way to understand people. The effect of one facet on another works both positively and negatively. If one facet is effected poorly, the others may be also. Conversely, if one is operating well it can have a positive effect on the others.

When an officer is physically injured on duty he will be affected in many ways. There is a tendency to feel depressed. Social contacts are limited. The drive for learning is depressed. And he may even question things in the spiritual realm.

A positive influence in the social arena, such as getting married, can have a positive effect on all other areas. An officer will feel happier, "on top of the world." He may have more physical energy and may be able to accomplish more in a shorter period of time. He may think clearly and feel more at peace with himself and his life.

As a society, we are probably least knowledgeable in understanding emotional responses. From everyday encounters, the awareness that people are different is inevitable. They have different values and interests and make different choices. This can be seen in the cars they drive, clothes they wear, movies they attend, television shows they watch, and so on.

We accept all these differences in people, and yet we refuse to accept the fact that people may respond differently to specific emotional events. We would be surprised to walk into a room and see everyone wearing the same kind of suit and tie, or dress. But we assume that everyone will respond emotionally like us to events such as death, divorce, marriage and promotion.

Our reactions to physical trauma are similar to one another. The same stimulus (cut finger, arm slammed in door) produces the same responses (blood, broken arm). They are seen and observable. But we tend to respond differently on an emotional level, and for a variety of reasons. We have been raised in various parts of the country with unique parents, during different time periods, and have developed a variety of values.

Consider two individual police officers experiencing divorce. One may have emotional reactions of quiet, anger and remorse. He may be sad, depressed and find it difficult to get through the day. The other officer could have entirely different responses. He could feel happy, almost giddy, even elated, and appear more open and carefree in his lifestyle. Two people have the same stimulus—divorce—with two different responses; depression for one, elation for the other.

Officer Harry S. was extremely casual about his marriage, which is to say he messed around quite a bit with other women. He didn't think much about the consequences. However, when his wife announced one day that she was leaving him, he just fell apart. He cried to the department psychologist: "I don't know how I can go on! I don't know how I'm going to survive!" He couldn't handle being the rejected one, couldn't cope with the fact that he wasn't in control of his wife any longer.

Officer Francis M. came home one night and his wife informed him that she had ordered expensive carpeting for a house that they were renting to another couple. Francis complained, half kiddingly, "How can you spend 15 bucks a yard for carpeting a rental unit? What're you doing?—screwing the carpet salesman?" Whereupon she broke down crying and admitted that this was exactly what was happening. Francis was stunned. He didn't know how to respond, and his well-tended macho image dissolved on the spot.

Such differences in emotional responses can be confusing for people who expect everyone to respond the same way, or who see a response different from theirs as inappropriate, wrong or a sign of weakness.

Statements such as: "I just don't understand today's police officer reactions"; or "Maybe they aren't tough or strong enough to handle some of the difficult parts of the job," illustrate that people often misunderstand others' emotional responses because simply they are different.

How much stress can we handle? Our emotional-tolerance levels are varied as our physical-tolerance levels for such things as pain, alcohol, etc. While one worker may take criticism from a supervisor in stride, another may take it as a personal attack and sulk for weeks. Present any new safety regulation to a group of officers and you will certainly see a variety of emotional responses!

Police officers, police managers and citizens should understand individual differences and emotional responses that may result from the same type of action. Police officers are not robots and all do not respond in the same way to every situation. To have effective police officers, and get the best results, fellow officers, managers and citizens must recognize and accommodate to the individual officer and his uniqueness.

Who are the police? How do they act? What is their personality? Their role in society? The answers to these questions will hopefully become clearer as we begin looking at law-enforcement officers throughout the various stages of their careers. There are a multitude of personality types among the police, as there are in other professions. In our attempt to understand police, there is a tendency to categorize them, to find a composite-model police officer.

The average officer, however, is really nonexistent. Officers can be very different than the "norm" and still be very effective.

For example, if we were to study the average height of cadets entering the police academy, we would find individuals ranging in height from 5' 2" to 6' 10." The average height for these cadets may be 5' 9¾." To establish this average, we used everyone in the population. There may not be a single cadet who is actually 5' 9¾," yet this height is used to describe the model cadet.

The difficulty in establishing personality norms is even harder. Personalities are developed from a multitude of factors—heredity, childhood experiences, parents' values, etc. Although there may be some general personality traits that attract people to certain professions there are a myriad of different personality types in all occupations. Each of us is unique.

Likewise, police have a unique position in society. Cops are more in the public eye than any other single group. They are easily identified by the uniform, gun and baton they wear, and the cars they drive. Although there may be

differences in the uniform color, insigna worn, etc., there
is a tendency to see all police as one type, with one personality. At times, they are classified in the same way.
Statements like, "It figures, he's a cop," or "That's what
cops do," reflect this. No one police officer fits all these
stereotypes. Yet they all must deal with them.

Cops are under close scrutiny—they have enormous
power. This power to limit citizen's freedom is both feared
and misunderstood by the public. Although there are concerns about legislators, judges, lawyers and doctors, they
are not nearly as much in the public eye as the police. The
fact that police work often involves violence, combined
with the fact that they have control over people's lives in
a direct way, focuses attention on law enforcement by the
media as well as many other segments of society. This
emphasis on police is, in part, the result of our society's
interest in authority, violence and crime.

Police officers affect people in many ways. At times
their role is rewarding, (saving a victim from a burning
car, delivering a baby). Other times it is traumatic and
tragic, (killing a suspect, removing multilated bodies from
plane or car crashes). How the public, media and others
view the role of the police officer may be different than the
officer's perception of his or her own job.

Two murder suspects were on the loose and had put
out the word that if any cops wanted to catch them
they'd better be prepared to die. One night officer Hank
G. spotted one of the suspects on foot and began to chase
him. It was a long and dramatic pursuit—through
alleys, over fences, and out of buildings. Hank knew
that the suspect was armed and very dangerous, and at
several points Hank had a chance to draw his gun and
shoot, but he didn't. He just kept chasing, and finally he
caught up to the guy. They wrestled in the street, and
Hank could feel a bulge in the suspect's pocket which he
assumed to be a gun, but still he didn't use his own weapon. Instead, he finally subdued the man, disarmed him,

handcuffed him, and brought him into the stationhouse. The ensuing reactions to Hank's behavior were wildly varied. Citizens treated him as a hero. Other police officers thought he was foolhardy not to have gunned down the suspect or let him escape, rather than risking his own life. Hank's own reaction, however, was altogether different. He explained: "Hell, the guy committed a murder! Do you know how many subpoenas I'll get from him? I wanted to bring him back alive . . . he was just money on the hoof to me! I'll get so much overtime going to court and I really need the money!"

When cops make a mistake, everyone will hear about it. When a doctor, lawyer or judge errs, few people know about it. In comparison with most other occupations, the mistakes in law enforcement have serious consequences.

Police have different roles in an urban environment than in a rural one. Differences are dependent upon various factors—familiarity vs. unfamiliarity with the people, high density vs. isolationism, agricultural vs. industrial surroundings, etc. All require different responses on the part of the police.

What may be appropriate behavior for a police officer in New York, may be inappropriate in Los Angeles. Even within major cities, the actions and roles of the police may be different as the neighborhoods they work. In Los Angeles, a police officer may act very differently in Westwood, an affluent neighborhood with UCLA as its focus, than he would in a ghetto.

In upper-class areas, cops are expected to spend a good deal of time on each call because the citizens there expect that kind of attention. In ghetto areas, however, calls are expected to be handled quickly because there are always more calls to respond to. Policemen who are transferred from high-crime areas to low-crime areas have to adjust to the inactivity and can get into trouble for stopping people without probable cause.

Officers working in high-crime neighborhoods get used

to dealing with citizens who have a lot of street smarts—for example, knowledge about search-and-seizure laws. Citizens in low-crime neighborhoods, not used to dealing with the police, might kick up a fuss about being stopped for drunk driving, while a slum-dweller who has been arrested several times will treat a drunk-driving charge as no big deal at all.

Mexican-American communities offer their own unique challenges for the police officer. For instance, in a black or a white community a cop tends to be forceful in dealing with juveniles because any sign of leniency might be regarded as weakness. However, juveniles in a Latin community will balk if they feel that their *machismo* is being challenged. A cop who wants to frisk a suspect (especially if the suspect's friends are watching) might have better luck by saying something like: "Hey, will you please turn around and put your hands on the patrol car? . . . because I'm getting a little scared here, and, man, you look like a pretty tough guy."

These distinctions become even greater when we consider the differences between a highly urbanized vs. a rural environment.

On the island of Kauai, Hawaii, the population of approximately 20,000 people is mostly native, and people know each other well. The police are natives and know almost everyone on a friendly, first-name basis. There has never been an officer involved in a shooting in the history of the department. Marijuana is grown by many of the residents of Kauai, and some say it is the major export of the island. Obviously the role of the police officer on this island is going to vary from that of an officer who works in a major city where there are over 50 officer-involved shootings a year, strangers trafficking in drugs, organized crime and prostitution.

A city of 2,000 people in an agricultural area may have different expectations of police than residents of a larger city. If a family-disturbance call came in, the officer handling it may know not only the family, but may also know something about their problem. The approach he would take would be highly individualized. This became evident to me when training police officers of an eight-man department in a city of 2,000. In a training session on family disturbances officers remarked: "We're all different here"; "We all approach people differently"; "We do whatever we think is best."

These responses in a large department would not be allowed and might even be considered ridiculous. The approach to family-disturbance calls and to citizens in general is rarely individualized. It is much more regimented, with specific procedures that must be followed. This is for both the safety and benefit of the police officer and the citizens involved.

Often the media puts so much emphasis on the large departments that here is a tendency to forget that in the United States there are 40,000 police departments, consisting of 400,000 police officers. Many small departments sometimes get lost in the shuffle when law-enforcement procedures are discussed. What works in large cities may not work for smaller cities, and vice versa.

In some rural communities, police not only live in that community, they also use their own cars. They often have views and beliefs similar to the rest of the community. In a large urban department rarely do officers use their own cars, and often they do not live in the community in which they work. Their views and beliefs may be different than the community they police. They are often isolated from the community, initially by their patrol car, sometimes by race, language and culture.

Sergeant Bob C. worked in a large metropolitan department. He had stopped to admire the sunset outside the coffee shop where he had just eaten dinner. Bob remarked to the man standing next to him, "It's really a beautiful evening." The man next to him responded, "I have lived in this city for twenty years and you are the first cop that has ever said anything to me!"

Unfortunately, this happens all too often in large urban communities. There is often a distance that exists between the average citizen and the police officer. This tends to cause some apprehension and distrust by both.

How an officer approaches citizens in the community varies greatly according to the size of the community. For an officer from a large city to use the same approach as an officer from a small city, and vice versa, may be inappropriate. The roles they play must meet the demands and the values of the community they are protecting.

Too much emphasis is put on the violent, exciting and attention-grabbing aspects of police work. What appears most important is the officer's use of weapons, self-defense techniques and procedures for survival. What is left out are the social aspects of a police officer's job and his role in society.

Studies indicate that anywhere from 70% to 90% of a police officer's job is involved in interacting with people. Often little time is spent on how officers can more effectively communicate and achieve better results. This area includes how an officer treats, talks with and responds to citizens he encounters during the job.

Every person has his own way of looking at the police, influenced by his values, attitudes and interactions with them. The variety of expectations that our society heaps upon its policemen has been put this way by Professor Judith Grencik:

> To serve society, to protect them and enforce laws, to provide great amounts of public service, to be around whenever there is a crisis or emergency, to rescue cats in the tops of trees, to ask neighbors to turn their radios down, and in general to be around to do all the dirty work that I do not want to do or am afraid to do. We expect the policeman to quickly and effectively deal with

the family crisis which occurs next door, to safely rescue
hostages held by a scared, angry individual down to his
last-ditch effort to gain some control over his life, to pick
up the habitual drunk in the alley, to stop the fights in
the park, to answer the call of abused children, and to
keep the drunks off the road, but to leave me alone
because I am not doing wrong—it is the other person
who is causing the trouble. On top of all this, we also
expect our officers to fight crime and arrest dangerous,
violent criminals. Twenty-four hours a day, 365 days a
year, not only do his job on the street, but also go to
court at the drop of a hat, increase his education, participate in community affairs, be a good family man and
above reproach ethically and morally.

The role of the police includes at one extreme, social
aspects, and at the other, law enforcement.

Those who emphasize the social-services aspect may
openly acknowledge that it is acceptable for cops to have
some emotional involvements on the job. They would like
to see police officers and the department more involved
with the community. A strong enforcement believer may
want the officers to be emotionally detached and more isolated from the community. This would allow him to provide police services from an objective standpoint.

Neither view is right or wrong. We must come to grips
with what society expects of police officers. The confusion
that now exists causes frustration and distrust by both
the police officers and the community they are trying to
serve.

By exploring the historical perspective of our society,
the holistic approach, and values in general, a developmental pattern can be seen for law enforcement. Police do
not work in a vacuum. They are affected by a constantly
changing society which rarely has definitive answers. In
following police-officers' careers, we will see how these general principals affect them and our views of the police during stages of their lives.

REFERENCES

Alexander, F. *Our Age of Unreason.* Philadelphia: J. B. Lippincott Company, 1942.

Bachman, J. G. and Johnston, L. D. "The Freshman." *Psychology Today,* 13 (9), 1979.

Broderick, J. J. *Police in a Time of Change.* Morristown, New Jersey: General Learning Press, 1977.

Dollard, J., et al *Frustration and Aggression.* New Haven: Yale University Press, 1939.

FBI Uniform Crime Reports, U.S. Department of Justice.

Grencik, J. *The Experience of Stress in Policeman.* California State University, Long Beach: 1973.

Gurin, G., Veroff, J. and Feld, S. *Americans View Their Mental Health.* New York: Basic Books, 1960.

Harris, M. "Why It's Not The Same Old America." *Psychology Today,* 15 (8), 1981.

Horney, K. *Neurotic Personality of Our Times.* New York: Norton. 1936.

Katzenback, N. *Challenge of Crime in a Free Society: Report by the President's Commission on Law Enforcement and the Administration of Justice,* Department of Justice, 1967.

Levinson, D. J. *The Seasons of a Man's Life.* New York: Knopf, 1978.

Massey, M. *What You Are is What You Were When.* Farmington, Michigan Magnetic Video Corp., 1976.

Murray, J. P., Rubenstein, E. A. and Comstock, G. A. (eds.), *Television and Social Behavior, Vol. II: Television and Social Learning.* Rockville, Md.: U.S. Department of H.E.W., 1971.

Naisbett, J. *Megatrends.* New York: Warner Books, 1982.

Niederhoffer, A. and Blumberg, A. (eds.) *The Ambivalent Force: Perspectives on the Police.* Waltham, Massachusetts: Xerox College Publishing, 1970.

Sheehy, G. *Passages.* New York: E. P. Dutton, 1974.

"10 Forces Reshaping America" *U.S. News and World Report,* 3/19/84.

Toffler, A. *Future Shock.* New York: Random House, 1970.

Quinn, J. B. "Boom-Boom Economics." *News Week,* 6/18/79.

Watts, W. "The Future Can Fend for Itself" *Psychology Today.* 15 (9), 1981.

2

THOSE WHO WANT TO BE COPS—THE APPLICANTS

When asked to list the qualities most important for officers in his department to possess, a police chief replied, "Sure, that's easy—sensitivity, honesty, a caring about people, decisiveness, a high moral standing, devotion to duty. They should be personable, detached but concerned, should handle stress well, be even-tempered, and slow to anger."

The job of being a policeman is one of the few occupations that puts people in the position of being feared, sometimes hated, occasionally reviled, or even assaulted in the ordinary performance of their duties, while they are able to help others, save lives and assist in the battle against crime.

Police work requires officers to deal directly with people, whatever their feelings about those people. It also demands sound judgment under stress. Good mental health, flexibility and adaptability to new and rapidly

changing situations are essentials for good policing. With
all the screening processes for police applicants it's little
wonder that those who enter law enforcement are above
average in intelligence, physical fitness and emotional
maturity.

Are the police a separate and distinctive group in the
community? Are their socioeconomic and career backgrounds different? Some believe that police stand apart
from the rest of society and that this gulf is encouraged by
basic socieconomic factors, values, life and family
styles. These people might argue that the police force
neither is, nor considers itself to be, a group of ordinary
citizens in uniform.

Yet others claim the opposite. In 1929 and again in 1962,
England's Royal Commission on the police declared: "The
police of this country have never been recognized, either
in law or by tradition, as a force distinct from the general
body of the population." A deliberate policy of drawing
the police from backgrounds which mirror the general
population can be seen as a subtle technique of social control. Personnel policies may have been instituted in order
to reduce the risk of distrust between police and the people
over whom they are watchdogs. Policemen today are
drawn primarily from working-class origins. Their values,
ways of life and thoughts have generally been developed
in a family unit where manual or office work is a way of
life. A strong military background in the family is common. Policemen are generally drawn from the middle
class, and the top and bottom of the social scale are
somewhat underrepresented. The remarkable thing is that
there seems to be little in the socioeconomic picture of
policemen that would set them apart from the general
population. Two-thirds come from manual working-class
backgrounds, which is similar to the distribution in the
population as a whole.

The increasing need for personnel in nontraditional
police-work areas such as computer programming, air

travel and photography may account in part for the fact that recruits are being selected nowadays from a broader range of the population.

There is a relatively high proportion of policemen who themselves come from a police background. In England this difference is dramatic: Policemen constitute approximately 0.6% of the working population, yet 14% come from police backgrounds.

In the United States, men with police fathers tend to be particularly heavily concentrated in intelligence divisions and among the "brass"; inspectors, chiefs, etc. Police who come from police backgrounds do better within the law-enforcement structure. They achieve more status and easily adapt to police work as a life style. They may have learned as children the necessary police regimentation. This, of course, holds true for many other professions, as well.

The fact that most police entering the profession have moved up socially and economically from their own family background is supported by data on their educational attainments. Compared with other adults from working-class families, police recruits tend to do better in school. Twenty percent of children born in the late 1930's to lower nonmanual and skilled manual households went to grammar or independent schools, while half of the policemen did. Police also seem to be more likely to enroll in college preparatory programs. (Once they reach these programs, however, they do not perform as well as the average student. In general, they are not among the academic achievers.)

An orientation toward upward mobility is reflected in the aspirations that policemen's families had for them and that they have for their own children. Police recruits tend to have held at least one full-time job in higher-skilled occupations than their fathers. Most entered the law enforcement profession after holding jobs that were at least in the skilled category and most likely in the business area, such as clerical and sales.

Police are often said to have experienced only a limited set of work situations, which serves to insulate them from the general population and to incline them towards a disciplinarian outlook on society. Many entered policing at an early age and are likely to have done military service. However, this is changing today. More and more police recruits are coming from many walks of life, with a greater variation of skills, education, values, attitudes and little, if any, military experience.

In general, policemen have improved their educational status, but have not yet swung over to great academic success. They were socially upwardly mobile before joining law enforcement. They had held outside jobs showing a variety of skill levels. In the last ten years, the police have become more and more reflective of the general population in terms of social class, education and career development. They want to be viewed as professionals, and have begun to work toward that goal.

PAST APPLICANTS	PRESENT APPLICANTS
1. Strong dedication to phenmenon of law and order	More liberalized view of law and order
2. Practical experience rather than school educated	Higher level of education
3. Strong military background	Minimal, if any, military background
4. Verbally sophisticated	Verbally sophisticated
5. Blue collar family background	Wider socioeconomic background
6. Politically conservative	Middle of the road politics
7. High sociability	High sociability
8. Greater interest in crime oriented functions	Greater interest in crime oriented functions

9. Physically larger   Physically smaller

10. Authoritative family   More permissive family
    background   background

11. Greater respect for rank   More challenging of police
    and authority   organization

12. More conservative lifestyle   More affluent lifestyle

13. Generally white and male   More minorities and women

The differences between past and present applicants have created both confusion and growth for most agencies. The confusion comes in the areas of training, supervision, cop-to-cop interaction and ways of dealing with people on the street. The growth has come as a result of trying to understand the differences and finding ways to utilize the best insights from the past and new ideas for the future.

> Jimmy Breslin states: "There are a number of reasons why a young man in New York takes a job as a policeman, nearly all of which are the pension. The pension, half pay after 20 years, runs a policeman's life. It is the only thing he is afraid of losing and it is the only thing he wants out of the job. After 20 years, he retires and collects the half pay and works as a security man at a bank or a manufacturing plant somewhere. He starts his second job at between the ages of 40 and 45. He holds it until he can quit and collect Social Security. At the end, he is a terribly bitter old man who wonders if he has wasted his life."

If you believe that the only reason police are doing their job is for an early retirement, you could believe that police don't care about people, are not interested in their work, or the services they provide. Although recruits often choose being a cop for financial and security reasons, the primary reasons most applicants enter law enforcement are to help people to improve the community and to serve society.

Those who select police work for the most part do so consciously and with determination. Generally it is not a career into which one stumbles because he is a high school dropout and has nothing better to do. Nor is it a career one would choose because he needs some quick money for a few days.

Those considering the law-enforcement profession believe they know what the job is all about. Often, this is not the case. Knowledge about being a cop often is acquired through glamorized movies and television shows, spectacular cases presented in the media, and vicarious experiences relayed by friends. Expectations are high and idealized. Cops are heroes. Cops are respected. Cops are well liked by families and friends. A cop is what they want to be!

> One young policeman said: "It's an exciting profession and you get to help people and society. Being able to catch crooks and put them in jail is an added plus. Punishing the bad guy and helping the good guy is what it's all about."

> Another new cop put it this way: "You know, when I was growing up we didn't have a TV. Never saw one until I was 12. But every Saturday I'd go to the movies and watch the Westerns or gangster shows. I started identifying with the good guys in the white hats. It was always so simple to tell the good from the bad. I developed a tremendous respect for the courage and dedication of the good guys, and made up my mind that some day I would be one of the good guys and fight crime wherever it reared its ugly head."

Although the decision to enter the law enforcement profession may not be based on the reality of the job, the applicant knows that policing is one that is exciting without requiring a college degree.

Although the high-school degree requirement is generally true in both urban and rural police departments, there is a trend now to require education beyond high school. In some departments it is merely preferred. For promotional opportunities, further education is looked on favorably, with most applicants receiving additional points for their educational attainments.

By contrasting high-school graduates entering the police profession with those entering other careers, the reactions when expectations are not met can be drastically different. Consider computer programming as a comparative example. It, along with many careers in technology today, may attract young men and women who have no definite concept of what the work is really like. Some may base their choice on sound reasons such as an aptitude for systematic thought, a preference for solitary work, or a fascination with technology. Others may see it as a means to correct all the refined tangles of the bureaucratic world. This last approach to a computer career would quickly lead to disillusionment. They may begin to see the human limits within computer programmers or see themselves being reduced to a machine servicing the computer. They may also realize what a lonely endeavor they've started. But although they may abandon their careers, computer programmers are consoled by the fact that it is a new field and they really didn't know what to expect anyway.

Police recruits do not have this recourse. They have not entered a new profession. Law enforcement has a long history and is a profession that most people are quick to say they understand. Thus, the new recruits feel that their expectations are certainly what the career offers. Moreover, if their expectations are not met, they are less likely to abandon the career. Applicants are willing to go through the numerous and lengthy screening procedures and rigorous training because they believe they know what law enforcement entails and are determined to become police officers.

> Jack S. exemplifies this determination. He started thinking about being a cop when he was living in Oregon, and, after much deliberating, finally decided to pursue his career in Los Angeles. He promptly packed up and moved his wife and two children to L.A., and took a job driving a truck while he studied for the police-department exams. He failed his first departmental interview because of his lack of education, so he took night classes at a community college until he earned his high school diploma. He tried the exams again, but failed the written test. At this point, friends and relatives tried to talk Jack into applying to another department, but he was adamant. He insisted that his truck-driving job was merely helping him to get to know the city so that he'd be a better cop. He returned to night school to study English, took the departmental exams for a third time, and finally was accepted into the academy.

In exploring the motives that lead young people into law enforcement, studies have shown that the desire to serve society is very high on the list. In a study of over 800 cadets, 50% listed service to society, helping and working with people, as their foremost reason for wanting to be police officers. The second most common reason was financial and job security. The job itself, its variety, excitement and challenge was third. Academy cadets tend to have high moral values. The want to be of service through protecting and aiding the community. Officers anticipate rewards such as respect and praise from knowing that their efforts are appreciated.

> Whenever friends in the department began talking about pulling a strike or a slowdown in order to get more wages out of the city, Gil M. would say, "Forget the pay—just give me some work to do." This young cop also

resisted suggestions that he run for an office in the policeman's union. As he explained it: "See, I'm a company man at heart, and in this case I work for the people of this city. And I didn't make any deals with those people that they have to give me raises every year. The only deal I made was that I'd serve them honestly and to the best of my abilities. I intend to honor that deal, which I took an oath on, and you won't see me working against the people who run this town. Being a cop is as important as any job in this country. Someone has to keep the wolves away from the sheep, and if the wages are more important to a guy than the job, then he's in the wrong business."

A second motive for entering the profession is security, financial security, as well as the knowledge that one is involved in a lifelong career with opportunity for advancement, early retirement and excellent benefits. The militaristic structure of most departments provides a type of security that is found in a family unit. There are defined lines of communication, authority, ways to act, etc. The guidelines for retirement pay provides recruits a clear sense of where they are going.

The risky aspect of the profession, the element of personal danger, tends to be seen as exciting rather than as a deterrent to entering police work. Those drawn toward police careers tend to be action-oriented men and women. They are the doers among us rather than the thinkers.

James Lee Walsh discusses what he calls "police career styles." He sees three distinctive career styles: "street cops," "action seekers," and "middle-class mobiles." Each type has different needs and outlooks on police work.

The *Street Cops* are those who see law enforcement as a secure work environment. Street Cops tend to be married or in a relationship at the time they seek police work. Their goals in life center around the well-being of their wives and children. What attracts them to police work is the secure work setting and the family-oriented goals.

Charlie D. was the model street cop. He looked like W. C. Fields, with a big round belly and a cigar always hanging out of the side of his mouth, and he had a sense of humor to match. He often forgot to tuck in his shirt in back and had to be reminded by his sergeant. But these appearances were deceptive, because Charlie was the most concientious, dedicated and street-smart patrolman in the department. As easygoing as he was on the job, he always noticed things like a broken padlock on a garage door or a car license plate that he'd seen listed on the hot sheet. He seemed to miss nothing, to bring an immediate sense of authority and order to any situation in which he involved himself. He was considered the best training officer for recruits just hitting the streets. He had more patience than a priest and the ability to teach a rookie without wounding his pride. He almost never had to use force on the job, but seemed to have an excess of force in reserve. He was just a street cop—that was all. He refused to take the sergeant's exam and had no ambitions beyond being an effective patrolman. His only long-range goal was to retire after 30 years instead of the usual 20.

Action Seekers go into police work for other reasons. In general they are men who have knocked about a bit in other occupations or have been in the military before joining the police. Many are single at the time they join the force. They are drawn to police work by the excitement, the outdoor setting, and constantly being on the move. They want to escape the boredom of office-type jobs and believe they would be restricted or confined in such an atmosphere. They are men and women looking for "real" police work, which to them is defined by unforseen action.

Officer James M. said: "Sure, I want to help people, but what I really like about police work is the excitement and not having a regular daily routine. Every day is different, and I don't know what to expect from one minute to the next. It sure is more interesting than sitting behind a desk all day."

The Action Seekers only mention family-centered goals after their desire for excitement.

Middle Class Mobiles become police officers for still other reasons. They are achievement-oriented and see law enforcement as one of the few professions that does not require a college degree. Their personal goals center around promotion and the achieving of a higher and higher rank. They believe that the way to meet family goals is through achievement. Generally they are married at the time they enter law enforcement.

Although the reasons are varied as to why men and women choose police work, many of the reasons for entering this profession are the same as those for other professions. Many people, for example, become doctors for security, the excitement of life-and-death situations and as a means for social advancement.

Police are really very much like most people entering a new profession—full of idealistic goals, not having an accurate picture of their new profession, but feeling confident that they can do a good job.

The primary criteria for assessing police applicants have deviated little from the process used 150 years ago by the Metropolitan Police of London, England. Chenoweth described this selection process as follows:

> Of the first 2,800 men recruited into that organization, at least 2,238 (or approximately 80%) had to be dismissed from the force. All 2,800 officers had been hand picked by a very careful system of selection. Each candidate had to submit three written testimonials of character, one of these being from his last employer; the writers of these testimonials were personally interviewed. If the candidate passed through this stage, he reported for a medical examination which in practice meant an inquiry into both his physical qualifications and his general intelligence. Less than one in three of the applicants were successful in passing through this stage. Those who did were then interviewed by an ex-

perienced personnel officer who eliminated the candidates obviously not suited for police work and passed the survivors on to the first two Commissioners of the Metropolitan Police, who again interviewed the remaining candidate. The disapproval of either Commissioner was sufficient to reject the candidate.

Current police selection procedures consist of minimum and maximum qualification levels in the areas of general health, physical fitness, visual acuity, civil service "aptitude," character and sometimes age or residency.

The screening process determines the personality pattern of what the department considers a desirable policeman. To be successful, aspiring officers have to be intelligent, in good health, quick and strong. They cannot have had any serious encounter with the law. Their ethics and morality have to withstand intensive scrutiny. They must have shown stability at school and at work. If they served in the armed forces, they must have been honorably discharged with no evidence of serious maladjustment. All relationships, whether they be with family or friends, should be stable and normal. They must show no deviation in behavior, morally or sexually. Addiction to drugs or alchohol will eliminate them. And it helps if they are true-blue believers in the American dream of achievement, tradition and law and order.

The screening process varies from agency to agency and from state to state. The people who are finally selected to be officers also vary according to the needs of the particular department. Most police agencies utilize a series of steps in their selection process. Each step acts as a screen to eliminate applicants who fall short of a predetermined standard. These standards are fairly specific for each agency. An agency that has six officers and is in a rural environment is going to select a different sort of person than one which employs 5,000 officers and must deal with a large metropolitan environment. With this in mind, various physical standards, written tests, oral examinations, background checks and psychological instruments are employed.

There appears to be a wide range of physical requirements in agencies relative to applicants' height, weight and age. The minimum height ranges from 64 to 70 inches, with many agencies having no height requirement. Weight requirements range from minimums of 120–170 pounds to maximums of 180–250 pounds, and, again, some agencies are now dropping weight requirements. The minimum age ranges from 18 to 22 years.

Some departments require a physical agility test which must be passed by all applicants. The Los Angeles County Sheriff's Department has such a test based on what it was able to validate as the physical requirements of officers in the field. The department studied its field officers and found that in the course of their duties they were required to perform the following tasks: climb a six-foot wall, run a quarter-mile, transport a body 15 feet, walk on a balance beam for 15 feet, push a vehicle for 10 feet, crawl through a crawlway and run 220 yards with a shotgun. As a result, all applicants are required to pass this physical-agility test.

Civil Service, general intelligence, police aptitude and situational tests are some of the written tests used as screening tools. From 30% to 80% of police applicants are screened out by general intelligence or Civil Service tests. Even though the ability to perform specific job-related reading and writing tasks has been the guideline established by the Equal Employment Opportunity Commission, some jurisdictions continue to use measures of general intelligence as an important screening tool.

Several agencies have explored the use of police aptitude tests in predicting police effectiveness. An aptitude test developed for the St. Louis Police Department in 1954 by Dubois and Watson showed low to moderate correlations with academy grades. The New York City Police

Department used a battery of similar tests and found no relationship to ratings of on-the-job performance. In a recent court decision, Louisville Black Police Officers vs. the City of Louisville, the court ruled that although the Multi-jurisdictional Police Officer Examination was content-valid, there was no evidence that the highest scores would make the best qualified policemen.

Another approach which uses situational tests has become more and more popular since it was originally developed for use during World War II. More recently, these tests have been used in assessment centers. The situational tests place applicants in simulated situations and test their responses to various situations. An example would be the Clues Test which requires one to search the desk of a hypothetical missing man and then complete a questionnaire. Although these tests appear to be helpful in assessing where the recruits need training, again they do not appear to be able to predict success in job performance.

Oral interviews are conducted under Civil Service guidelines by a combination of law-enforcement officials, commission members and citizens. Such boards will evaluate the applicants in many areas and attempt to determine their potential for police work. The interviews may also contain situational questions to test the applicants' common sense. As with other screening procedures, the validity of an oral interview to predict job performance is questionable. A validity study by Landy in 1976 concluded that hiring recommendations by the typical group-interview "oral board" had no relation to job performance.

Many law enforcement officials and behavioral scientists believe that the best predictor of behavior is past behavior. Background information, they believe, offers useful input into predicted future job performance.

The prior history of applicants will be investigated to make sure they do not have criminal records, or backgrounds of activities which would make them unsuitable for the job.

In 1970, the New York Police Department conducted a longitudinal study investigating the accuracy of background investigators to predict future job performance. Since applicants for the New York Police Department could be hired regardless of background-investigator recommendation, there was a unique opportunity to study this predictor. Job-performance data on sick days, termination for cause, awards and commendations and training failures were collected on 396 applicants. Of most interest was the finding that the percentage of false negatives (individuals once predicted to fail who succeeded) was greater, 94%, than the total hit rate (individuals correctly predicted to fail who did fail and those predicted to succeed who did succeed) of 82%.

Even though the value of background information as a predictor of future police performance appears questionable, it is probably the best measure available. This type of screening has become more difficult because a large majority of today's applicants have limited life experiences, having spent the majority of their time in school and (often because of the economy) having continued to live with their parents.

"On a warm day in 1964, a tall 15-year old boy, regarded by his classmates as well-mannered but a shy lone wolf, calmly shot his grandmother to death with two bullets to the head. When his grandfather returned from the grocery store, the youth murdered him in a similar fashion. He then telephoned his mother and reported what he'd done. His explanation was, "I just wondered how it would feel to shoot Grandma." After six years of penal and psychiatric institutionalization and treatment, he was released. In September, 1972, two psychiatrists reported, "He has made an excellent response to treatment." One was so convinced that he said, "I see no psychiatric reason to consider him a threat to himself or any other member of society." Tragically, four days before this psychiatric evaluation he had murdered a 15-year-old girl. Before his capture in May, 1973, he had murdered and dismembered six young girls. Three days prior to confession to these murders, he bludgeoned his mother to death with a hammer and strangled one of her friends. A total of ten human lives were taken by Edmund Kemper before his personal reign of terror ceased." (Stenz & Hassel)

If, after seven years of close observation, psychiatric treatment and testing, this was the best the experts could do in their psychological assessment, we have a long way to go in being able to predict human behavior.

Although psyhological testing may be important, it is the job of evaluators to show that they have the knowledge and tools to assess those emotionally suited for police work.

To date, there has been no systematic correlation of tests or interviews with an individual's subsequent behavior and success or nonsuccess in law enforcement. However, psychologists and agencies continue to reject candidates on the basis of unvalidated strategies whether they be tests, clinical interviews or both.

To determine the effectiveness of psychological screening there must be an increased emphasis on the correlation of test data, interview questions and psychological examinations with an officer's subsequent performance. The evaluators and their tests must be carefully examined to determine whether their use is ultimately detrimental to the individual, society and law enforcement. I am not advocating the abandonment of psychological testing for law-enforcement applicants. Rather, I'm suggesting a more scientific approach, greater understanding of the issues involved, and caution by all.

Screening and selection are the two general approaches used to determine who should be hired.

Screening is the process of evaluating an applicant's

fitness within acceptable psychological limits. If this can be accomplished, screening appears to be the more appropriate procedure, professionally and legally. Levy has summarized the following drawbacks to a screening approach: (1) The mere absence of unwanted qualities prior to employment does not guarantee a continued absence after employment; (2) Psychological tests have not been demonstrated to have predictive value; (3) The definition of emotional suitability for law enforcement remains undetermined; and (4) Some traits which are often deemed pathological may be essential for the stress tolerance needed in effective policing.

In the selection approach, applicants are chosen for their optimal potential on the job. Some psychologists claim to have developed methods to determine specific traits seen as important in police work such as logical reasoning, decisiveness, organizational compatibility, self-confidence, sensitivity, stress tolerance, nonverbal impact, positive motivation, behavioral flexibility and others. However, with the documented inability of psychologists to predict even extreme behavior such as violence, the chances of more refined predictions of behavior seem remote. Psychological instruments as tools to assess non-pathological traits are extremely limited, with clinical interviews fairing not better.

Given the state-of-the-art in psychological evaluation of police applicants, psychologists should be limited to screening out the pathological and leaving the determination of selection to other aspects of the application process. The subsequent months of intensive training and observation by the training academy and the continual evaluation during the officers' probationary year provide a more logical opportunity by police personnel to make final judgments about an individual's capacity to handle the job on certain identified dimensions.

In the current process of screening or selection, psychologists in the same geographic area—using the same test data in conjunctuion with interviews—sometimes reach different decisions on the same applicant. This also happens in other areas of the criminal-justice system wherein psychologists called as expert witnesses in competency and sanity hearings emerge with conflicting assessments.

Psychologists must make theirs a more exact science by discarding arbitrary tests and subjective interviews that make arbitrary and subjective predictions and decisions about people and human behavior.

They must be able to determine through their screening procedures, not only a "healthy" cop personality type, but also a healthy cop personality type which will remain healthy.

The major problems with psychological screening are that there are no validated tests on police to confirm the psychologist's evaluation of the candidate. Often there is a lack of knowledge on the part of the psychologist about police work and what it requires of an individual, and the instruments used were not developed for evaluation or screening but rather to determine pathology, or to provide descriptive personality traits. To simply use these instruments to select applicants for police work needs further scrutiny.

When using psychological instruments as screening tools, it should be in conjunction with a personal interview. Tests alone do not give the evaluator the opportunity to query the applicant on issues that tests may indicate as reasons for refusal.

Applicant John S., scored high on hypochondriasis (an overconcern about his body) and feminine interest. Without an interview, he would have been disqualified because of these results. With an interview, the examiner might have learned that John had been in surgery many times, had been expected to die twice, and was told he wouldn't live to be forty. Though extremely healthy now, John would be foolish not to be concerned about his bodily functioning after these experiences. Furthermore, while he was sick John read a lot, and later he attended college and received an M.A., in history. He had a wide range of interests (movies, plays, art, poetry, gardening, classical music, etc.) and because of this scored higher in feminine interests. Both scores on the psychological test were appropriate in light of his experiences.

This holds true for other events that happen to people. Depression, anxiety, paranoia and other reactions may be explained and appropriate for the applicants in view of their experiences.

By using unvalidated tests along with one 15-minute to one-hour interview, psychologists measure the ability to handle stress, interpersonal skills, emotional control, violent or aggressive behavior and many other traits. Sometimes, their decisions seem questionable.

Edward L., a ten-year policeman in a medium-sized Midwestern city, applied to become a police officer for a large Southern California city. In his ten years in the Midwest he had fired his weapon only on one occasion, after waiting until the last second to shoot. His actions were never questioned and fell well within department standards. The psychologist for the Southern California city said that Edward was psychologically healthy, but was not organizationally compatible. The psychologist's rationale for disqualification was that the department was under tremendous media pressure because of officer-involved shootings and, since Edward had been involved in a shooting while working for another police department, he would not be acceptable in the organization he wished to join.

Should psychologists assess organizational compatibility? Should this be the criterian used for psychological fitness? Or should psychologists simply judge applicants according to acceptable psychological standards, and then leave it up to the individual and the department to determine their compatibility?

Even after the lengthy procedure (written, oral, background, medical, etc.) have been completed, some psychologists have disqualified 40% to 60% of applicants as psychologically unfit. It's hard to believe that, with the numerous interactions the applicant has had with various police officers, such a high percentage is disqualified on psychological grounds.

Some psychologists appear quick to claim an ability to evaluate police officers but hesitant when it comes to assessing themselves or other professionals in critical occupations, whether they be psychiatrists, surgeons, airplane pilots or others who dramatically affect people's lives. One can only imagine the reaction of psychologists if they had to be psychologically tested and interviewed before graduation or *licensure*. Many would consider this approach ridiculous or would be offended. The fact that none of these other careers requires this type of screening speaks for itself.

The police applicant certainly has a long road ahead of him, whether he be applying for a position in a rural town or a large metropolitan city. Whether his screening process consists of answering a newspaper ad or hours of testing and interviews, it's essential that he and his family understand the rigors of police work. This will help the applicant make a decision which will mean success for him whether it's in the law-enforcement field or not. By carefully examining our applicants and allowing them to examine their own motives, we can have a more qualified and satisfied police force.

"What is a policeman?" Perhaps Paul Harvey sums it up well:

"A policeman is a composite of what all men are, a mingling of Saint and Sinner, Dust and Diety. Culled

statistics *wave fan over the sinners,* underscoring
instances of dishonesty and brutality because they are
'news.' What that really means is that they are exceptional, unusual, not commonplace. Buried under the
froth is the fact: less than .5% of the policemen misfit
that uniform. What is a policeman made of? He, of all
men, is at once the most needed and the most unwanted.
He's a strongly nameless creature who is "sir" to his
face and "fuzz" behind his back. He must be such a
diplomat that each will think he won. But, if the policeman is neat, he is conceited; if he's careless, he's a bum.
If he's pleasant, he's a flirt; if he's not, he's a grouch. He
must make an instant decision which would require
months for a lawyer. But, if he hurries, he's careless; if
he's deliberate, he's lazy. He must be first to an accident
and infallible with diagnosis. He must be able to stop
bleeding, tie splints and above all, be sure the victim
goes home without a limp, or expect to be sued.

"The police officer must know every gun, draw on the
run and hit where it doesn't hurt. He must be able to
whip two men twice his size and half his age without
damaging his uniform and without being "brutal." If
you hit him, he's a coward; if he hits you, he's a bully.

"A policeman must know everything and not tell. He
must know where all the sin is and not partake. The
policeman must, from a single human hair, be able to
describe the crime, the weapon, the criminal and tell you
where the criminal is hiding. But, if he catches the criminal, he's lucky; if he doesn't, he's a dunce. If he gets
promoted, he has political pull; if he doesn't, he's a
dullard.

"The policeman must chase bum leads to a dead-end,
stake out ten nights to tag one witness who saw it
happen, but refuses to remember. He runs files and writes
reports until his eyes ache to build a case against some
felon who'll get dealt out by a shameless Shamus or an
honorable judge who isn't. The policeman must be a
minister, a social worker, a diplomat, a tough guy and a
gentleman. And, of course, he'll have to be a genius for
he'll have to feed a family on a policeman's salary."

REFERENCES

Breslin, J. "The Policeman." *NEW YORK POST,* September 9, 1968.

Check, S. and Klein, J. "The Personality of the American Police:A Review of the Literature." *Crime and Et Justice,* May, 1977

Gettinger, S. "Psychological Testing." *Police,* 4(2), 1981

Harvey, P. "What Are Policemen Made Of?" October 27, 1967.

Labour Research "The Police and the State." 30(2), February, 1975.

McNamara, J.H. "Uncertainties in Police Work: The Relevance of Police Recruits' Backgrounds and Training." In Bordua, D. (Ed.) *The Police: Six Sociological Essays.* New York: Wiley, 1967.

Poland, J. "Police Selection Methods and the Prediction of Police Performance. *Journal of Police Science and Administration,* 6(4), 1978.

Reiner, R. *The Blue Coated Worker.* Cambridge University Press, Cambridge: 1978.

Rhead, C., Abrams, A., Trosman, H. and Margolis, P. "The Psychological Assessment of Police Candidates." *American Journal of Psychiatry,* 1245(11), May, 1968.

Saxe, S., Reiser, M. "A Comparison of Three Police Applicant Groups." *Journal of Police Science and Administration,* 4(3), 1976.

Smith, B. *The State Police.* New York: The Maxmillian Co., 1925.

Stentz, T. and Hassel, C.V. "The Sociopath," *Journal of Police Science and Administration,* 7(1), 1979.

Territo, L., Swanson Jr., C.R. and Chamelin, N.C. *Police Personnel Selection Process.* Indianapolis, Indiana: Bobbs-Merrill Publishing Company, 1977.

Westergard, J. and Resler, H. "Class in a Capitalist Society." London: Heinemann, 1975.

3

GETTING READY— TRAINING

In no other area of police work can one have greater influence on young officers than in training. Until they enter the police world, their thoughts about a police career are shaped by personal experiences, the media and their own educational processes. The values and attitudes they have about police work may be very consistent with the realities of the job, but more likely they are filled with myths, exaggerations and a great deal of misunderstanding.

It is the department's responsibility to give the cadets a balanced foundation and shape them into successful police officers. In most departments, this is done through some type of formal training program. How young cadets are influenced and prepared for their future assignments is vital, since this is the time their attitudes, values, behaviors and perspectives of the job are molded.

Each of us establishes our own view about "good cops"

based on one's values and experiences. Interaction with parents, peers and the police effects how we view the role of police.

If we were to ask a group of people their view of the role of the police we would get a variety of responses. For example, city-dwellers have more contact with the police than do rural residents, and they seem to have a more cynical view of how effective and honest policemen are. Nevertheless, city people readily admit that they would be afraid to walk the streets if the police weren't available.

People in minority and low-income neighborhoods tend to see the police as representing the establishment's desire to repress them. They might resent and even hate cops, and yet they might call upon them in siuations where middle- or upper-class citizens wouldn't. For instance, the police will often be summoned for medical emergencies because slum-dwellers realize that private ambulance crews will then be more likely to come, knowing the city will guarantee that they get paid for the run.

Residents of rural areas, on the other hand, see the policeman's role as much more limited. They tend to settle disputes among themselves rather than relying on the authorities as much as urban-dwellers do. Rural people usually know the policemen who work in the area, and they have more respect for officers than do city people.

There are two philosophical extremes. At one extreme, the officer is regarded as a person who weeds out evil from society; the emphasis is placed on enforcement. At the other, the officer is seen as helping the whole community; this approach emphasizes service. Both approaches are trying to reach the goal of a healhier society, even though they are in conflict. How a department and individual officers determine their roles affects the whole area of training.

In the 1920's and 30's, most police irrespective of department, received little, if any formal training. The Wickersham Commission in 1931 reported that of the 383 cities surveyed only 20% conducted any formal training. Even so, historical reports indicate that law enforcement has experienced a continual increase in the amount of training as well as the number of those trained.

An untrained police officer is almost unheard of today. Most citizens place great value in the fact that police receive extensive training. Despite this, there still are untrained police officers placed directly on the street by some departments in the United States. This occurs when the state law requires that an officer must have a specified number of weeks of training within the first year of employment. For economic reasons (it is a waste of money to train him if he stays around for just a few months), the department allows him to work for a while so he can be observed. If he performs well for about nine months, the department then provides him with the required training. Chiefs and administrators of these departments should be concerned about negligent training and vicarious liability. If an officer acts inappropriately, and with training the officer would have performed more appropriately, the chief and city can be held liable.

Training is essential for all police officers. However, the methods of training, and the curricula, are dependent upon what administrators and those developing the training program see as the police officer's role.

Only by talking to fellow officers, being told what to do by the chief, or being told or shown by an "old-timer" would the recruit of the early 1900's to the 1930's learn what to do. As formal recruit training became established more formalized methods of instruction were developed.

In addition, police departments tried diligently to hire veteran soldiers and armed forces personnel. There existed state statues, such as West Virginia's, which in the 1920's enjoined the appointing authority to give preference "whenever possible to honorably discharged soldiers, sailors and marines." A Texas statute stated,

"Preference shall always be given to honorably discharged soldiers." At times, such acts caused the virtual exclusion of all except the members of the preferred class-military personnel.

With the many similarities of the police to the military; wearing uniforms, carrying weapons, being of service to one's country, and with the recruiting and preferential-treatment to military personnel, police training reflected both military format and values. In the 1910's and 20's because of the heavy demands upon their time, police in many states were required to live in police barracks. There were frequent transfers throughout the state. All these factors operated to make the service unsatisfactory to one who was bound by family ties. Many states during this time found it necessary to prohibit the enlistment of married men. This exteneded even further to the point that the state of Pennsylvania, in 1917, ordered that any member of the force entering into marriage should be honorably discharged.

Though it is logical and understandable how policing might start from a very strong military base with its command structure, this did create problems. When the Colorado Rangers were established in 1917, the individual chosen to head up this new police organization was a former National Guardsman. He was identified with the suppression of violence in an industrialized area which had had problems for many years. He saw to it that his organization was subjected to intensive military drill, but paid little attention to the training or the more subtle aspects of the line policeman's job. At times, it seemed as if they were operating under imposed martial law, and it is apparent that citizens' civil rights were often violated.

Although the military approach was the preferred approach in the '20's and '30's, it still had its detractors. These were people who felt that any method of training which focused on the powers and authority of police, virtually ignoring their responsibilities, might ultimately create an efficient but altogether ruthless machine.

After World War II, the country favored military veterans and personnel. They continued to receive extra bonuses or points when applying for police work and the training continued in the basic military fashion. Throughout the late '40's and early '50's, the police were still highly regarded. Police prestige and respect was at its peak after World War II and has continually declined since then. As a result of the turbulent '60's more and more focus was directed not only to what police were trained to do, but also how they were trained. At this time, people looked more closely at the military approaches to see if they were the most effective methods to instruct and train police officers.

The military approach is a stress approach and includes such things as: strict military procedures and atmosphere; a superior-inferior relationship between cadets and trainers, with minimal interaction or support; doubts openly expressed about cadets' abilities with frequent recognition of their inferior status; isolation and/or extra work for failure to comply with accepted standards; loud public verbal abuse and public discipline; punitive physical training for mistakes; and requirements that cadets speak in a loud, commanding voice and at times command and control the training class during marches, drills and in the classroom.

Proponents of this approach believe it is effective for a number of reasons: Subjecting a cadet to stress builds his tolerance for it and shows his superiors he can take it; the recruit learns both his endurance capabilities and his weaknesses; he learns he can extend his physical capabilities; it promotes individual organization; it strengthens cadets' abilities to operate effectively together in a crisis; it teaches officers to follow the chain of command and to follow orders without question.

One day the drill instructor asked Cadet Phil M. what

he thought of the police academy and Phil said, "Well, I think it's just great, and all the people are great!" The D.I. then asked, "What does your wife think of this training?" Phil replied, straight-faced, "Sir, my wife thinks that this training is absolutely ridiculous and she thinks that you, sir, are a jerk. But I happen not to agree with her, sir." The other cadets burst out in laughter. Almost every day after that, the D.I. asked Phil what his wife had to say, and Phil, using his wife's name, called the D.I. everything in the book, from a homosexual to a pompous ass, and it was a way for the whole class to let off a little steam. Of course, every time the cadets laughed, they had to do push-ups, but they figured it was worth it.

Detractors of this approach point out that most of the police officer's actions are performed independently and without supervision. Today's officers must exercise the broad powers conferred on them, using their own judgment and discretion.

Training officers are role models for the cadets. Thus, when cadets trained by the stress method become officers they tend to treat the citizens as they were treated by their training officers—namely, as inferiors. These officers might abuse citizens verbally and administer harsh public discipline. While stress training may teach the cadet how much he can take, it may also teach him how much he can give out.

There are certain times when strict military procedures are needed, such as riots, in dispersing large crowds and in other highly visible police group actions. However, in some situations other approaches to people may be more appropriate.

Proponents of stress training must also look to see if the stress inflicted on the cadet in a learning situation is similar to what he experiences while being an authority on the streets. Although it may be stressful to the cadet while in the academy, the question remains as to the relevance of this approach to the stress experienced by the line officer in his various daily functions.

The nonstress approach includes such things as a relaxed, supportive atmosphere; a regular and consistent schedule with no unpredictable changes; friendly and supportive relationships between cadets and training officers; private counseling about problems and mistakes; normal tones of voice used by everyone, and different leadership roles being performed by the training staff.

Proponents of this approach believe that there should be more of a college atmosphere in police training today, since most applicants have at least some college education. They believe the stress approach is becoming outmoded, since very small percentages of today's applicants have military backgrounds. They also feel that it is time for law-enforcement trainers to try new approaches, hopefully adapting to the cadet rather than forcing the cadet to mold to the traditional ways of the department. They tend to view stress-training methods as silly and childish games. Because statistics indicate that 70% to 90% of police work deals with police-citizen interaction, they feel a wider range of skills and responses can be learned by the cadet in this nonstress atmosphere.

Detractors of nonstress training programs see them leading to a deterioration of police effectiveness and integrity. They argue: Without discipline, standard procedures and similarity of response from all officers in given situations, there will be a breakdown of police teamwork and effective operation. The chain of command and the following of appropriate orders (rather than questioning them) are seen as appropriate in specific field situations. There is the fear that with nonstress training the ability to rely on one's fellow officers will deteriorate over time so that individual officers may end up doing it "their own way."

One critic of nonstress training ridiculed it in this

way: "For a while there at the academy they had people coming in with towels on their heads and turbans—they had pimply-faced Nazis and Muslims and Hare Krishnas and every kind of freak and dispossessed person you can imagine coming in to talk to the officers so that the officers would be familiar with their viewpoints, and it got to be a circus atmosphere. But a stress academy, on the other hand, leaves you for years with the thought that whatever you do is going to be closely scrutinized. When we went through they told us that we couldn't even talk while we were within ten miles of the academy. I car-pooled with another recruit, and I remember once on the way home he said something to me without even moving his lips, and then the very next morning one of the drill instructors came up to me and accused me of talking on the way home the day before, and I almost shit in my pants. And I'm sure that carried over, because after that every time I did anything in the field I'd think, 'Can this possibly come back and bite me in the ass?' Whereas the nonstress-trained cop seems to be much more casual and careless. He does whatever feels right at the time, without thinking about the consequences."

One's belief about police training, be it stress or non-stress, is dependent on how one sees the role of police. Should police officers be trained to react or to think? Do we want police to react by shooting when they hear a gun fired or do we want them to look for appropriate cover and then proceed in the pursuit of a suspect? When a police officer receives a man-with-a-gun call, do we want him to react by driving as fast as he can to the location and pulling up in front of the suspect, or do we want him to go at a slower pace and consider various alternatives and protective cover while driving to the location? Should the primary emphasis be for cadets to have one appropriate response or a variety of responses, depending on the situation, before taking action?

The type of community, the department organization and the defined role of the officer (enforcement or service orientation) will determine the type of training new officers receive. The needs of the small rural community where everyone knows each other will be different from the needs of the urban centers with their large populations and diverse ethnic makeups and economic stratas. There is more crime in large cities. The larger and more diverse the population of our large metropolitan areas, the larger the variety of actions the officer may be expected to perform.

The people who make the decisions in a community determine to a large extent the role that police play. This obviously effects the type of training they receive. In performing a variety of tasks—i.e., settling family disputes, notifying people of relative's deaths, catching suspects, calming emotionally distraught victims, delivering babies—plus knowing the legal requirements of every situation, the police have been looked on at various times as doctors, lawyers, medics, psychologists and social workers.

The variety of situations and tasks an officer may be involved in, and hopefully prepared for over the length of his career, are almost too numerous to list. While a police officer may be expected to perform many professional duties in service of his community, the time he is currently given to master these skills ranges from a few short weeks to an upper limit of about six months. The applicant is expected to learn all of the laws relative to his enforcement and service-oriented duties in less than half a year. Doctors, lawyers and other professionals are given as much as eight years of specialized training. We expect the police to give a myriad of professional services with little more training than is given truck drivers, plumbers, electricians or carpenters.

Often, academies must push very hard to see that the cadets receive all the training mandated by law, to say nothing about other special areas of instruction. These special areas are often the more complicated areas of the job, such as dealing effectively with people, stress management, and so on.

A typical curriculum today includes laws related to: alcohol and beverage control, arson and explosives, burglary, trespassing, robbery, the Constitution, dangerous-weapon control, disorderly conduct and crimes against the public peace, laws of arrest, juvenile laws and procedures, use of force and firearms, civil disputes, miscellaneous crimes, rules of evidence, search and seizure, theft and violent crimes. Other things taught are a history of law enforcement and the department's organization, knowledge of the broader justice system, prisoner rights and responsibilities, and the interrelationship of various law enforcement agencies.

Officers must know about the collection, identification and preservation of evidence; courtroom demeanor and testimony; field show-ups; fingerprinting; interview and interrogation techniques; handling of missing persons; preliminary investigations and countless other procedures.

Firearms training is another vital area, including such things as combat and night shooting; using the firing range; special combat training; tear gas training, and so on.

In relationship to line operations, officers are expected to learn how to approach and contact suspects or suspicious persons; handle barricaded suspects and hostage situations; to book and release both adults and juveniles; to run breath tests for drunk drivers; to know vehicle codes, issue citations and conduct traffic examinations; to control and search for contraband; to handcuff and transport prisoners; to handle crimes in progress such as burglary and robbery; to master crowd and riot control; to handle disasters and other unusual occurrences; to know emergency plans, first aid, childbirth and CPR. The recruit is taught how to deal with disturbances, injured and rabid animals, major traffic offenses, mentally ill people, news-media relations, off and on-duty officer survival, officer shootings, patrol and observation, prowler calls, pull-over and approach procedures, radio procedures, vehicle searches, sniper-ambush techniques, and to direct traffic. In addition, recruits need a good percentage of time for physical conditioning and training, as well as firearms training and various role-playing exercises.

It is amazing that as much knowledge is imparted in the relatively brief training period, and understandable why information related to interpersonal relationships and communication skills may be at a minimal level if even existent.

Some people believe that the training should be reflective of the knowledge and skills the officer needs on the streets. A close examination of police work reveals that the majority of activity involves social interaction with people, whether it be pushing a car off to the side of the road, giving a ticket or a warning, or helping someone cross the street. These contacts require sensitivity and the ability to communicate with other people. This behavior, however, is almost at the polar extreme of the way police work is presented in the media as well as in war stories in locker rooms and even at the training academy.

Often what is presented are the criminal aspects of the job—arresting felons, putting people in jail, using firearms, and so on. Because these are threatening and dangerous assignments, police receive an enormous amount of training in this area. Much time in training academies is spent on laws of arrest, individual rights, firearms training, pull-over and approach, etc., and often a resultant lack of training in the area where police function the great majority of the time: effectively communicating with citizens.

Communication is a recognized factor in law enforcement, and yet it is often given a low priority because it is assumed that everyone is automatically able to communicate, without recognizing communication as a very involved and difficult process.

By inappropriate language, behavior and physical presence—body language—police officers can inadvertently heighten anxiety in a situation or take a situation that is hostile and make it even more so. Conversely, if they are effective communicators, they can take an emotional situation and lower the anxiety and nervousness not only for themselves but for others. Two examples of officers heightening anxiety through poor communication, are related by Patrolman Curtis Mc.:

> "We had a lady that came into the station one night— her clothing was disheveled and she had a large swelling over one eye, as if she'd been beaten up. The desk officer asked her, 'What's the problem here?,' and she said, 'I was raped.' He inquired, 'Where?,' and she looked at him, perplexed, and said, 'Well ... in my pussy!' So the officer laughed—he couldn't help it—but that just caused the poor lady to break down crying. She became hysterical, and it turned out to be a big issue that shouldn't have happened at all.
>
> "Another situation we had. this guy approached a bunch of officers on the street and he was real upset. He wasn't mad at the police—just at life in general—and he was screaming and yelling and everybody was trying to get him to quiet down. Well, it was raining at the time, and one of the officers had glasses on, and they were getting all wet, so the officer took them off. Well, as soon as he did this the man stepped back and assumed a combative stance. Because he figured, when a guy takes off his glasses he's getting ready to fight. And the whole situation got farther out of hand than it should have."

The complex nature of communication and the extent to which it involves self-awareness has long been recognized in other fields. Psychologists, psychiatrists, social workers and others in the helping professions spend years at school trying to understand the most effective methods of communication and to increase their understanding of themselves and the people they will be dealing with. Police get very little training in this area.

When people hear the term communication, they often identify it exclusively with talking. Yet verbal communication is only a small part of the communication process. Much of our communication is a result of the way we present ourselves—our self-image, body language, facial expressions and attitudes. A significant determinant in communication is our attitudes and/or prejudices, which can be so deeply seated that we're unaware of them.

For instance, what officers believe about violence affects how they see the citizens or criminals they deal with in the street and how they approach them. If they see them as naturally bad, incompetent or worthless, assuming that nothing can be done because by nature they are the way they are, they will approach people in a certain way. Similarly, if they believe people are the way they are as a result of their education or their experience, they may try to alter the way people look at things through communication and interaction. It appears that if police officers really believe that people are bad by nature, the only alternative left to them is to weed the bad out of society by incarceration. On the other hand, if they believe that people are the way they are as a result of their upbringing, they can attempt to influence the individual by trying to understand and work with him so that he may act more appropriately in the future. The second position involves communication, understanding of self and others. The first position excludes communication. Officer Bill A. relates this story:

> "When I was working the Chinatown district my partner Jim introduced me to the strangest couple I'd ever known. Bongo was a tall skinny black man who played the bongo drums so well that he could have been a professional musician, and he also walked around

with a spider monkey on his shoulder. His old lady, Pat was a white girl who'd run away from home when she was 15 and had been introduced to both prositution and hard drugs by Bongo. At first I couldn't understand how my partner could be so friendly with this pimp and his hooker. But then I realized that everyone liked this couple, and after a while I got to like them, too. Bongo turned out to be a very intelligent and well-read person— quite shy, actually. In fact, he was a real gentleman, if you can call a pimp that, and Pat was a real nice young lady. She and Bongo never stole from anyone, never sold drugs. They did just enough hustling to support themselves and to live in a small hotel room with that monkey.

"We knew Bongo and Pat for three years, and then one day Bongo died of a heroin overdose. The monkey died too, but no autopsy was done to see if he had o.d.'d, too. Anyway, Pat was a total wreck for weeks. My partner Jim and I took up a small collection to pay her rent for two months, and everybody—cops and street people alike—told her to go back to Idaho where she'd come from and start a new life. Instead, she hooked herself up with a new pimp and went back to hustling. But this pimp was a different sort than Bongo, and after a couple of months she was beaten up, half-starved, a real mess.

"Finally my partner picked her up one night and took her to the city jail. Jim told her he wanted to ask her some questions about Bongo's death, but instead he threw her into the holding tank with five older and very hardened prostitutes. Jim had worked out a deal with the vice sergeant and five hookers, and the deal went like this: If the hookers could scare Pat into giving up prostitution and going home to Idaho, then the charges against them would be dropped.

"Well, it worked. Two days later we gave Pat a ride to the bus station, bought a ticket for her with some money that we'd collected in the neighborhood, and said goodbye. Jim even got a little choked up when he put her on the bus, and he kissed her on the forehead. When we got back to our patrol car he said: 'I had to get that little bitch out of town or I'd have wound up marrying her myself, just to get her off the street.'

"Jim was the kind of cop who could communicate with anyone."

On a supervisory assignment, a professor had an experience observing a student psychologist counsel his client. At the conclusion of the counseling session, the student psychologist was asked his view of the session. His response was, "I knew in the first ten seconds that my client had nothing going for him." If in the first ten seconds the student knew this, then the way the client was approached and subsequently treated would be a result of this impression. The client happened to be living in a board-and-care home and receiving aid to the totally disabled. If this student worked from the assumption that all humans are worthwhile and have meaning in their existence, the outcome of that session may have been much different.

A different professor briefed a group of student psychologists on a particular family situation. The information given was that there were four children living with their grandmother; two of the children were 13 and 11 year-old girls. Their concern was mounting because their father was to be released from jail shortly. The reason for the concern was that the father had sexually molested the 13-year-old and both she and her younger sister were apprehensive about the father's return to the home. In addition to the two sisters, the grandmother was worried as well. The student psychologists were told that they would be seeing the family the following week. The only information given the students was the above explanation. However, one student psychologist heard in the illustration that the family was of a particular race when there had been no mention of race. The student who "heard" the race of the family may have a tendency to deal with or approach this racial group differently than he would other races, as he appears to have certain biases or attitudes about the way certain ethnic groups live.

Two girls friends recently saw each other and began talking about their lives. Because they had not seen each other for a while, one of the friends invited the other over for dinner, particularly after hearing that she had a new boyfriend. The girl friend accepted the invitation, explaining that her boyfriend would probably be very interested in joining the party. The person issuing the invitation then asked what the boyfriend did. On hearing that he was a police officer, she hastily explained, "I'm terribly sorry, but we do not allow those people in our house." Another clear indication of certain attitudes, values and biases about a different segment of society.

These illustrations point to the fact that all of us have biases, attitudes and prejudices which effect how we see things and how we interact with others. Police officers' must know their attitudes about others so that they can avoid acting inappropriately in the field. Officers should also have an understanding of how they come across to others so that they can be effective communicators. Besides understanding themselves they must also understand the variety of people they may come in contact within their day-to-day work in the community.

Many studies indicate that various theoretical approaches used by people considered experts in communication or human interaction are not nearly as important as how they actually interact with the clients that seek their assistance.

In these studies, members of the helping professions who had the most success with their clients were people who communicated:

Respect—Recognizing human beings as worthwhile and capable of determining their own destiny.
Emphatic Understanding—The ability to genuinely feel

and understand how people become involved in various situations.

Genuineness—Being honest and sincere with others, sharing reactions, beliefs and values.

Self-Disclosure—The ability to share experiences with the client which identify the helper as having similar struggles and problems.

One study showed that people who had professional degrees scored lower than lay people with no professional training. Thus it appears that when members of the helping professions receive education and enter authority positions they can forget some essentials of human interaction. They may not feel it is appropriate in their professional role to relate with others in such ways.

What is true for members of the helping professions such as psychology would also be true for police, since much of what they do is "helping." Anyone involved in communicating with other people knows that if the relationship goes well, invariably it is a result of both people. Like others, the police have an effect on how successful or worthwhile the relationship is between themselves and the people they interact with: family, supervisors, citizens and suspects. They have the ability to raise anxiety, to heighten emotions, to add fuel to the fire, as well as the ability to defuse hostile situations and guide them to a successful outcome. How law-enforcement officers communicate and relate with others has long-lasting effects, not only on their individual interaction but also on the public's long-range view of police.

Given the fact that much communication is nonverbal and a result of other aspects of behavior, paying attention to the difference between CONTENT—what is talked about—and PROCESS—what is going on—can be helpful. Often people talk a lot and do very little. There is a tremendous difference between a citizen making boisterous complaints or threats to the police (the content of what he is talking about) and becoming violent or aggressive.

Often we react to words rather than to what is happening. Paying attention to behavior is as important as listening to what is being said.

Imagine two officers encountering a group of juveniles or a family dispute where the leader or husband becomes boisterous and belligerent, threatens the officers, and makes assaultive statements. The content in this situation is assaultive and threatening in nature; however, the process is one of saving face. Being attuned to these differences, and providing a chance for the individual to save face, could be useful. An officer who responds immediately to the content rather than observing the process could easily escalate the situation into a physical altercation rather than a verbal discharge. Being called a "pig" is very different from being treated like one.

In recent years there has been a shift of emphasis in the expectations of police. Until recently, the emphasis has been on the arrest and prosecution of criminals—the hook-and-book approach. The emphasis on social interaction—calming potentially explosive situations, getting suspects arrested and to jail with as little hassle as possible is called the walk-and-talk approach. Once an aggressive action has been taken by the police officer there is no turning back. Once it is decided to assault a location or arrest an individual, the officer must proceed. However, there are many options available before the assault or arrest is made. These can entail talking with the suspect, trying to understand him, and seeing if there are alternative methods of having him arrested or going to jail.

This is exemplified in hostage situations when, once a location has been secured, the officer's job is to apprehend the perpetrators. The perpetrators can be caught if law enforcement attacks or takes other types of offensive action. However, if the officers wait and talk to the suspects, apprehension may occur without any aggressive action, avoiding harm to suspects, hostages and officers as well as damage to buildings.

Those who believe the challenge of police work lies in using the brain rather than brawn can alleviate altercations and physical encounters. It is relatively easy for anyone with a little bit of muscle and proper authority to hook-and-book people and cart them off to jail. Walking and talking takes more talent, is more difficult, may take a little more time, and can be more rewarding.

What to train police officers is a complicated issue involving the department, the officers and the community. To access the effects of training, we could ask, "is the police officer currently successful in the streets in the eyes of both the department and the public?" If the answer is yes, then the department may have a successful training program. But if the answer is no, some changes may need to be made so that police officers have a chance for a successful career and citizens have trust in their police.

Military or stress training teaches the "best" methods of accomplishing various tasks. Nonmilitary or nonstress training provides more varied approaches. Each department must decide which approach to use.

With stress training, classroom instruction usually consists of a straight lecture program, a very detailed orderly predetermined approach. Somehow, there is a tendency to highlight the dramatic emphasizing those stories that add to one's macho view of self. And cops, being action-oriented people, are interested in the more dangerous and often traumatic aspects of life; they like to listen to "war stories."

This is reflected by the strong emphasis on hostage-negotiation training during the late 70's. The course was exciting, the lecturers were good and the material had suspense and drama. Even if other subjects were more important to the officer's safety, hostage-negotiation training was chosen because of its dramatic nature and life-saving features.

So it is possible in academy training to emphasize the dramatic, the violent and shocking and, as a result, minimize interpersonal skills and abilities required to work effectively with people on the street.

More than just straight academic information is imparted, of course. The young cadet who is idealistic and at times naive is influenced in numerous ways. In any type of intense training like this, many values and attitudes are gained though not expressly taught.

Consider the patrolman who is afraid to wear his uniform to his son's kindergarten class because he was told only to wear his uniform at work. Or the officers who drive home a different way every night, sit facing the door at restaurants, and never let their uniforms be seen hanging in the car.

One time while I was giving a talk on social aspects of police work at a police academy, a cadet interjected, "What you are saying up there is all well and good, but here we are trained that once we get in that black-and-white car everyone who isn't in a black-and-white is our enemy." Or, consider the following statement of the wife of a recent cadet: "Those cadets sure change a lot when they go through the academy. He's only been there six weeks and I'm trying to find a way to let him know that the kids and I are not 'assholes' or 'pieces of shit!'"

Training programs must be examined regularly to make sure they're having the intended impact—both explicit and implied—on the developing attitudes, values and behaviors of new officers.

Take an officer who is responding to a family-disturbance call. Besides the basic information he's been given, he is also responding with his own perceptual set, which includes his attitudes, values, mood, prior training, etc. This perceptual set is much like a filter. How the officer responds to the call will depend on what he sees through his filter. If, for example, the call is in a certain ethnic neighborhood, one that involves his prejudices his response might include a large amount of fear, anger, stress, etc. Whether he will overreact to a family-disturbance call and have complaints filed against him, or underreact and perhaps put his life in danger, depends both on the information given and his filtering process.

One officer, Fred C., was asked to handle a family disturbance call and, after having talked to both the husband and wife, was able to leave feeling relaxed about the situation. However, he was called back a second time. He didn't use precautionary techniques and instead walked straight to the door, knocked, identified himself—and then was shot and killed. Who is to say how this officer's filter worked that day—his moods, values and prior training. These may all have been part of the reason for his inappropriate actions.

The training academy's job is to make officers aware of their filtering process. It is a process which, when used properly, can help an officer add humanness to a tragic situation, or, if used inappropriately, can add to tragedy.

Historically, police came from the military and, when training new recruits, trained them in a traditional military manner. The cadets of the 80's are individuals who, for the most part, have not had military experience, but instead have attended some college, with many obtaining degrees. Some older training instructors are even referred to as "D.I.'s"—drill instructors. Their teaching approaches may be very appropriate for high-school graduates, but may not be sufficient to teach people who have been instructed with a variety of methods.

Initially, everyone wants to impress one another. The cadets want to learn and the instructors want to train. Observing cadets on their first day in the academy, words like fear, excitement, anxiety and challenge come to mind. The emotions are mixed and highly charged. The new cadets have been through the often-times long application process and now are ready to begin their careers. This is a job they hope to have for at least 20 years, so they are impeccably dressed, their hair recently cut, their shoes polished to a shine. They are anxious to make a good impression on the academy staff. The academy training staffers are also impeccably dressed, in uniform, their hair perfectly cut and trimmed and their shoes shined. It is important to them that they be model officers for the new cadets they are about to train. Both the cadets and training staff want to impress one another.

As time passes, the recruits become aware of different aspects of the training. They notice mottos on the wall such as, "the more you sweat here, the less you'll bleed in the streets," or bulletin boards that dramatically display the headlines of accounts of officers killed by their lack of caution or not following accepted law-enforcement methods. Ideas and ways for officers to survive are also displayed. This is all compounded by the rigorous academic requirements. The cadets begin to see certain aspects of the law-enforcement profession they may not have considered. With each day's progress, they begin settling in and at times may experience disillusionment.

At this point, there is probably a direct relationship between the superficiality of their preconception of the job and the extent to which they develop a healthy attitude about the profession. The more idealistic their perception of police work was originally the rougher the first weeks in the academy will be.

As days move into weeks, the cadets who remain feel that they're on firmer ground. Although perhaps still timid, they are glad that they have chosen law enforcement as a career. Those applicants who believe their career choice is wrong or who are unable to meet the stringent demands of the academy usually leave in the first few weeks. In fact, in large metropolitan areas, approximately 15% to 25% leave within the first six weeks and, after that, between 5% and 10% do not finish the academy.

Meanwhile, the training staff is scrupulously watching the new charges for any indications that they might not have the necessary physical condition, motivation or emotional stability to handle the job. They tend to be aloof with the cadets, since they want to be as objective as possible during their initial evaluations.

The trainers have to be exceptional people. Not only do they have to be streetwise and willing to share their practical experiences, they also have to be academically oriented, possessing knowledge of training approaches and programs in a wide variety of subjects. Additionally, the officers must push for new ideas and be open to new approaches in training, even from those they may be training. The trainer has to be a combination of educator, advisor and confidant. These roles may at times be in conflict, thus it takes a very capable person to handle them.

The exact training-academy curriculum is changing along with society and the people who make up the law-enforcement profession. As society changes and there are questions about what is right and wrong, the group that is most affected by this confusion is the police. Society changes faster than the laws do, and the well-trained officer is caught in the middle. He enforces the too-slowly-changing laws as much as he tries to adapt to the too-quickly-changing society. Most of the officer's actions are open to public scrutiny, and, no matter which position he takes, he is criticized by either the people who think all laws should be strictly enforced or those who think laws should be applied more leniently. The pace of change in American society over the past 25 years has been extremely rapid, socially, economically and politically. On the cutting edge of his change stands law enforcement, attempting to preserve order and to be neutral between the competing forces.

In a study of members of the American Society for Training and Development almost 60% of the trainers indicated that "increased technical awareness" and "increased knowledge of the behavioral sciences" were emerging as important requirements for the various occupations in which they train. This finding seems especially true for law enforcement.

The spouse and children must be considered in any training program. It is easy to see that training is an extremely intense time for the cadet. So, too, is it for the spouse. For many, getting through the academy is very much a joint process. It is a husband-and-wife team effort, and consequently they view law enforcement as their career. In fact, the spouse must sacrifice and bend as much as the officer. It is important that the spouse be involved in the training process because, the more one spouse changes in comparison to the other, the higher the chance for marital discord. I believe that a cadet's chances of completing the academy could be determined if we could measure the spouse's attitude, supportiveness and willingness to learn and understand law enforcement.

At the graduation ceremonies, the group that receives the most applause is the cadets; secondly, it's the training staff; and, many times, the spouses are not even mentioned. If spouses were mentioned they would receive almost as much applause as the cadets. At least they should. Because in most cases officers cannot complete the academy without the support received from the spouse, family or friends.

Throughout training the cadets continue to change, as do the spouses and training staff. Camaraderie continues to build as the cadets and training officers work hard to be the best class ever. Fellow cadets having difficulty in particular areas are helped by other cadets. The push toward deep and solid relationships is cemented in the sharing of similar trials and tribulations. The closeness of this bond is evidenced by the fact that relationships developed in academy training often continue throughout an officer's career. In agencies that utilize spouses-training programs, similar camaraderie develops.

Since the pressures on law-enforcement personnel and thus on their spouses cannot be eliminated, it is valuable to consider ways in which departments can aid in making the situation more productive. Growing awareness of the need for departmental support has led to the development of special programs in several departments throughout the country.

The Spouses Training Program developed by the Los Angeles County Sheriff's Department, outlined in Figure 1, consists of eight classes which meet once a week. The spouses are given an overall look at the programs within the department and the duties their law-enforcement spouses will be performing. Such a program increases understanding and awareness for the spouses. Further, it provides actual participation in some of the activities that their officer spouses will be performing throughout their careers in law enforcement. The program interjects a personal touch as it gives spouses interaction with the sheriff, undersheriff and other top administrators, who have consistently made themselves available for classes.

An important aspect is the honest, open exchange between the instructors and the participants. There is no attempt to glorify the job; the realities, problems and concerns are all open for discussion and suggestions.

All spouses of new cadets entering the academy and any spouses who married officers of the department during the current year are invited to attend. The program is held in the training academy facilities, which lets the spouses get a feel for the training experience as well as meeting the instructors who train their husbands or wives.

Statistically, over 98% of the cadets who had spouses participating in this corollary program graduated from the academy. Out of the 1,000-plus ratings from student spouses, the program was evaluated as: Excellent 61%, Very Good 33%, Good 5%, Fair 0%, Poor 0%.

While all segments of the program were seen as valuable, several significant overall factors seen by the spouses as important were: feeling that the department

Figure 1

SESSION	TOPICS COVERED	LECTURERS
Session 1	Orientation to Sheriff's Department Organizational Structure and Functions Sheriff's Department Training Procedures	Sheriff or Undersheriff Captain of Training Academy Department Psychologist Academy Staff
Session 2	Various Functions within Department Divisions/ Special Department Programs/Tour of Custody Division	Chief of Custody Division
Session 3	Law Enforcement's Role in the Criminal Justice System	Sergeant from Training Academy
Session 4	Marital and Occupational Pressures/Resources Available to Department Employees and Spouses	Department Psychologist Spouses of Deputies for over 5 years
Session 5	Investigative Techniques/ Gathering of Evidence/ Ballistics: Sheriff's Comprehensive Rape Program: Methods of Self-Defense	Criminalist Female Deputy from Training Academy
Session 6	Personal and Home Firearm Safety Use of the Firing Range	Range Staff
Session 7	Patrol Ride-Along	Patrol Deputies
Session 8	Review, Summary and Graduation	Assistant Sheriffs Captain of Training Academy Department Psychologist

values the spouse as an important contribution; allaying the fears and apprehension the spouses hold about firearms by learning safety techniques and actually firing a gun; and the opportunity to experience patrol in realistic situations as opposed to what is generally portrayed on television and in the movies.

Following are some written responses from individual spouses who have attended the program:

"It helped me realize that you are not the only one having problems. It rather relieved the tension that had been building up inside. It was nice to air out problems that others had in common with you."

"Lessened the fear I have for this type of law enforcement work. The more you know about something, the less you usually will fear it."

"The friendships that developed among the spouses were really great. It helped to make the spouses more enthusiastic toward their husbands' work, which, in turn makes it easier to understand problems they might have involved with their work. Also, I know that I now don't feel so 'apart' or 'distant' from my spouse's work experience."

"They made me feel that I'm not just a wife, but am important to the department because of my husband. If his home life is happy, he will be a better deputy. It's hard to say how much I appreciate all you've done; this class will always be a pleasant experience."

"These classes are so informative, and to me it took a lot of pressures off of us. I felt I was working along with my husband. I was pleased and don't have to lose touch with what my husband is doing."

"The department seems much less impersonal and, by this program's very existence, seems to care much more about spouses and family than I ever thought they did."

"I feel really good about my husband's job now. Being involved in this class has brought my husband and I closer together. I feel I can communicate better with him on his job. Looked forward to coming every week."

This favorable response is in line with the reported responses of agencies that have established spouse programs in other parts of the country.

In addition to all the training that is now provided for law-enforcement officers, other approaches—such as awareness and stress-reduction techniques, crisis-intervention techniques, and police/citizen interaction —have proven helpful to individual officers.

Training should be given to an officer every time he is assigned to a different aspect of the job, whether it be from forgery to robbery, from patrol to homicide, or being made a supervisor. In addition, the demands and functions of the job will constantly change to meet the challenges of a changing society. There should be advanced-officer training periodically to update officers on various changes and new procedures developed.

The final determiner of how much and which type of training the police will receive is the taxpayer—in short, or by the dollars available.

Training needs should be properly identified at both operational and supervisory levels. If training needs are assessed correctly, the training selected will meet department needs while at the same time fulfilling societal needs.

It's helpful to remember that most cadets will make it. Having a positive attitude, asking questions and remembering that they are part of a select group and wouldn't be there unless their skills and strengths were recognized can help cadets through what may seem like a long and tedious training period. Encouraging spouses to attend spouses' classes, if offered, will help communication and help them understand the responsibilities of an officer's job.

The training academy staff need to: be open to learn from others, even cadets; spend time "on the street"; attend classes, seminars, or talk with other teaching professionals; learn as much about teaching, its methods and techniques as possible; include the cadets' spouses in the program; talk about the importance of communicating with spouses; periodically examine the program; make sure the academy is teaching for today's cadets and an ever changing society; include evaluations of the program, and be open to hearing how it might be improved.

Because of training's importance, the department needs to: be committed to the training program and be willing to support it financially and emotionally; choose the training staff carefully; have executives participate in the training program; encourage on-going training throughout the officers' careers in the form of seminars, workshops, conferences, etc., and encourage the training staff to be avid learners.

REFERENCES

Bard, M. "Role of Law Enforcement in the Helping System." In Monahan, (Ed.), *Community Mental Health and the Criminal Justice System.* Elmsford, New York: Pergamon Press, Inc., 1976.

Carkhuff, R. R. and Berenson, B.G. *Beyond Counseling and Therapy.* New York: Holt, Rinehart and Winston, Inc., 1967.

Carkhuff, R. R. *Helping and Human Relations: A Primer for Lay and Professional Helpers, Vol. II.* New York: Holt, Rinehart and Winston, 1969.

Carkhuff, R. R. *The Development of Human Resources.* New York: Holt, Rinehart and Winston, 1971.

Carkhuff, R. R. *The Art of Helping.* Amherst, Mass.: Human Resources Development Press, 1973.

Coughlin, A., Hern, S. and Ard, J. *You Know You're a Peace Officer's Wife When.* Peace Officer's Wives Club Affiliated of California, 1978.

Earle, H. H. *Police Recruit Training: Stress Versus Non-Stress; A Revolution in Law Enforcement Career Programs.* Springfield, Illinois. Charles C. Thomas, 1972.

Elliot, J. F. *The New Police.* Springfield, Illinois: Charles C. Thomas, 1977.

Flaherty, J. J. *Inside the F.B.I.,* Philadelphia, J. B. Lippincott Co., 1943.

Harris, R. N. *Police Academy: An Inside View.* New York: John Wiley and Sons, 1973.

Kinton, J., ed. *Police Roles in the Seventies.* Ann Arbor, Michigan: Edwards Brothers, 1975.

Muir, W. K., Jr. *Police: Street-Corner Politicians.* Chicago: University of Chicago Press, 1977.

Stratton, J. G. "The Law Enforcement Family: Program for Spouses" *FBI Law Enforcement Bulletin,* 45(3), 1976.

Truax, C. and Carkhuff, R. *Toward Effective Counseling and Psychotherapy,* Chicago: Aldine, 1967.

Walsh, J. L. "Career Styles and Police Behavior." In Bagley, D. H. (ed) *Police and Society,* Beverly Hills: Sage Publications, 1977.

4

ON THE STREETS— THE INITIAL YEARS

Idealism, eagerness and naivete are words that might be used to describe rookie cops. They know they are the cream of the crop. They've passed all the tests and are now ready to face the real world. Under their outward confidence may be all types of fear, but rarely will this show. In fact, they have learned well from the academy staff and know that it's important to keep everything under control—which means keeping all emotions hidden.

The spouses and families are glad that the strenuous demands of the academy are over. They're proud of their officers and glad that now their lives can return to "normal." Typically, they expect an adjustment period but are sure that soon they'll have their mates back home regularly. It seems impossible to them that any job could be more difficult than getting through the academy.

The rookies enter a world which will begin to shape their lives. The changes that will happen begin slowly but in most cases are everlasting. How they understand and handle these changes may be the key to whether they are successful cops or not.

This chapter could be termed "The Rude Awakening," "The Formative Years," "From Idealism to Cynicism to Equilibrium," or maybe even more appropriately, "Hitting the Streets and Bouncing Back." In other words, the young cadets now encounter the realities of the profession. Confronted with so many different destructive human activities, often encountering hostility on the part of the public, and physically strained by the long hours and emotional stress, the fledgling police officers may begin to form an invisible shield. This they use with increasing skill to protect themselves from undue battering, both emotional and physical.

There are many officers who emerge at the end of their initial years with the necessary critical objectivity to handle their job with self-assurance and refined judgment. The following years they experience the satisfaction and pride of achievement and, for the most part, cope well with the inevitable difficulties and frustration. The job, to them, is a learning experience and one they enjoy.

But for some officers the impact of the job has negative effects, both personally and professionally. The job is extremely demanding, both physically and emotionally, requiring much more of an individual than could possibly be anticipated. Perhaps this is the first step to understanding the changes that young officers go through.

Let's look at these changes as a natural progression, and then see how these changes can be used to an officer's advantage.

As discussed, the initial training program primarily addresses the area of law and law-enforcement techniques, with necessarily less emphasis in the behavioral sciences. The training is presented with little ambiguity and almost no room for questioning. In each situation presented there is a right and a wrong way to do things, with very little middle ground. The academy staff assures the cadets that if they work hard during their training period they will be able to handle anything that they meet in the streets. After all, they've been there, they should know!

Upon completion of the academy, cadets are highly charged to go out and be the perfect cops. After their assignment to their field training officer, invariably the first words addressed to them by the officer are, "Now that you're through with the academy, forget everything you learned. I'll show you how to really do the job." For, indeed, the field training officer is aware of the bookishness of the academy and would like to speed the process of bridging the gap between what the rookie hasn't learned and what he'll need to know. The officer may even question the training academy's staff and their street knowledge. Often the field training officer feels that the academy staff doesn't know what it's like to be on the streets anymore. The field training officer may have an entirely different approach to the job.

"Before we leave the parking lot, there's a couple of things I want to talk to you about. This was always Officer Jack W's opening lecture when he was assigned Field Training Officer (FTO) Duty with a recruit fresh from the academy.

"I see you did pretty good in the academy. You'll do pretty good in the street too if you try. You're going to make mistakes, all rookies do; in fact all cops do once in a while. Just make sure the mistakes you make won't be serious enough to cause somebody to get hurt or killed. I'm real easy to get along with, and I'll tolerate a lot of mistakes. But the mistakes that have to do with guns I won't tolerate. Whether it's checking the shotgun, which I want you to do now, and every shift we work, or whether it's in a situation where we might have to use weapons. I want you to remember everything you were taught about handling weapons. There's no room for mistakes with guns.

"A lot of field training officers will tell you to forget everything you learned in the academy and get used to the way the real world is because the people in the academy haven't been working on the streets for quite a while. But some FTO's will tell you it is safer to stick strictly by the book because it is safer that way. I think both sides have a good argument and I am in the middle of the road about your training. You need the information and knowledge you got from the academy but you will need a lot of street experience before you can apply what you have learned to real situations. The real key is common sense and good judgment.

"That's hard to teach, but experience is the best teacher. Now, I could lecture you for hours about using common sense, then when something comes down where you have to react without time to think it over, all that information goes out the window and you have to rely on your instincts and judgments. During training, I want you to learn what I think is best because I want you to live and enjoy this crazy and exciting job."

However, young officers equipped with an idealistic image of police work, and wanting to be accepted, may hurriedly model themselves too closely to their field training officer, and may indeed have to in order to be accepted. They may adapt manners, attitudes and approaches which may well be legitimate for their senior but are not completely appropriate for their own personality. The more unconsciously this occurs without reflection or self-examination, the more likely they are to acquire habits which do not bring out the best in them. But it's important for young officers to be accepted. As one young officer wondered, "Will we ever be friends?" He feels like an outsider and must find ways to enter what he perceives as the elite circle of seasoned cops. One way to do this is to actually become one of them by imitating as closely as possible their ways of thinking and handling the job.

If the trainee did not have contact with anyone actually involved in law enforcement as he grew up, his most vivid impressions were most likely obtained from the mass-media portrayal of the police. This is also true for many of the civilians he will subsequently be policing. Many authorities believe that the media presentations may well shape the officer's image of himself even after he is on the job. He comes to feel that he should be as invincible or tough as any cop portrayed on the tube.

The No. 1 television show in the country in the late 1970's, for example, was a dramatic series entitled "SWAT." This show presented a special police unit presumably performing its routine duties. In any given episode these officers would handle three or four major assignments that may never be required of actual SWAT officers, or perhaps might occur only once or twice in their entire career. In addition, numerous people were killed and/or injured by this special unit. Americans watched this show and many believed it represented the true picture of a SWAT team at work. When the public saw actual SWAT teams appear in their communities they would tend to get anxious and nervous. This reaction is tragic when one considers that statistics do not at all concur with what is portrayed on television. For instance, over the last 12 years members of the Special Weapons Team (SWAT team) have fired rounds less than once in every hundred call-outs in the most dangerous and difficult assignments.

News reports of real police-citizen encounters only highlight the most dramatic aspects and present the resolution. In one case a barricaded suspect fired repeated shots into the streets, then retreated behind drawn blinds and closed doors. A lengthy period of silence followed and, after much consideration officers concluded that the man might have fallen asleep. With great caution, Special Weapons Team members approached the house and, sure enough, found the man sleeping. The headlines the following day simply reported, "Thirty deputies required to get sleeping man out of the house." Neither the danger to deputies and the community, nor the planning and concern involved in bringing the man safely out of the house, were explored.

So the media presents a very biased picture of police work. But for some young officers this was the only picture they had until they reached the academy. One of the first things the cadets learned in the academy was that it was important to keep their feelings out of the way. But they might not have known the distinction between *acknowledging* their feelings, particularly negative feelings such as fear, anxiety or doubt, and *denying* them. And now, when they enter the streets, not only do their field training officers again repeat this warning, but they model it for the young officers. The rookies, knowing their field training officer is considered a good cop, models his behavior.

The young officers have had minimal, if any, psychological preparation for the traumatic situations they will encounter. They have had no training to cope with the considerable emotional drain involved. They may not even be able to acknowledge it, thinking something may be wrong with them personally if some aspect of the work bothers them. After all, their field training officer tells them, "It's no big deal—it's all part of the job." For cops who are trained to believe that they can handle any emotional reaction to some incident on the streets any thing may be seen as a weakness. Instead of finding ways to deal with it, they may ignore it until it reaches crisis proportions.

Officer Frank D. entered the law-enforcement profession after having spent ten years as a salesman in a local department store. He was intrigued by the anticipated action and excitement and felt that this was a career that would challenge him. His family supported his decision to enter law enforcement because they saw it as an opportunity for him to do something he really enjoyed. The training staff viewed Frank as a caring man whose maturity was sorely needed on the streets. After about two years on the job, Frank became overwhelmed with feelings of anger, fear and depression. He attributed these feelings to the amount of violence he was now seeing in the world. Frank felt totally immersed in it through his job, the radio, the television, and the newspaper he read in the evening. He became fearful for his family and insisted they take *numerous precautionary measures which they considered unnecessary.* He became concerned about his wife driving at night. He asked her to call him at work when she left, and then again when she reached her destination. Frank required his teenage children to be home at a very early hour and wanted to know their friends' families well. His wife said, "Sometimes I have great difficulties with Frank. When we go to restaurants he has to sit at a special table so he can have his back to the wall and see everyone who enters the place. He's beginning to think people are out to get him, so he's constantly on the watch. He even drives home a different way every night. I'm beginning to be concerned that he won't even leave the house. And I don't know how to help him!" It got so bad for Frank that he would sit at his desk and just cry. What he had anticipated in the job were not the realities he now faced.

No other representatives of society are so tirelessly available to provide services such as marriage counseling during family arguments; settling neighborhood disputes; searching for lost children; aiding stranded motorists; giving emergency first aid, and assisting people who are frightened, sick, hungry or homeless. Situations which a person in the normal course of living would find deeply distressing are faced repeatedly by police officers. At one time or another, every officer sees bodies shattered in automobile accidents and mangled deliberately—the aftermaths of murders, riots, rapes and robberies. Even more disturbing are cases of child-battering and starvation. Officers are the ones who must counsel rape victims and notify families of victims of violence. They might be sniped at, slugged, clubbed, beaten and spit upon. They might be killed when they least expect it.

An older officer related this story. "We had a young officer, not long off training, who came in damn near tears. He had received a call from a person who was concerned about a neighbor in her 70's or 80's who was being housed by her granddaughter. When he reached the house he found this old woman virtually a prisoner, locked into a portion of the house in a room that didn't have any toilet facilities. There was no food or water available to her and the granddaughter hadn't been around in days. By the time the kid got there, the old woman was dehydrated and couldn't move. She was senile and hysterical. The room was filled with defecation and the odor unbearable. An ambulance was called.

You know, they talk about cops as hard guys, devoid of feelings. Well this kid was truly upset. He wanted someone to go to jail for this unhuman act upon an old woman. If she had been a dog, he said, he could have arrested the granddaughter for cruelty to animals. Or if a juvenile, the arrest could have been for child abuse. But there was no penal code for being cruel to relatives— especially old people. He ended up writing an attempted murder report.

Considering violence in the abstract is so different than meeting the reality.

Robert F., a patrolman for two years, came upon a man approaching a group of people with a long knife. In the short time available, the only thing the officer could do to save his life and others was to shoot the suspect. In discussing the incident later he responded, "Two years ago when I interviewed for this job, I was asked if I could shoot someone and I replied—yes, if it was a life and death situation, or a citizen's life was in danger and I had no other choice, I could. But my expectations then and the realities I've experienced are totally different. It really bothered me . . . shooting that stranger. I can't quit the department because of financial reasons, but I know I don't want to work in assignments where there's the possibility of killing someone—and that's almost impossible in police work. I want to work where my chances of shooting someone are minimal, and hopefully I'll be able to leave law enforcement in a few years. It's just no fun killing someone. It's not at all like what I heard in the academy or from my field training officer. In fact, no one *ever* talked about how you feel when you shoot someone."

Feelings are rarely talked about among police officers. The new officer learns this quickly. Unfortunately, he or she may interpret this as meaning good cops don't have feelings. By trying to imitate those they perceive as being successful on the job, the new cop may be denying a very important part of himself—his feelings. This can be carried into his home life, which will create additional problems. Acknowledging feelings and then moving on is essential for a healthy, well-balanced human being. Although this may be difficult for a cop, it is still essential if he wants to maintain his humanness.

The constant stress and the exposure to life-shattering experiences often create disillusionment and loss of respect for society and its members in the officer's years on the job. His contact with society in the criminal aspects of the job is primarily with suspects—the law violators, drug addicts, burglars, pimps, prostitutes, drunks, murderers, and their victims. All too often, even the victims seem to be ungrateful individuals who are unable or perhaps unwilling to protect themselves in the most elementary ways, but who expect the officers to lay down their lives to protect them. Policemen deal with almost all people in their worst moments. For the young cop who has

come into the job to "help society" and who sees himself
as a "knight" willing to rescue all people, both the suspect
and the unappreciative victim might dispel these illusions. The cop may begin to wonder whom he's really
helping.

A rookie might typically think that in order to be one of
the boys, not only must he hold his emotions under control, he must handle every incident with precision, understanding and skill. He has heard the "war stories" at the
end of the day which help cops keep their equilibrium and
balance, and soon he becomes part of the game of one-
upmanship in which police relate their most harrowing
experiences. Rather than understanding this process as a
way of releasing tension, fear and emotion, the young cop
may become taken by the game itself.

Many officers will admit to nightmares about particular
incidents; yet they must somehow master the greatest job
demand: to retain a "cool head," nonemotional responses
and quick, alert thinking in a wide variety of situations.
This can be more difficult for novice officers whose
increasing public contact may not conform to their
expectations.

While young officers are struggling with the disillu-
sionments of the job, they soon become aware of another
important one. They, as police officers, have lost their
individuality.

In dealing with the police, most people, while insisting
on recognition of their unique problems, are sublimely
unaware of the problems or individuality of the police
officer. At best, they expect him or her to be some sort of
super-hero, impervious to any personal attack, verbal or
otherwise, swift and unerring in his actions. At worst, the
public sees police as their enemy, or as merely emotionless
and lacking in compassion.

The officers' role, by necessity, is authoritarian. He
must enforce the laws which have been determined by
legislative bodies representing the people. For the rookies,

the ways in which he can handle this authority may be confusing. He has at least two options: One is to come on very strong in the beginning, which will hopefully show the officers' strength and eliminate any possiblity that a suspect will try to overcome what he sees as a weak cop; or the officer may come on as the "good guy" to show people that he's non-authoritarian and friendly and doesn't want any trouble. Often a young officer chooses to come on strong, particularly because he's still very unsure of himself. He's learned to take the offensive.

This pattern of behavior has been referred to as the John Wayne or Wyatt Earp syndrome, a common affliction among some young officers. They are the ones who take their job too seriously and consider everybody a suspect. They cannot give out a traffic ticket without putting their hand on the holster.

In some respects, the way a police officer handles authority can be compared to that of a school teacher or an athletic coach. Often teachers and coaches decide to 'come on strong' during the initial part of the year to gain both control and respect from their students. This allows them to loosen up towards the end of the year and be more human. The philosophy implies that if you establish control, that control will remain unchallenged while you allow your more human side to show. But there's a difference—teachers and coaches deal with students on a daily basis for nine months. Police officers are usually dealing with people they don't know—and who could run the gamut from model citizen to dangerous criminal. Although the public applauds the strong teacher and coach, many times they question this same behavior by the police, often failing to see the possible gravity of the situation.

For young officers, the issue of authority is a particularly difficult one. It is essential that they understand themselves and how they come across to others. The rookies have had little time on their own to test their authority skills because they have been busy imitating training academy staff and their field training officers. Once they are on their own there is a possibility that they will make mistakes in their use of power and authority. The excitement, combined with their own fear and bestowed authority, can cause the young officers to become overly impressed with the amount of power they now discover they have. They become all too aware that they had little power with the academy staff and field training officers, and now find this power exciting. This adjustment of being on one's own can cause problems for the officers, their families and the department. At this stage of their career they may become too carried away with being cops, and it can appear to all around them that they eat, drink and sleep police work. Arriving to work early, looking for problems while off-duty and asking for overtime are typical behaviors of these officers.

Handling even a minor confrontation such as a traffic citation appropriately can present a dilemma for a new officer. Very few, if any, citizens are pleased to receive a ticket. If the officer is friendly and calls the offender by his first name, he is viewed as hypocritical. If he acts rigid or aloof, then the recipient wonders why he is being treated as a criminal. As one wit put it, "I have never met anyone who was stopped by the police for speeding or whatever, who had been doing wrong!"

People stopped for traffic violations almost invariably blame the officers. The cop was "out to get them," or needed his quota of tickets filled, or it's said that "cops harass solid citizens instead of catching real criminals." Not only does the officer generally encounter antagonism when fulfilling his duty in citing a traffic offender, the irate citizen may file a complaint leading to an investigation, which may be particularly trying to the officer if he knows he wasn't out of line. Even cops who are not directly involved in giving the ticket are called on the line by their civilian friends.

Officer Doug S. explained his feelings well when he said, "I received a call just recently from a girlfriend of my wife's about a ticket she got. She swore up and down that she hadn't been speeding and even went so far as to say that she was going to complain about the cop because he wasn't nice to her when she challenged him. She said that he had a bad attitude even though she admitted coming on strong. It seems her husband wasn't too fond of her getting all these tickets.

She proclaimed her innocence by explaining that she had received a ticket about a month ago and had been nice to the cop because she knew she was guilty. Thus, it was OK for her to be belligerent to the cop this time because she wasn't guilty.

I felt like asking her, but didn't because she is a friend of Anna's, if she wrote a commendation to the first cop for being so nice to her when he gave her the ticket. After all, she was certainly willing to write a citizen's complaint for the other cop.

And they call quite frequently, especially with these tickets. I think you could arrest someone for a murder they didn't commit and it wouldn't irritate them any more than a ticket.

Recruits have generally heard about the breakdown between laws and new social trends, but until they're on the streets they don't experience the frustration this may cause. The current marijuana laws typify the breakdown between legislators, members of the community and law-enforcement officers, a situation which is a constant source of frustration to officers who get the brunt of the public resentment. For enforcing legislated marijuana laws, police must treat as offenders a large group of casual users who may otherwise be law-abiding. But the police, rather than the legislators, get angry reactions due to their immediate visibility. The result is that sometimes a negative image of the police is held by even law-abiding citizens.

Victimless crime is another area of conflict. Vice operations are often criticized by certain segments of the population. Consenting adult homosexuals, prosititutes and gamblers all defend themselves with the contention that they are not harming anyone and have the consent of all involved. Any attempt to enforce laws forbidding such practices is conceived as harasssment, and thus another segment of the population views the police as their enemy. Their anger is not allayed by the known participation of organized crime in these activities nor the fact that other groups of society are opposed to them.

These are only two examples of how some current laws put police, and particularly young police, in a very difficult situation. Other problems emerge as the laws slowly change to meet the changing mores. And, though all segments of society have never agreed on any issue, all must abide by the will of the majority. Thus a vicious cycle is often created in relation to these unpopular laws, with the community becoming increasingly alienated and hostile toward the police and the police becoming equally alienated from the community. This is often much different than the young officer had anticipated.

Officer Ken B. was excited about his promotion from patrol duty to the vice squad as second-grade detective and went to a tavern to celebrate. There he ran into three civilian friends and told them the good news, but he was disappointed at their cool reactions. One of the friends said, "So you went and joined the pussy posse, huh? I guess now you'll be out harassing and arresting hard-working, honest citizens who just want to relax and play around with cards and fast women and slow horses. Well, don't forget, Ken—I knew you before you became a cop, and you used to go out with us to the after-hours joints and gamble, and you paid for some pussy a few times yourself. Aren't you being a hypocrite now? Who's being hurt by this vice that you're going to be cracking down on?" Ken was taken aback by this scorn, and he tried to explain that seemingly harmless vice operations were actually going to support violent mobsters and heroin pushers. But Ken's civilian friends weren't impressed, and he left the tavern after one drink. After that, he did his drinking only in another bar whose patrons were mostly cops and ex-cops.

Another cop frustrated about his job in general and particularly about being blamed or disliked for carrying out the laws of society and the justice system made these comments. "We cops are also at fault because we don't explain to these people that we are simply doing what we are supposed to be doing. And, honestly, we can't strictly obey all the edicts of the Supreme Court.

We should tell the public that we can't arrest that guy standing in front of your house calling you a "mother fucker" because the Supreme Court has decreed that profanity in the presence of women and children is no longer a crime. Or explain that we can't go arrest John who lives down the street for burglarizing their house until we get a warrant.

The public needs to hear our frustration with the system, and stop directing their anger towards the most visible people—the cops. I think more of that is being done lately as more and more criminals are being released from jail and then they go out and rape someone or commit some other crime.

The true folly of our system which opened the public's eyes was watching Hinkley live and in color on television, shoot the president, kill a police officer, screw up the press aide, then plead insanity. For this he was put in a mental institution rather than prison where he belonged. The Onion Field killers, and Sirhan Sirhan and Dan White raised the public's ire. But for each of them there are hundreds who have beat the system and have been just as vicious or more so.

Because of the antagonism that police often feel from the public, there is a strong tendency for the police to categorize people. This may happen particularly with the crime-oriented strata of society. Generally, in the criminal aspects of the work, police deal with two to five percent of the population—the unsavory part. They are constant witnesses to degrading acts and the emotional toll these acts have on the victims, their families and friends. Young officers may find themselves developing tunnel vision where they see only good or bad and justify all their actions by this dichotomy.

Officers and their families tend to lead isolated, separated lives. They find that if they stay together they are not questioned by people on general police-related questions. They become a kind of a new minority group—the minority in the middle, damned by one side for taking actions, damned by the other for not acting enough.

Officers are further isolated from the community by the use of patrol cars which can deny them the opportunity to get to know the people in the area. Many young officers are placed in difficult neighborhoods, which complicates things even further. Often they grew up in different environments than the ones they're patrolling. This is not true for many rural officers who have known their neighborhoods since childhood.

Officers are further prevented from interaction because they're set off by their uniforms, badges and guns. And the police-car radio, while necessary, keeps up a steady stream of calls describing crimes and tragedies which tend to reinforce an alienated view of society.

Consequently, when dealing with the public, it is no wonder that young police officers often have difficulty developing the special knowledge of sensitivity required by various situations. The limitations of the job further force police into a police oriented life style. The shift work, the overtime, the court appearances in off-hours, the weekend and holiday work—all limit their ability to relate to others outside of the law-enforcement profession.

Oftentimes, while trying to socialize, the young officers find they run the gamut of social commentary, from "pig" to sly innuendo. They may be ostracized for what they do.

Many times they may find themselves becoming defensive. They may invent stories about their occupation, or say merely, "I work for the county."

The easiest solution—not the best, but the one often taken by young officers—is to avoid all situations where they might be criticized.

> During his first week off training, Officer Mike G. stopped at a hot dog stand while working a one-man unit in a minority community. While walking to the counter he noticed a real cute little girl peeking at him from between her Momma's legs. He said something to her like "Hi, sweety," or "How are you today?" She said "HI" after which her mother grabbed her and turned her around and told her not to talk to the pig. Mike was really pissed off and felt like taking her mother to jail, but fortunately didn't act on that feeling. However, he was quite hardened by the experience.

Even in circumstances where they might not be held personally accountable for their professions' reputation, in some ways the young officers can never completely be just one of the group. For instance: at a party where illegal acts such as the smoking of marijuana or underaged drinking occur, most people need not be concerned, but police officers are required by law to take action. Most officers choose to leave the party rather than questioning or arresting anyone. If they decide to stay, the officers risk consequences which could include losing their jobs.

This type of thing may be very difficult for young idealistic officers who until recently were very much a part of the youth culture. This culture emphasized individuality, but now these young officers have moved into a different culture with contrary values and goals. However, the police culture is something they have wanted to be part of, and now that they've made it the young officers will do almost anything to remain.

Rookies may find themselves increasingly excluding themselves and their spouses from most socializing because they feel the need to protect them from the realities of work life and to shield them from criticism. Thus, very few officers, especially those who work for a large metropolitan agency, live in the communities in which they work. They have a tendency to live and congregate within certain areas, which, naturally, further deepens the isolation. They begin to have a very microcosmic view of the world.

Spouses and children find it difficult to build meaningful relationships outside the boundaries of this "Blue Race." While the officers' meaningful contacts are with their work life and fellow officers, the spouses find themselves even more cut off from the world. They often seek communication with other police wives or anyone who has the time to listen to them. This type of pattern may have much to do with reported high rates of divorce during the initial years of officers' careers.

For policemen, the department and fellow officers symbolize security, protection, stability and order. Society is increasingly viewed as insecure, threatening, unstable, unordered and in a constant state of conflict. They come to view the people with whom they deal as symbolizing the failures of judges, lawyers, parole and probation officers, doctors, psychologists, sociologists, psychiatrists, prisons, welfare and housing programs; in short, the failures of society. The resulting view is that law enforcement is the only segment of that society concerned about law and order and upholding traditional views.

If one were to contrast the psychologist, his background, his views and his day-to-day life with those of the average police officer, they'd see two different worlds.

Dr. David P. lives in an "ivory tower world." His reality is based on a great deal of academic education; his associates are fellow professors and professionals connected with the university whose views, like his, are basically liberal. In the thick of the McGovern-Nixon 1972 presidential campaign he believed McGovern would win. His friends believed it, the newspapers he read seemed to indicate this, and everyone he knew would be voting for McGovern. The reality was that McGovern carried one state!

Officer Jimmy K. lives in a "black and white world." His formal education ended with high school—and that's when he contends real learning began. He has worked the streets for several years and often sees things as either right or wrong. His theories are based on the practical experiences he gets daily. The people he deals with are either those who are breaking the law or his fellow officers who seem to understand him. His views are politically conservative and he supports those who believe in "law and order." In the 1964 Johnson-Goldwater presidential race he believed Barry Goldwater would win. The literature he read supported this, his friends agreed, he believed that it was the only logical conclusion that the average voter could reach. Yet Barry Goldwater, like McGovern eight years later, carried one state!

This distortion of reality can occur not only in politics but in other aspects of an individual's life. Attitudes towards fellow man, crime and violence can cause a misperception and overreaction.

During their first years on the job, officers may see all their expectations distorted. They may even become bitter if the disillusionment is too great. They suffer from the ambiguity of their role, ambiguity that they never knew existed. They may increasingly internalize the "macho" image their uniform so often evokes. They can become badge-heavy, feel that emotions are unhealthy and keep their feelings locked inside under tight control.

Suffering from the discrepancy between expectation and reality, young officers may resent the modifications they must make in their perceptions of the job instead of understanding them. This type of resentment may be carried onto the streets and affect how they deal with people.

Although it appears that there is a good possibility that most young officers will become very negative seasoned cops, this is not usually the case. There are many well-rounded caring cops at all ages and places of employment.

Young officers need to remember that they are probably going to be in law enforcement for a long time. Everything will not be accomplished in the first few weeks. This includes being patient with innovative ideas. As the newest kids on the block, they may not be listened to. They need to first establish themselves as competent cops before trying new ideas. However, they are important and their ideas need to be shared.

The sharing of career experiences with spouse and family is important for young officers. They need to spend time with their families and communicate their feelings about day-to-day work. Too often young officers who devoted all of their time (perhaps with their spouses' assistance) to getting through the academy continue this pattern (much work, little family) during their careers. Yet communication and time together are essential ingredients to most successful marriages. And officers should also keep and establish friends outside law enforcement. This is important in keeping a more balanced picture of the world.

They need to learn to balance their idealism with their new reality, keeping a part of both. Although the older officers may smile with a know-it-all attitude, they are actually impressed and motivated by younger officers. Rookies should take time to laugh about themselves, and most important allow themselves to be human—to have feelings, make mistakes and smell the flowers.

It is the responsibility of *all* of us to keep police officers healthy and well-balanced. Too often it is left on the shoulders of the individual cop, and this becomes an added burden, at times an impossible load to carry.

Departments must be aware of their role in keeping cops physically and emotionally sound.

Departments should choose their field training officers carefully. Not only will these officers break in the cadets, they will be the ones to help young officers integrate their idealistic thoughts about the profession with the reality of the streets. These men and women need to appreciate the skills brought to the department by the young officers and be open enough to share with them their ideas and *feelings* about the job. It should be regarded as a learning process for both.

Departments should encourage young officers to continue their learning—be it at seminars, conferences or at a local university. This learning will give the department people who know and understand a variety of values and who will have a variety of ways to communicate with citizens.

Administrators need to provide avenues of communication from the bottom to the top. Too often young officers feel frustrated because they feel they are not heard. This may mean riding patrol and talking with the young officers to get a sense of the changing values within the department and on the streets.

If the young officers pay close attention to themselves and the changes they experience, there is a tendency to become more self-assured again. Their shell may diminish, as may their unhealthy view of society. They will regain their closeness with their families, and their sense of humor. As they mellow into the job, they will feel less vulnerable and cease to take themselves and every passing remark so seriously. Then they will have developed the critical distance which allows them to function at their best and take interest once again in things outside the department.

At this point, many officers are able to see that there are large groups of law-abiding and supportive people that have no relationship to the people the officers have encountered on the job. However, the tragedies experienced do not vanish easily; and the police officers have a tendency to remain cautious, skeptical and conservative in human relationships other than with their fellow officers.

Police and other members of society travel over the same streets and occupy the same spaces; however, their experiences are as different as if the people were traveling in two different worlds. Understanding of other people's experiences and perceptions is always difficult, especially if we come from different backgrounds. But we need to keep our minds open to this. When minds are open, then those who are seeking understanding have a better chance for change. We must not categorize or stereotype people because they wear uniforms, carry guns, travel in black-and white-cars with a siren, or live in a certain neighborhood, or because they are black, Mexican-American or white.

Understanding the law-enforcement officer is an elusive and perplexing task, a task made more difficult by the masks we have placed on them and the masks they must assume. However, under the masks, we find that policemen are as human as everyone else.

REFERENCES

Bordura, D. J. (ed.) *The Police: Six Sociological Essays.* New York: John Wiley and Sons, Inc., 1967.

Kirkham, G. L. "A Professor's 'Street Lessons'." *F.B.I. Law Enforcement Bulletin,* 43 (3), 1974.

Klien, H. T. *The Police: Damned if They Do—Damned if They Don't.* New York: Crown Publishers, Inc., 1968.

Kroes, W. H. *Society's Victim—The Policeman.* Springfield, Illinois: Thomas, 1976.

Niederhoff, A. and Blumberg, A. (eds) *The Ambivalent Force: Perspectives on the Police.* 2d ed; Hillsdale, Illinois: Dryden Press, 1976.

Reiser, M. *The Police Department Psychologist.* Springfield, Illinois: Thomas, 1972.

Wilson, J. Q. *Varieties of Police Behavior.* Cambridge, Massachusetts: Howard University Press, 1968.

5

THROUGHOUT ONE'S CAREER—
STRESS

In exploring the various struggles faced by applicants, cadets and street officers, it becomes evident that police work is a stressful profession.

For many years, both the public and the police have viewed officers as impervious to experiencing emotional or physical distress. Traditionally, they have been expected to handle any situation and move from one emotionally charged scene to another while remaining detached superpersons. This may seem somewhat admirable, but it is not at all easy to fit into the shoes (or the boots) of a cowboy sheriff who blows away a barroom full of villains and then returns to his poker game to win the next hand without a change in his expression. The chubby little European night watchman with his tasseled cap and candle or the British bobby may present a less glamorous image, but they are functioning under less pressure. It is doubtful whether the real Wyat Earp was as cool in every crisis as Henry Fonda made him out to be on the movie screen, but in any case it is not our purpose to examine the glorification of reality that has transpired with the Western hero. Suffice it to say that the myth has shaped the expectations of Americans, and this has become the role that awaits the young police officer.

When our superheroes face situations they did not anticipate, they may be unprepared and stressed. While no occupation is free of job-related stress, research has shown that law-enforcement personnel are at the upper end of the spectrum when stressful jobs are measured.

Stress is a hot item these days. You can't pick up a newspaper or turn on a TV without hearing something about it. Not only does everyone have a cure for it, they also have a multitude of definitions for it.

Life is largely a process of adaptation to circumstances. For those in law enforcement life is the process of adaptation to experiences encountered on the job. Because of the stress involved, it is easy to develop habits that are personally and professionally destructive to a successful cop and human being. We will explore stress and its implications for police officers—physically, emotionally and socially. Suggestions for reducing stress both individually and departmentally will be found in Chapter 12.

Although police officers are healthy, normal individuals when they enter the profession some studies indicate that by the time they leave they are below average in terms of physical and emotional health, and longevity and have high suicide and divorce rates. In addition, the presumptive clause in California and many other states presumes a heart attack (85% of which are attributed to stress) to be related, if officers have worked five years or longer. The Connecticut Supreme Court has ruled that if officers have heart attacks on or off duty, they should be compensated and, if they die, their families should receive compensation.

Stress is an inevitable part of life and is not necessarily detrimental to health. A certain amount of stress accompanies all change. A change in work assignments, even when desirable, produces some anxiety. Stress is associated with pleasant as well as shocking experiences. Spectators of sports look forward to the uncertainty and resulting stress attached to football, basketball, horse racing and other events which would be meaningless if the outcome were known beforehand. A certain amount of stress can also help to stimulate people to achieve their goals. While the spectators derive pleasure from the tension of a close football game, the players experience stress that improves their performance. In this manner, stress can contribute to an individual's performance.

Stress that improves performance and provides life with zest is considered to be positive and is referred to as eustress. However, certain types and amounts of stress are negative, inhibiting achievement and producing health problems. This is called distress.

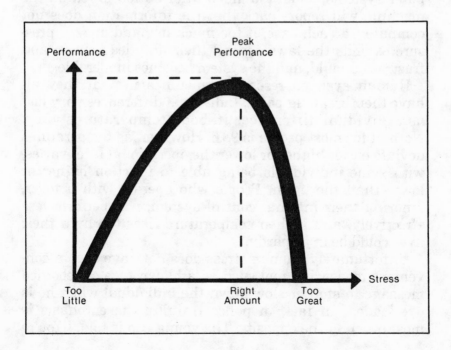

In our analysis of officers stress, we will consider the amount of illness or disease within the police occupation, especially since doctors attribute anywhere from 70% to 90% of all illness as being related to stress.

For this discussion, stress will be defined as a demand on a system. Every system, human or mechanical, operates on a formula of laws which enables it to handle the demands and pressures placed upon it. However, if these laws are pushed too far, tension and frustration build.

Electrical sockets are designed to put out a limited amount of power, and when more energy is demanded than can be released by the system the circuit is broken or a fuse is blown. The United States telephone system normally operates better than any other; but in attempting to place a call on Mother's Day or Christmas, chances are a recording will announce that "all circuits are busy— please hang up and try again." Even with advanced computer systems, when too much information is fed in, the machine will report back that the information does not compute. In each case, if too much demand and/or pressure extends the laws beyond their abilities tension and frustration build, and the system becomes inoperable.

Human systems resemble machines in that they all have their breaking point. Individual differences vary just as individual differences in body temperatures vary. Normal for most people is 98.6. However, as temperatures deviate either higher or lower the operational level varies, with some individuals being able to function higher or lower than the norm. People who operate with a fever, ignoring their internal control system, will perform less effectively; and if their temperature rises too high their lives could be in jeopardy.

Unfortunately, human stress does not have such a convenient measuring tool such as a blown fuse or recorded message to stop or slow down the individual when he is overloaded. In fact, in police training the emphasis is most often on the opposite. The young cop is told: "You're the last line of defense. You're out there to handle it. It's tough, but that's what you get paid for." Often there is no discussion of the possibility of an officer having difficulty and at times not being able to handle one or more aspects of his/her job. Nor is there any discussion of the possibility of an officer being overloaded, experiencing weakness in certain situations or having incapacitating emotional responses to a particular event or combination of events.

Alan M., a married officer with one child, was involved in an incident in which he performed his police function very well. However, during the incident his partner of several years, and another officer who occasionally worked with them, and the suspect as well, were killed, and Alan received a minor injury. Back at the station, Alan's fellow officers commended him on his good work and tried to encourage him to accept that he had done all he could, and that the two fellow officers' deaths were out of his control. But Alan could not accept this. Driving to and from work he would suddenly start to cry. Passing the area where the shooting occurred brought the occurrences back anew to preoccupy him for days on end. When camping, he would hop into a boat, paddle away and drink a six-pack of beer before returning to his family. Sometimes he would send his wife to the store just so he could be by himself and cry. For four years, he would physically shake each time he put on his weapon and got ready for work.

These reactions, though not abnormal, may be considered as such in a male dominated world where such difficulties are never talked about. This man's behavior was not unusual given the tragedies he experienced. However, the way he chose to handle his problem could have been detrimental to him, his wife and his family. The first time Alan ever mentioned his difficulties was *seven years* after the incident. Never had the officer confided in his colleagues or his wife, even though the nightmares and the shakes had increased to a point where he was barely able to tolerate them. If he had talked to anyone about it, he felt he would have been seen as weak, and this was not acceptable to him.

> Officer Dick U. was wounded in a fight with a gunman that left Dick's partner dead. He was laid up for months, and when he returned to work he was uncharacteristically ill-behaved and incorrigible. He beat up a suspect who had handcuffs on; he got into one jam after another. What's more, he treated the department's internal investigators like a bunch of jerks and refused to show up for polygraph tests. It seemed to other officers that Dick was trying to get the department to fire him, and eventually he accepted early retirement. Fellow officers believed that Dick was haunted by guilt because the gunshot which killed his partner had actually been intended for him.

In law enforcement, facing a life disturbing situation demands adrenalin from the system. When this occurs, officers experience an autonomic nervous system response which increases heart rate, blood pressure and muscle tone. The normal response is a fight or flight reaction, which would enable individuals to strike out at the stress agent or remove themselves from the scene. Unfortunately, officers cannot do either; the job simply does not allow for either attacking or running away.

Regardless of the ways in which stress in an individual is manifested, there are some general basic biological interpretations of how stress occurs within the body. Selye's General Adaptive Syndrome presents stress occurring in three stages: alarm reaction, resistance, and exhaustion.

The alarm reaction, sometimes called the emergency reaction, refers to the physiological changes that the body undergoes in response to stress. This reaction consists of a series of complicated bodily and biochemical changes.

There is the autonomic (automatic) nervous system response which increases the heart rate, blood pressure and muscle tone. There is also the adrenal (emergency) gland response; biochemical changes which include increased hormone secretion of adrenalin from the adrenal glands. It is adrenalin that spurs every nerve and muscle into immediate action when faced with a crisis. Because the adrenal glands pour forth adrenalin in time of physical danger or emotional crisis, continued mental or emotional tension overworks these emergency glands to the point where nerves and vital organs are constantly kept keyed-up to fever pitch, thereby sending the powerful adrenalin hormone into the bloodstream when unneeded. In addition, the adrenal glands release cholesterol into the bloodstream. The overworking of the adrenal glands, caused by physical danger, emotional crisis or continuing psychological tension, can cause bodily disorders characterized by fatigue, excessive need for sleep and marked mental lethargy involving lack of concentration and inability to think clearly. Diseases such as arteriosclerosis, coronary thrombosis and cerebral hemorrhage may be the result of constant over-stimulation of the adrenal glands. In addition to having numerous high voltage chemicals put into our system, we tend to: increase our pulse rate, perspire more, tense our forehead and neck muscles and experience eye strain, fluttering eyelids, irregular shallow breathing, cold hands, curled toes or fingers, and "butterflies" in our stomach which impede digestion and increase the sugar in our systems. (Fig. 2)

During the alarm stage the human organism is totally aroused and all resources are focused upon the stress agent. When exposure to a stress-producing situation continues for some time, the alarm stage is followed by the phase of resistance. Here the body seems to develop a resistance to the stress that provoked the alarm reaction, and the symptoms that occurred during the first stage disappear, even though the disturbing stimulation may

Figure 2

Effects of Stress On the Body
The specific biological and chemical reactions stress cause, in our bodies are illustrated in Fig. 2.

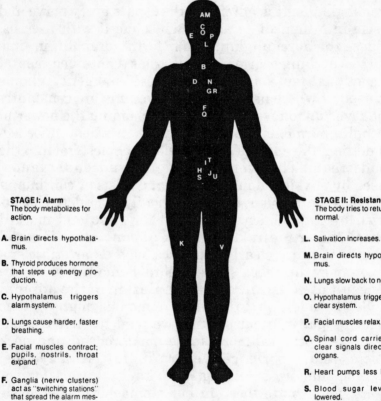

STAGE I: Alarm
The body metabolizes for action.

A. Brain directs hypothalamus.

B. Thyroid produces hormone that steps up energy production.

C. Hypothalamus triggers alarm system.

D. Lungs cause harder, faster breathing.

E. Facial muscles contract; pupils, nostrils, throat expand.

F. Ganglia (nerve clusters) act as "switching stations" that spread the alarm message from the spinal cord to the organs.

G. Heart pumps more blood.

H. Blood sugar level is elevated.

I. Stomach, intestines, bladder relax; digestion slows to crawl.

J. Adrenal gland secretes hormone which helps liver, pancreas, kidneys, spleen and large blood vessels take on extra workload.

K. Sweating increases.

STAGE II: Resistance
The body tries to return to normal.

L. Salivation increases.

M. Brain directs hypothalamus.

N. Lungs slow back to normal.

O. Hypothalamus triggers all-clear system.

P. Facial muscles relax.

Q. Spinal cord carries all-clear signals directly to organs.

R. Heart pumps less blood.

S. Blood sugar level is lowered.

T. Stomach, intestines, bladder swing back into action; digestion speeds up.

U. Adrenal gland stops secreting hormone that regulates liver, pancreas, spleen, kidneys, large blood vessels.

V. Sweating is retarded.

continue. In short, the body adjusts to the situation, and in many cases this is within the individual's control.

Once the resistance level is passed, the third stage of exhaustion sets in; the defenses against stress give way and the effects of stress become dominant. Many of the emotional responses that originally appeared during the alarm reaction stage begin to reappear at this time. Severe physiological and psychological problems may occur once the individual's defenses have collapsed to the exhaustion stage.

Normally, the body biologically copes with an emergency, utilizing the extra fuel and strength provided for specific coping reactions such as escaping from the danger, fighting it, or exhibiting fear. Because the officer's role does not permit these alternatives, the adrenal glands continue to pour forth adrenalin and cholesterol into the bloodstream, the heart is overworked, frustration is high, nerves and vital organs are keyed up to a fever pitch, muscles are tense and the required response,—calm detachment—does not allow the mechanisms to return to their normal levels. If the stress persists, or the person fails to adequately cope with it, more chronic depression, feelings of fatigue or alienation may become evident, causing health problems. In such situations, the individual may maintain an extreme level of physiological activity over a much longer period than is usually true with emergency reactions. If this state continues for a sufficiently long period of time, tissue damage may occur, and this damage may take on a permanent form, the most common resulting diseases being heart disease, ulcers, high blood pressure, headaches, gastric disorders, arthritis, allergies accompanied by emotional problems, rheumatic reactions and kidney disease. In fact, if the stress is not acknowledged and continues to mount until it completely takes over, it might lead to functional psychosis or even death.

Individuals vary in their stress threshholds and recovery

Figure 3

Stages of Stress Reactions

People generally react to stress in 3 stages as described by Hans Selye.

Stages	Symptoms	Capabilities
I. Alarm	Individual alerted to impending difficulty or threat.	Vulnerable, but has great personal reserves available for use.
II. Resistance	Alarm symptoms replaced with greater control; though adjusting, will also show fatigue, anxiety, tension and extreme irritability.	Ability to withstand effects of stress climbs to an all-time high; able to perform sanely.
III. Exhaustion	If the individual does not adapt during resistance stage, the symptoms can increase to cause physical or emotional illness.	Energy to adjust is used up; with no reserves left to draw on, ability to perform diminishes and finally ceases.

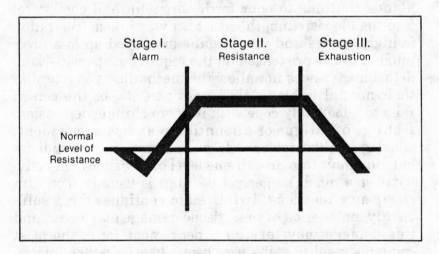

rates. Some officers may have an enormous capacity to absorb intense stress over a short period but be less able to cope with minimal stress over an extended time. Other officers may exceed their stress tolerance level quickly when exposed to a single instance of extreme stress, yet they may be comfortable with steady pressure below their maximum tolerance limit.

What can officers do and what can be done for them? Is there a preventive course to steer? By examining the various pressures, from within and without, which any officer is likely to experience, we will be able to better determine what is inevitable and what can be averted or changed, either by heightened awareness on the part of the officer himself or by changes in departmental policy.

When considering stressors (anything that produces an autonomic nervous system response), one's attitude is an essential factor. Control also is important. If one is in control of the specific stressor he can change it or change his reaction to it. But if he can do nothing about the situation, the individual must find a way to "let go" or else he'll become frustrated, angry or depressed. Since often we have no control over a stressor, we must revamp our attitude toward it in order to avoid stress. The often-stated Prayer of St. Francis presents a low stress approach: "Lord, give me the strength to change what I can and endure what I must, and the wisdom to know which is which." However, too often officers become upset about issues they have no control over or can do nothing about.

Think about using a car battery effectively. One can run through life at 90 miles an hour with the air conditioner running, the radio blaring and headlights on, and the trip will be over in a relatively short period of time. Or one can choose to run the same car up the road of life at normal speeds, with attention to the ways energy is used, obviously this will make the trip (and the battery) last much longer. It is a matter of choice. The same is true about ourselves: We can speed through life, ignoring our health, or we can practice good health habits, get regular check ups, and adopt a positive attitude enabling us to live a longer and more productive life.

Stressors are dependent on one's perceptions. If someone believes something is a stressor, then it is—even if it isn't a stressor for anyone else. If one heard he was going to meet with the training staff at the Sheriff's Academy, the stressfulness of the event would depend on the individual, his function, and his role. The sheriff or training academy captain may well be relaxed and at ease, whereas an applicant or new cadet may anticipate the encounter with tension and trepidation. The stressfulness of an event is dependent on how one perceives it and subsequently reacts to it.

One trait which creates some of the stress officers experience is being dedicated professionals, with the drive and desire to do the best job possible. This sense of urgency can drive officers into a crusader-like frenzy of activity. Their work becomes more important than anything else in the world. They may lose touch with their own physical and emotional limitations, work grueling shifts, be unable to shut off after work hours, and begin to suffer from extreme fatigue. This may be aggravated by their families, which, although compassionate, have their own difficulties coping with irregular hours and exhaustion. If officers continue at this pace without providing breaks or time to collect themselves, they may ultimately become burned out.

There are a variety of other stressors that affect individual officers having to do with being married, being a minority officer, alcoholism, supervision and promotion, or being involved in a traumatic incident. These are discussed in a broader and more detailed way in individual chapters on these topics.

Although some stressors are applicable to any assignment, function or experience in a police department, our present discussion on stress will relate first to the line officer and later to the detective.

In law enforcement, stressors have been identified in various ways. Many authorities have tried to categorize the stressors impinging on law enforcement. Though stressors are not the same for each officer, the following ones have brought about autonomic nervous system changes.

EXTERNAL STRESSORS

The Court System: Officers know when they have a good arrest. So when they watch a suspect get off with a light sentence because of lenient decision from the bench—or when the suspect goes free altogether—the officers often see it as a revolving door—a process in which, they enter the subjects into the system, while the judges let them out. This can make officers cynical and cause them to question the advisability of making an arrest. Court decisions (such as the exclusionary rule) which restrict officers in their daily activities are a stressor to many. Officers may know when criminal behavior is occurring, yet they feel they can do nothing because their hands are tied by the decisions of the court. A survey of decisions for the Syracuse City Court, revealed that of misdemeanor offenders cited, only 24% were fined and in third-degree assaults cases 75% were dismissed or acquitted and 12% were suspended. When dedicated police professionals view the results of their citations and arrests, at least some degree of frustration and disappointment is inevitable.

As two officers walked out of the courtroom the younger man turned to his partner, a veteran of 16 years, and said: "I have to hand it to you, Frank. You never get upset when you get a case thrown out. It really gets to me to see them throw a case out the window on a stupid technicality like searching the wrong part of a car." Frank didn't reply immediately, but then finally said: "You're wrong about my not getting upset. I just don't show it anymore. If I don't put this crap out of my mind it eats at me to the point where my ulcer acts up, and it could cause me to do something really dumb, like trying to become the law instead of just enforcing it. The whole system seems to be geared for the criminal and against the police, but the bigger issue is how you let it affect you and your work. I just do my job and never worry about what the prosecutors or the judges or even the detectives do. I don't worry about the sentences or the appeals or any of it. If the system's fucked up, I didn't fuck it up, and I'm not going to lose any sleep over it."

Officer John G. speaks: "When people come on the force they have these expectations about serving and protecting the community and all that. But then down the road they realize that generations of cops before them were out serving and protecting, but they hadn't really altered the goddamn community one bit. It's like shoveling against the tide, because they'll put people in jail and then other people are released to make room for them, because the prisons can only hold so many. So, if a guy's original intent was to make the community a safer place to live, it doesn't take him long to realize that he isn't really doing that. He is only changing the population of the state prison system. So the cop just tries to have fun on the job and not worry about serving anybody. Just like a fisherman—he doesn't think that his harvest from the sea is going to vastly alter the environment of the ocean. He probably just fishes for the sake of it, and I think that is why cops do what they do."

Court Scheduling: An officer drove 500 miles, leaving his family on vacation to testify in what he considered an important case, and then returned the 500 miles back to his family. He knew that if he failed to appear in court the case would be thrown out and the suspect would be released. Very often, court schedules do not take into consideration the commitments of the arresting officers—even though, the judge or one of the lawyers is going to be out of town, the case is rescheduled. Officers who may have been working a late night or an early morning shift are expected to report to court at 9 a.m. Then it becomes like the army: "Hurry up and wait." The waiting could go all morning or into the afternoon before the officer gives his half hour or less of testimony. And during his testimony he might begin to feel as if he were the one under attack by the defense attorney, while the suspect is presented as an innocent victim.

Negative or Distorted Media Accounts: Many officers involved in situations reported by the media are often amazed when reading, listening to, or watching news reports of the incident. Newspapers have to be sold and ratings increased, leading to an emphasis on dramatic and violent aspects of the event rather than the more sensitive and underlying aspects.

Police are dismayed by the media's judgment. For example, on the day that a funeral was held for a police officer killed in the line of duty, another officer shot and killed a citizen/suspect. The front-page headlines were "Police Kills Citizen." The story of the officer's funeral was one paragraph on Page 22.

Community Attitudes: Many negative attitudes about the police are reported by the news media or portrayed in fictional stories. Even though police enter the profession to be of assistance and to serve society, in the course of their duties they find they are feared by some, hated by others, and reviled or assaulted in the ordinary performance of their duties. Police have even been set up for ambush. Conflicts will always exist between those breaking the law and those chosen to enforce it. No one likes to be told he is doing something wrong, and generally the person to do this is the officer. In the late '60's and '70's the most frequent complaint by police was the lack of respect citizens had for their authority. It is very stressful for officers when there is such conflict or disagreement with the people they police.

Officer Tom C.'s wife expressed surprise and disappointment when he told her he was getting out of law enforcement. "It's not like you to give up like this," she said. "What's happened to you?" Tom replied, with amusement in his voice: "You know, I never realized I was going to join the minorities when I joined the force. But the good citizens out on the streets are just as scared of us cops as they are of the criminals we're trying to protect them from. They seem to think that, because we have to work with violence and corruption, we must be violent and corrupt, too. I used to think, or at least hope, that the average citizen liked me, but they seem to be going out of their way just to tolerate us. They don't see us as part of their own structure, and I, for one, don't feel like being an outsider or a minority. We cops seem to be mistrusted and mistreated by people on both sides of the law, and that's not where I want to be for the next twenty years of my life. I've had about all I can stand."

Adverse Local Government Decisions: Decisions made by the local governing authority regarding the amount of funds available for the police department can have repercussions for everyone. The amount and type of manpower, the quality of support personnel and the equipment for law enforcement are all affected by the amount of money allocated. To fight their war on crime and do the best possible job, officers need the latest and most upto-date equipment. When this is not available, it becomes another stressor for the dedicated officer.

Ineffective Referral Agencies: One day a police officer asked a psychologist, "Have you ever referred somebody to Dr. M., or to the Child Guidance Clinic, or the Family Counseling Service?" Upon hearing a negative he stated, "I've tried to keep people out of the criminal justice system by referring them to various agencies—but inevitably the police are called in to deal with the same people again! After a while you begin to wonder if referrals are of any value at all." There are many officers who would prefer to refer people to an agency and help them stay out of the criminal justice system, thus avoiding the negative aspects of arrest and incarceration. Too often, though, officers come to the same conclusion as the officer quoted above—that the agencies, for whatever reason, are simply ineffective.

Ineffective Interrelationship Between Various Agencies in the Criminal Justice System: A police officer in a shooting who has criminal charges filed against him by the district attorney can really begin to question the role and function of the district attorney in the total law-enforcement effort. So, too, can the officer who knows he has a good arrest only to see it rejected by the D.A. for various political reasons. For effective law-enforcement service the police and the district attorney must work closely together.

Similarly, probation and parole officers often recommend short sentences, believing it's best for the individual to never leave the community, or to return to it as quickly as possible. The police often disagree more strongly with probation and parole officers on these issues than with the D.A.

A sadistic murderer who called himself "Son of Sam" had randomly killed six to eight people in New York City. New York Police officers were working twenty hours of overtime a week plus donating their own time to try and catch this man who followed the "orders of a dog." The community was anxious and citizens were becoming more and more afraid to be out at night. On a lucky break, the officers were able to arrest one David Berkowitz and have him incarcerated. Just when the city was beginning to return to normal, an independent probation agency in New York recommended that Berkowitz be released on his own recognizance because of his lack of a previous criminal record, because no arrest warrants were outstanding against him, and because of his nonverified community ties. In the space set aside for aliases, the probation agency official wrote, "Son of Sam."

Fortunately, the recommendation was not heeded, and eventually Berkowitz was convicted of the murders.

This was an enormous error by someone in the probation agency. However, in less dramatic ways events like this happen daily to officers during their interaction with the various components of the criminal-justice system.

In reviewing these external stressors it can be seen that in many, if not all, instances the stressors reported are way beyond the control of any individual officer. These external stressors may be addressed by the sheriff, the chief of police, or the Police Officers' Association, and even then the amount of change may be minimal. For officers to become frustrated and obsessed by events beyond their control is at best an ineffective effort, and may lead to some of the devastating effects of stress. It may be more appropriate and healthy for the officer to develop a new attitude about these events or at least change his reaction to them.

INTERNAL STRESSORS

Poor Training: We discussed how officers will be less stressed if they are prepared appropriately for the events they will encounter. The more perfunctory and rigid a department's training program is, the more anxious and therefore ineffective its officers will be. Effective training is essential. It affects how officers see their role and respond to various situations. If over or under reaction results it can be detrimental to all. A variety of learning approaches should be employed including lecture, multi-media, small group discussion, role playing with as much experiential knowledge as possible presented.

Poor Supervision: The major stressor for most line officers is the first line supervisor—the sergeant. Secondly, it's the administration. Whatever the reason, weak or authoritarian supervision at all levels of police management creates stress for police officers and will be discussed later.

Poor Career Development Opportunities: Police officers want to do a good job and get ahead. They want more say in the department and its direction. The problem occurs when more people want promotions than there are positions. Large agencies, having more personnel, generally have more promotions because of the movement that naturally occurs in a big organization. However, there has been less upward movement lately because, as budgetary constraints get tighter, the span of control or command for the supervisor seems to widen. Combine this with a move toward civilianization (having civilians rather than police personnel to perform jobs not requiring a sworn person, i.e., budgeting, payroll, personnel), the upward movement in these larger agencies slows even more. Small departments have only one chief, perhaps a captain, and maybe a sergeant, with the rest of the officers performing line functions. This makes promotion even more difficult.

Often departments will select individuals who are ambitious, outgoing, like to take charge and have high energy, and then will place them in a situation which denies them the opportunity of moving up the organizational ladder. There are few opportunities for aspiring officers, and as a result they may laterally transfer to another department for perceived opportunities or they leave law enforcement altogether.

The Harbor Patrol boat tied up alongside a salvage boat and the two patrolmen stepped aboard. The diving boat's skipper asked the officers into the galley for a cup of coffee, and the younger cop asked him if there were any openings for divers with his company. The skipper replied, "Yes, as a matter of fact I have got an opening— if you're sure you want to leave the force." The officer told him: "It's not really a question of my wanting to leave police work. It's just I don't think I'll ever get where I want to be in the department. I'm doing police diving for $1800 a month while your divers are drawing down about $2900 a month for the same kind of work. If I stay with the department for another fifteen years, which will give me twenty, I'll be lucky to be a lieutenant. And I'd still be making a lot less than one of your new divers. So—why don't you give me a job application and I'll return it tomorrow."

Inadequate Reward and Reinforcement System: Cops are expected to perform well under all circumstances. Exceptional performance is often the standard expected by everyone: supervisors, peers, city and department administrators, and the community. Everyone knows when an officer makes a mistake. If they don't read about it in the paper, hear or see it on the news, they'll hear about it via the grapevine. But what about the officer who performs well? Does the administration say anything? Does the immediate supervisor acknowledge the performance? Since the supervisor can't give a raise, commendations are acceptable, as are words of appreciation for a job well done. Do fellow workers recognize the performance or do they, too, just go on about their day? There aren't many people who don't like hearing nice things said about them or receiving a pat on the back, whether it be from a citizen, administrator, supervisor or fellow officer. And, yet, this rarely occurs.

Officer Earl C. showed me a letter he'd received from

the office of the mayor commending him for his heroic efforts in risking his life to save the lives of four citizens. The officer didn't want the letter, stating, "It was rubber stamped. In fact, I don't think the asshole even knows about it."

Offensive Department Policies: Periodically, decisions are made by administrators which are experienced as stressors by the line troops. These inappropriate policies, (as viewed by officers) are different in each department, whether it be a new shift rotation plan, the lowering of height and weight standards, a manual of policy and ethics changes, or whatever. The more input that line officers have about such decisions, the more chance they'll have of being accepted. In surveys of line officers and chiefs, both groups see that one of the major problems confronting police officers today is the lack of administrative support. Officers have to make numerous independent decisions, some of them enormous in consequence. Often they don't feel supported or backed by the chief, particularly if the wrong decision was made. And yet they see the administration demanding support on all of its decisions.

Excessive Paper Work: Police are outgoing, energetic people who are doers rather than observers. They want to be involved, where the action is, not sitting at a desk doing paper work. However, every instance, from arrests to merely listening to a complaint, must be written up. On a busy night a policeman and his family can almost be guaranteed that there will be a few hours out of their time together because of necessary paper work.

Poor Equipment, Poor Pay: Everyone is tied to budgetary restraints. You can only cut the financial pie into so many slices. Administrators make their money by planning and allocating appropriately. Each dollar put into equipment, facilities, support services, benefits, etc., takes away from the dollars available to put officers on the street. And yet for officers to be effective on the street they need adequate equipment support services, etc. Striking the right balance is extremely important—and it's frustrating when administrators and officers alike know the cops salary is less than that of a trucker or a journey-man in most trades, and the cop's equipment is inferior to that used by criminals.

Security—Arbitrary And Political Terminations: In some cities and counties throughout the country, police officers are not considered part of the Civil Service system. The average stay for a police chief is three to five years. When an election occurs and the incumbent is defeated, supporters of the old sheriff or chief are often requested to leave the department. In such situations, policemen can hardly avoid feeling anxious.

In considering internal stress, one can again see that many of these stressors are beyond the control of any one officer. However, police associations working together with administration may be able to come up with healthy solutions. Clearly in some instances an administrator can take some direct steps to reduce the stressors affecting their officers.

THE WORK ITSELF

Role-conflict Services Vs. Enforcement: It is particularly important for administrators and officers to have similar views of the officers' proper role when they are faced with ambiguous situations where there is a discrepancy between law, police and community standards, and personal loyalties. Police officers must perform adquately not only to meet their own role definitions and those of their supervisors; they also must meet the expectations of citizens and critical elements of the media.

Shiftwork: Rotating shifts place extra demands on individuals and their biological clocks. These shifts can leave officers cut off from their families and other normal social interactions. In the family, two schedules must be maintained: one for the wife and children, the second for the husband and father. Cooking separate meals, keeping the children quiet, answering the door or phone quickly—all come with the changing shifts.

Officer Katie S. said:
"I think it's pretty well acknowledged that everybody who comes into law enforcement realizes it's a 24-hour-a-day job. They know that it's going to stress them physically—it certainly stresses me when my shift is changed, for example. And when shifts are changed it doesn't only affect the officer, it also affects the officer's family and children and friends, even. Whole lives are altered by the stroke of a No. 2 pencil."

Fear and Danger: The bodily reactions one goes through when in particularly stressful events have been well documented. Police officers must constantly be on the alert so that they don't drop their guard and become another officer killed. However, quite often the police officer's job can also be boring, with little to do. Yet when the call comes they must move into a totally alert posture instantaneously. These extremes of experience produce wear and tear on officers.

Absence of Closure: Modern society has made us comfortable with the idea that everything fits together, has its place, and each event has a beginning and an end. For police officers, this often is not the case. They know there was a crime committed, but they have no suspects. They apprehend or arrest suspects and may never find out what happened to them. They rush a child, an elderly woman or a rape victim to a hospital and never find out if they lived or died. They are involved in the process but not the conclusion.

When the sergeant reprimanded Officer William B. for wasting department time and resources by phoning hospitals, driving past victims' homes to check up on them, and doing other unauthorized follow-up calls, William replied with an unusual vehemence: "Look, Sarge, as far as I"m concerned I'm not wasting time by showing a little human feeling for the people I deal with! It so happens that I work for the people of this town! That's what I get paid for! I've been programmed since high school to be neat and orderly and well-organized. I've always hated to start something and have someone else finish it. What am I supposed to do?—forget all about a guy that loses his leg in a wreck I'm called on when all it takes is a phone call a couple days later?"

People Pain: Police see people experiencing a great deal of pain. Day after day, week after week, seeing so much depravity and sadness can "play with your head," as some officers put it. They may begin to wonder, "What's society coming to?" Besides personally experiencing various human tragedies, officers hear about countless others over the police radio. The result can be the same as experienced by others in the helping professions—namely, burnout. People only have so much to give to one another, and cops (as well as doctors, nurses, psychologists and social workers) need to know when to step back and ask for a breather. Hopefully, with the understanding and assistance of supervisors and administrators, this can happen when necessary.

Patrolman Ell S. relates this incident: "One morning at about 1:00, we were driving south on a viaduct in a driving rainstorm. I was driving while my partner was resting his eyes and was barely able to keep my eyes open myself. I was suddenly snapped out of my drowsiness by a late-model Buick which passed at a speed I estimated at more than 100 miles per hour. I immediately gave the new Plymouth we had been assigned all the acceleration it had, correcting a little for the fish-tail as we lost traction on the slick pavement.

"At first, I didn't think we could catch up, but as we gained speed and I noticed the speedometer needle passing 105, it looked like we were matching his speed, and as we reached 115 I could tell we were gaining. I held top speed, managed to get past the Buick, and then started slowing as I pulled right, forcing him to slow down too. The Buick seemed to slow to about 60, then the driver attempted to turn right into an open parking lot, which caused the car to spin around, and it came to a stop with the right rear wheel in a ditch.

"While my partner approached the passenger side of the car, I opened the driver's door, reached in and turned off the ignition, and pulled the young man out of the car. As he stood up, I was almost sickened by the smell of booze and vomit emanating from the interior of the Buick. I didn't think the young man was going to be hostile, and I could see that he was so drunk he could barely stand, so I almost caught a well-thrown right fist that glanced off the side of my head, knocking my cap into the mud. I put the suspect on his face beside my cap, handcuffed him, and hauled him to his feet. When we got him in the back seat of the patrol car, I noticed the suspect had on a pair of military dress trousers, a military belt, and dog-tags. I asked him if he was stationed nearby. He said, 'Yeah, in nearby 'Nam. I'm home on leave.'

"Since my partner and I had both been in the service,

we had a certain amount of sympathy for the young man, especially since we had both been hard drinkers while in the service ourselves. But as we were listing the charges he had accumulated—which included Reckless Driving, Driving While Intoxicated, Attempting to Elude, Speeding: 105 in a 40 zone, Resisting Arrest and Assault—there did not seem to be much we could do to help him. After we finally got through to the suspect that he was in pretty serious trouble, his attitude started to change. He no longer seemed angry, but rather very despondent. When I told him that we would talk to the sergeant and see how easy we could go on him, he surprised me by saying the charges were not important. He just wanted to get it over with so he could continue his 'celebration'. When we asked him what he had been celebrating he looked like he was trying to smile, but then his face crumpled and he tried unsuccessfully to fight back tears. 'I was celebrating the birth of my wife's son, officer. We always wanted a son, ever since we got engaged when we were in high school together. But not like this.'

"What do you mean, 'not like this', soldier? Isn't the baby healthy? I asked him. 'Look', he replied, 'I don't want to try to make any excuse to you guys, but I'll give it to you straight. I flew in from 'Nam about 16 hours ago after getting emergency leave. I'd heard from a friend that my wife was going into the hospital, but he didn't know why. I was almost ready to come home anyway, and my lieutenant fixed up the papers in four hours, and I didn't have time to call home. When I got to my wife's parents' house, nobody was home, so I rushed to the hospital and that's where I found out she was having a baby. I didn't get to see her at first, and couldn't find her folks, so I went across the street to have a drink and start my celebration. I was really happy till I got halfway through my beer. Then I realized what was going on: my wife and I had gotten married a week before I left for 'Nam. But I had been in 'Nam for 13 months. I couldn't believe it, but I'd got shot out of the saddle while I was over there. I found my wife's mom and dad in the hospital cafeteria and they didn't have to tell me anything. The look on their faces told it all. I didn't talk to them, and never went up to see my old lady. I split and started drinking until I was able to figure out what I should do. At first I wanted to kill my wife. I called the hospital to find what room she was in, and that's when I was told the baby was a boy. But I couldn't kill her and I couldn't look at her or the baby. After getting drunker, it seemed the best thing I could do was kill myself. So I got in the car that my wife had been keeping for us, and was looking for a good place to crash and burn. You know the rest.'

"I asked my partner to step out of the car for a minute with me. Since I was the senior officer, any decision regarding the handling of the suspect would ultimately be my responsibility, but I wanted him to know what I was going to do and, hopefully, have his backing. He did not agree, but reluctantly went along with the plan. I radioed the precinct to inform our sergeant that we would be about a half hour late getting in, with no explanation as to why. Then we got the Buick out of the ditch and my partner drove it, following me with the suspect in my car. We first went to my apartment, cleaned the young man up, gave him an old but clean pair of pants and shirt, then drove by the hospital. The duty nurse confirmed his story about the baby boy. Then we took him to a restaurant where I knew a waitress was working who owed me a favor. She agreed to keep an eye on the young man, give him all the coffee he could drink, and call us if he tried to leave. I explained to him that I would be back shortly after 4:00 to take him to his car. By this time, he was starting to sober up somewhat and assured us that he had no intentions of harming himself or his wife. He still did not know what he would do, but he seemed rational and more in control of himself.

"When I arrived back at the precinct, the sergeant was

boiling. He refused to accept my explanation and threatened to have me fired if I did not come to my senses and bring the suspect in for booking. At any rate, I picked the soldier up at 4:30 a.m., took him to his car, which we had left in front of my apartment, and he left. I never followed up on the incident and just hoped the soldier never did anything crazy that would make me regret having helped him. As for my sergeant, he forgave me the next evening when I arrived early and informed him that there were two fifths of his favorite scotch in the back of his pickup truck. All he said was, 'You sure have a different way of doing things, son, but once in a while you do the right thing'."

Responsibility For Other People's Safety: A belief of many experts in the field of stress is that the more you feel responsible for other people, the more stress you experience. Police have a tremendous responsibility over others' lives and are given a "sacred trust" in this matter by the community. They must act appropriately in events that affect the welfare of others in spite of any anxieties they might have about their own welfare.

Officer Bob B. was called to the scene when a man climbed to the top of a tall oil tank and was threatening to jump. Even though he was afraid of heights, Bob had to scale a ladder to the top of the tank and talk to the man, and eventually he wrestled the man onto the ladder and forced him to climb down with him step by terrifying step. When they reached the ground, everyone cheered and hailed the officer as a hero. But Bob was still so shaken up, so afraid, that when he stood there over the man who had caused him so much agony, he simply lost control and kicked the man, hard, in the teeth. The officer had to be restrained, and he ended up getting days off for using unnecessary force.

Consequences Of One's Actions: Police officers daily

must make a variety of independent decisions in ambiguous situations: whether to cite an individual or give him a warning, to arrest or not, to shoot or not, etc. Most decisions in police work are not clear-cut. It is inevitable that certain mistakes will be made, and officers can lose their jobs or even have criminal charges filed against them. As with few other professionals, officers must face the consequences of their actions. When this is combined with the feeling that there is no administrative support, the pressure can be unbearable.

Policing is stressful. However, there are also many joys officers receive, whether it be from delivering a baby, saving a life or seeing a frightened face turn to a smile. There are many other ways officers receive rewards for their work.

Just before retirement, Officer James D. looked back over his career and expressed these satisfactions:
"I've made some tremendous friends because I was a cop, whether they were victims or in some cases suspects. I wouldn't ever invite them to my house, but I enjoy the relationships I have with the dings in my area. The guy, Chain Man, who comes in with chains welded all around him—I give him a cup of coffee and he provides me with a war story about what's going on in the streets, and I really look forward to seeing him. Or I get a call from a woman who's in the mental hospital, and she's entertaining to talk to because she's a ding and she's got things to say that I'd never hear from anybody else. There are just a huge number of dings who are interesting, and I feel sorry for people who are in any other line of work where they basically meet the same type of people day in and day out. We cops get really intimate contacts with a wild variety of people because we're called in when things have gone completely awry and people's veneers are stripped away.

"There is a tremendous amount of satisfaction in bringing an old woman her television set back, or finding a lost child, or delivering some woman's baby in her living room. God, sometimes the parents even name their kids after the cops who delivered them! And other officers who work with gangs know those kids by their first names and achieve a certain amount of . . . well, you couldn't really call it friendship, but certainly a mutual respect, I guess, that's a two-edged sword between them. The cops know these kids and their Mommas and Daddies, whereas civilians pay good money to go to a movie about gang life. All in all, being a cop is very rewarding."

PERSONAL STRESSORS

Incompetence: Within every organization there are some individuals unable to perform certain aspects of the job, whether it be the ability to shoot, to take charge of a particular assignment, or to perform effectively in a variety of assignments. Incompetence is dangerous in a police organization, and when it exists it not only affects the individual but the entire organization. But where do you go when you feel you can't cut it? To your wife? To the sergeant? The captain? And what will occur when you talk to them? A person who feels this way must be able to get some non-judgmental guidance. Supervisors must also understand their responsibility to keep abreast of their employees' performances.

Fear: What do officers do when they're afraid to shoot? What is the pressure like for them? We know that all of us respond to a set of events differently, making it more difficult to understand what makes one of us afraid. Policemen who are afraid will tremble; their faces will break out; their toes will curl up, or they'll experience other unsettling responses. It has happened to cops who've been on the job for a few weeks, a few months or years—for even 20 years. Often their fear is understandable and the situation is treatable or correctable.

Officer Patrick W. remarked:
"The man who doesn't know the meaning of the word 'fear' probably doesn't know the meaning of most other words either. Only the most stupid, drunk, drugged or enraged man doesn't experience fear when he's in a dangerous situation. Fear is a natural response to danger which gives us that necessary shot of adrenelin. I don't think courage is the absence of fear, but rather the ability to control fear and maintain composure in the tightest of jams. The only problem that certain officers have in working with these extreme emotions is that they can get addicted to the adrenelin 'high' that they feel in danger situations. Then they actually 'go on the hunt'—they go out looking for danger in order to feel that rush of excitement."

When discussing fear it is difficult to make the distinction between paranoia and reality. One officer had been involved in two incidents where he would have been killed except for a weapon malfunction and another where a part of his finger was shot off. Was this man paranoid when he said he was afraid to go out and work because he feared being shot? Or was he simply being realistic?

Fear, if it grips the officer and goes untreated, causes him to be inefficient, a high risk, and detrimental to himself and the department.

Non-Conformity: Those who are in the minority, not because of race or sex but rather as a result of their ideas and views, can experience additional stress. Police tend to stick together and prefer others who have the same point of view. Officers tend to react poorly and slowly to change, yet if we look over the years there have been major changes and advancements that have benefited police performance. Some of these new ideas or approaches have come from those with a little different point of view, those who dared to be different. Still, however, unless one conforms, goes along with the crowd, he is often isolated and left alone.

The Minority Officer-Ethnic And Female: Law enforcement is based on teamwork and reliance on one another. Whenever overtly or covertly, an individual is made to feel he or she is not wanted, additional pressure and frustration are put on the officer.

Personal Problems: Whether they be related to marriage, children, finances, having too many commitments, or whatever, our problems can overwhelm us. We have just listed the many general stressors facing police officers, and then when we add pressures from their personal lives we can see how they might become overloaded and how their performances can deteriorate both at work and at home.

If things are difficult at work, the stress can spill over to the home and family, and vice versa. A factor often correlating highest with an officer's performance is the stability of his home life or lack of it. For this reason law-enforcement agencies should make an active effort to foster family support.

Officer Peter S. and his wife Linda separated when she discovered he was having an affair. His repeated pleadings and promises never to see the girlfriend persuaded Linda to return. The home situation was tense for children and parents. These difficulties affected Peter's work, but imagine how he performed after the girl friend and her baby arrived at the wife's house.

CRIMINAL INVESTIGATOR STRESSOR

Criminal investigators have some stressors similar to those of any policy officer: the courts, shift schedules and inadequate support in terms of personnel and equipment. Yet, while being an integral part of the police effort, they are less likely to receive public attention for their efforts. Most of their daily duties are the behind-the-scenes activities which are crucial but generally not perceived as highly stressful in the continuum of police work.

Time: Investigators are required to handle many cases simultaneously within a limited time span. Receiving numerous bits of information regarding several cases, they must be highly organized and master jugglers of information. Investigators may find it harder than patrol officers do to leave their work behind at the end of the day; it may constantly prey on their minds. When caseloads are enormous, completing any case thoroughly becomes difficult.

Prestige Of Assignment: Within detective assignments, there are those which receive more acclaim, such as homicide, narcotics and vice, and others which can be seen as minor, although important to those involved, i.e., school problems, stolen bicycles, juvenile investigations, etc. Detectives with these latter assignments can sometimes question the value of their work.

Increased Caseloads: With the quick time frames established by law, the investigators must work rapidly to establish sufficient reason for continued detention. This pressure continues to heighten with the increasing crime rate. The sheer number of cases can overwhelm some officers.

Fishbowl Experience: In highly publicized cases, the police department and its investigators are under constant scrutiny, with expectations that the case will be solved quickly. As time passes, they are subject to news media criticism for not releasing enough newsworthy items or for not yet having solved the crime.

Role Conflict: In many investigative cases that involve surveillance, there is often much tedium while waiting for suspects to perform their illegal activity. For officers who are by nature active and aggressive, the boredom of waiting can be tension-inducing, especially, if they sense that there will be no results.

Lack Of Cooperation From Citizens: Generally not at the scene when the crime occurs, investigators depend on public cooperation, whether from witnesses or victims. Many people are hesitant to give information and at times will not even report crimes because of a fear of involvement or hostility toward authorities.

Officer Daniel S. commented:
"Not infrequently you find yourself liking the crook better than the victim. A case in mind is one in which two kids burglarized the house of a major political figure. The two burglars and I developed a rapport, and the parents of these two kids were also very nice and really concerned, and I wanted very much to do the right thing for the kids. I could see them as something besides just burglars. On the other hand, the victim of this crime gave me a list of stolen items that was just absurd. I knew the kids hadn't lifted most of the things that the victim listed—hell, he was just trying to rip off the insurance company. And suddenly the shoe was on the wrong foot—I was taking the side of the burglars against the victim. As it turns out, the politician had a great deal to do with my department, so my feelings put me in a tough spot. But sometimes it just happens that way. You like the bad guys despite yourself."

Although this list is not complete, it is easy to see that police work, whatever one's assignment is stressful.

Some police stressors are analogous to pressures encountered in other professions. Teachers, for example, might also be frustrated by inadequate pay, or by a system which doesn't allow them to implement their own ideas but expects conformity of style and method. Teachers may feel locked into their role as classroom authoritarians and find it difficult to relate to some of the children who might require more individual attention or whom they might simply prefer. Likewise, television writers are often caught in a dilemma between what they would consider an original screenplay and what they must produce to be commercially successful. The pressure on corporate executives to perform helps to keep our hospital coronary units well occupied.

We'd be hard put, though, to think of a job other than police work that carries so much responsibility for the lives and safety of other at this pay level. To cope with the danger of their jobs, police officers typically develop a defense mechanism which corresponds closely to what psychologists call reaction formation, i.e., the repression or driving into one's unconscious of thoughts which are unacceptable and the conscious assertion of the very opposite. Like an old maid who compensates for unacceptable sexual impulses by expressing intense prudery, police officers can express a defensive facade of confidence and aggression as a means of coping with underlying feelings of fear and anxiety—elements which could incapacitate and immobilize them were they conscious of them. The inadequacy of this defense mechanism is twofold: Excessive aggression may lead officers to perform in unprofessional ways, and if the defense mechanism breaks down unprepared officers may not be able to function effectively.

Persons who attempt to underestimate the danger involved in police work often point to the greater proportion of time spent on activities where the danger level is low. However, officers have no way of knowing the true danger of a situation beforehand, and must approach most calls with caution. This fear, in turn, might lead to abrasiveness and conflict between the officers and the citizens they're supposed to be serving.

Officers can cope with this problem by establishing appropriate ways to readjust to a situation after their concern for personal safety has diminished.

In light of the kind of work the police do and the nature of man, the goal of eliminating fear is both undesirable and unrealistic. Fear in dangerous situations can be controlled to the point where it does not cause impropriety or inaction by officers. Fear can be used constructively to motivate officers to learn from past experience, to improve their conduct and to develop habitual responses to cope with danger. Officers need to remember that, in the face of danger, it is more important to exercise sound judgment than it is to be fearless.

Police officers, whether naively expecting to be fearless, or more conscious of what lies ahead, will still be unable to turn their emotions on and off as easily as putting on a uniform or getting into a black-and-white car. If they were better prepared, if the system were more supportive, if they were less isolated as time went on—indeed, if they were suited for the job in the first place—their chances of success would obviously be greater.

To meet the demands placed upon them, officers can keep too tight a rein on their emotions, can isolate their feelings and become uncomfortable in expressing them. They can become like pressure cookers that have been tightened down so the steam can't escape. Eventually, there's bound to be an explosion.

Underlying several of the common emotional problems are the officers' strong dedication to the job and to the principle of public service. This commitment, though admirable and desirable, may add to pressure on officers as they become frustrated in accomplishing their goals.

Police officers show a strikingly high incidence of stress-induced illness such as coronary heart disease, ulcers, arthritis and allergies, in addition to emotional problems. Research has indicated that law enforcement personnel commit suicide two to six times more often than the norm and some report that alcoholism and divorce may be more prevalent than has thus far been publicly acknowledged. More basic, and not so widely reported, are such things as family problems, breakdowns and milder stress-related phenomena. As a result of the concern about stress and how it is dealt with, studies have been conducted concerning its effects on the officers. Here are the sobering results of a few such studies:

> Kroes, Margolies and Hurrell in 1974 found that all 100 police officers interviewed in their study stated that the job adversely affected their family life. Digestive disorders were reported by 32%, and 24% reported headaches while compared with 14% of the civilian population.

> Richard and Fell's in 1975 examined hospital records and revealed that the suicide rate for police was very high. There was an extremely high number of "premature deaths" for every age group from 18 to 64 in the officer population, and admissions to hospitals were significant in the areas of circulatory and digestive problems. No significant difference was found in the frequency of use by officers of mental health facilities.

> In 1973, Grencik found that the onset of strain occurs early in an officer's career. This study focused on police officers who were 35 years old or younger who had worked in patrol for 5 years or more. The findings: 15% of the officers had levels of cholesterol which rendered them twice as prone to coronary heart disease. Triglycerides, often related to large alcohol consumption, were elevated in 27% of the officers. Some 45% of the

officers were from 6 to 20 lbs. overweight, while 28% were more than 21 lbs. overweight. Some 86% of the officers performed little or no exercise, with 14% exercising three or more times a week. The Health-Heart Index categories in relationship to coronary heart disease found:

Low Risk	11%
Average Risk	62%
Medium High Risk	25%
High Risk	2.5%

The summary of this study, tragically, seems to be speaking about law enforcement officers all over the country. It reads as follows:

"The evidence presented in this index indicates that the officers are overweight, tend toward high cholesterol and triglyceride valves, smoke excessively and do not get enough exercise. They eat larger amounts than needed; they eat too much of the wrong kinds of food; and their daily eating schedules are not in accordance with good health practices."

In yet another study, Jacobi, in examining Workmens' Compensation cases in 1975, reported that police officers submitted six times more claims than other employees. Approximately 30% of their claims were concerned with lower back pain, with about one third of those estimated to involve psycholgical problems. Some 50% of all claimants had high blood pressure, an early indicator of coronary heart disease.

In addition to these physical problems just mentioned, there are other problems or behaviors that are related to the stress of the job.

Workaholism: When we combine dedication and excitement with the challenging aspects of police work, they become job addicting. The satisfying feelings of solving crimes or apprehending criminals, eliminating menaces from the community and preventing crime, become the sole goals for many in these circumstances. The growing isolation from other events around them, the feeling that they can be truly "themselves" only around their colleagues, and perhaps also alienation from their families and spouses, can add to the vicious circle. The more they work, the more they only feel well working. They can ultimately reach the point where they are obsessed with work, and lose a feeling for their limitations, and perhaps their ability to objectively judge situations. This over-zealous attitude can strain their systems to the breaking point and have the results on the job that are diametrically opposed to their intentions.

Exhaustion Syndrome: Stress is cumulative, causing individuals to become "burnt out," cynical and disgusted. Officers who have experienced too many setbacks and been continually frustrated, often without even realizing it themselves, may lose all incentive. Their only remaining motivation is sticking it out until time for retirement and the pension money.

Sergeant Eddie E. had been a fairly productive employee whose work performance began to deteriorate. With 18 years on the job and two left until retirement, he informed his captain that he lacked all motivation, but would stick around until his 20th year. In the encounter with the captain, Eddie also informed him he had not been performing some of his daily assigned tasks for as long as a year. With this knowledge, the captain encouraged Eddie to seek professional assistance.

Eddie had really given up, to the point of not cleaning his house, cutting the grass, washing his car, or even keeping his clothes clean. This had gone on for almost three years. The only thing he had managed to do was to keep his uniforms clean, as he had to be presentable at work. In addition, Eddie had not sent his income tax in for over three years. After several counseling sessions, Eddie began to regain his motivation. His car was washed and polished, and he even managed to launder his clothing. And, finally, the income tax forms were filled out, which culminated in a $6,000 return. The two year deadline until retirement given the Captain had passed, Sergeant Eddie was anticipating working an additional five years.

Hyperaggressive Street Behavior: Officers often face hostility, which can cause them to slip into hyperaggressive attitudes which perpetuate themselves. The tougher they act, the more aggression they provoke. To them it most often seems that they are merely reacting by necessity rather than contributing to the hostility.

Alcoholism: The most socially acceptable way in the United States of relating with other people is in the presence of alcohol, and so an acceptable manner of commiserating with fellow sufferers is during the consumption of toxic beverages. This can become a habit or pattern not easily broken, and can lead to alcohol being increasingly seen as a substitute for other forms of relieving pressures. While many view alcohol as a shortcut to alleviating the negatives in life, it is a clearly established medical fact that alcohol is a depressant: Continual consumption of these beverages only increase one's depression.

Statistics from the National Council of Alcohol and Drug Abuse indicate that one out of every ten people in our society has a drinking problem. It is logical to assume that law enforcement has the same percentage of employees with drinking problems as found in other professions, and in fact the programs operating in police departments around the country to rehabilitate alcoholic officers support this assumption.

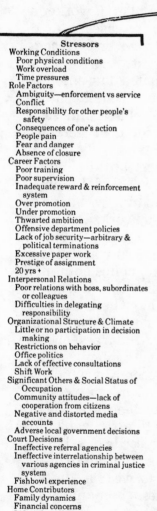

Stressors
Working Conditions
  Poor physical conditions
  Work overload
  Time pressures
Role Factors
  Ambiguity—enforcement vs service
  Conflict
  Responsibility for other people's
    safety
  Consequences of one's action
  People pain
  Fear and danger
  Absence of closure
Career Factors
  Poor training
  Poor supervision
  Inadequate reward & reinforcement
    system
  Over promotion
  Under promotion
  Thwarted ambition
  Offensive department policies
  Lack of job security—arbitrary &
    political terminations
  Excessive paper work
  Prestige of assignment
  20 yrs +
Interpersonal Relations
  Poor relations with boss, subordinates
    or colleagues
  Difficulties in delegating
    responsibility
Organizational Structure & Climate
  Little or no participation in decision
    making
  Restrictions on behavior
  Office politics
  Lack of effective consultations
  Shift Work
Significant Others & Social Status of
  Occupation
  Community attitudes—lack of
    cooperation from citizens
  Negative and distorted media
    accounts
  Adverse local government decisions
Court Decisions
  Ineffective referral agencies
  Ineffective interrelationship between
    various agencies in criminal justice
    system
  Fishbowl experience
Home Contributors
  Family dynamics
  Financial concerns
  Life cycle
  Developmental phases
  Significant others

The Individual
Genetics
Unique Personal History
Developmental Phases
Psychological Makeup
  Level of anxiety
  Level of neuroticism
  Tolerance of ambiguity
  Type A behavior pattern
  Minority Officer—ethnic & female
  Non-conformist
  Alcoholic
  Workaholic
  Overly Aggressive
  Traumatic Experiences
  Incompetence
  Fearfulness

Effects
Job Performance
  Attendance difficulties
  Arrives late—leaves early
  Frequent days off for vague ailments
    or implausible reasons
Job Satisfaction
  Fellow workers complain
  Overreacts to real or imagined
    criticism
  Lacks motivation
  Undependable statements
  Avoids associates
  Job dissatisfaction
State of Physical Heath
  Complains of not feeling well
  Sick days and hospitalization used
    more than average
  Minor injuries on job
  High blood pressure
  High cholesterol level
  High triglyceride level
  High heart rate
  Digestive problems
  Circulatory problems
Emotional State
  Negative—pessimestic attitude
  Unreasonable resentment
  Depressive mood
  Reduced aspiration
  Exaggerates work accomplishments
Increased Smoking, Drinking, and Drug
  Use
  Escapist drinking
  Other drugs
Family Adjustment
  Personal & domestic problems

As a result of the increasing discussion and awareness of police officer stress in the late 1970's and '80's,
there has been a steady rise in the number of worker's
compensation and retirement disability cases related
to stress in California, the only state currently recognizing psychological components to work related
injury. Cognizant of the dangers that a law-enforcement career can create, injury-on-duty benefits have
been awarded to officers for stress-related illnesses
ranging from heart disease to emotional or nervous
disorders and alcoholism.

Worker's Compensation laws were established to
insure that an employee who has an industrial injury,
as well as those who are dependent on him, will have a
means of support while he is unable to work. They are
also intended to provide a forum to decide disputed
cases as quickly as possible—and this is what sometimes drives a wedge between officers, police adminis-
trations, and the governments for which they work.

The issue is: How does one determine whether a person is really sick? In the macho world of law enforcement, people who are emotionally ill are seen as
"candy asses," complainers, malingerers, phonies, etc.
In the movie "Patton," there is a scene in which a
soldier is brought into an infirmary for minor wounds
and it appears as though he will be able to return to
the front lines shortly. When General Patton walks in
the young fighter is crying. Patton proceeds to yell and
berate this man, who says he "can't take it anymore."
Is this man a coward? One not fit to wear a United
States military uniform? A worthless human being
who is a disgrace to his family and country? Or has he
simply, for whatever reasons, reached his breaking
point?

Although this example may seem far fetched, the
issues in many worker's compensation cases are similar. The contention that an officer "can't take it any-

more" is frequently heard and is at the core of many stress related cases.

The claimants or wounded employees know they are sick, even though there may be no physical signs of their illness and some people think they are trying to "rip off" the system, get as much money as possible, and skip town.

Unfortunately, with the continuing escalation of these claims an adversary proceeding develops, with the employees hiring lawyers and doctors who believe they are sick, while the municipalities hire attorneys and doctors who believe they are well. This disagreement is finally decided by the Worker's Compensation Appeals Board after a lengthy process. Too often at the end of the process no one is happy and the interaction between the employee and employer is, at best, strained.

California Worker's Compensation law states that injury may occur as the result of repeated insults to the body or psyche over a period of time. These insults are known as micro trauma: minor incidents or events which over time culminate in injury. Law enforcement officers can make legitimate medical claims from numerous stress related micro traumas. California law also provides for benefits if the job aggravates, by injury or accumulated "stress and strain," a pre-existing condition. It's easy to see how the work a police officer does could result in stress and aggravate a pre-existing condition. Think of someone who periodically has minor mood swings such as depression or elation. Exposure to several tragic incidents could cause a predisposed depression to become a major depression. Conversely, too many "hot" calls to exciting events could cause some to go beyond excitability to a state of frenzy.

There is a great deal of money involved in worker's compensation cases. Officers who receive disability retirements will receive between $1,000,000 and $2,000,000 over their lifetime. The expenses to governmental agencies for abuses of police and firefighters disability pension systems is costing at least $20 million a year nationwide, according to the Better Government Association. According to some critics these pension systems are so poorly planned and so badly administrated that abuses are not only allowed, but encouraged.

Larry C. had worked eight years for a medium-sized city and had many of the problems discussed. He applied for an "injury-on-duty" stress-related injury because of emotional problems. After the lengthy appeals process the officer was awarded $100,000—and within a week he bought a Mercedes Benz with a license plate that read "STOLEN 1."

Police managers get upset with such apparent "rip offs." However, there are officers who are deserving of stress related compensation. How do you tell if the emotional problem is real? And job related?

If employees file a claim for stress related illness and the department questions them, they feel betrayed and quickly angered. It becomes even more complex when two qualified doctors give opposite opinions relative to the employee's condition and its cause. Unfortunately in too many of these cases the employees are almost forgotten among the medical and legal terminology, the disagreements and the squabble for money.

Chris W. is a 50 year old veteran. Divorced twice and looking forward to retirement, he is now looking for an easier assignment during his last two years with the department. Chris is involved in a serious relationship with a woman which is shaky at best. He has been on patrol in a particular metropolitan area for ten years and has requested a transfer which was denied. He has been having conflict with a particular ethnic group at work and now members of this group have started moving into his neighborhood. For a second time, he requests a transfer and again it is denied. This increases the pressure on his relationship and he begins having sexual-performance problems, which adds more stress. One day, in the middle of his shift, he drives into the station parking lot, walks into the watch commander's office and begins to tear up all the papers on the lieutenant's desk while yelling long and loud at the bewildered man.

Should Chris be disciplined for his actions? Should he be required to see a doctor? Is he a victim of stress? Should he be qualified for a work related injury, and if the symptoms persist, a disability retirement? Would your decision be any different if you were a street cop? A lieutenant? The chief? A lawyer or doctor? Did work cause or aggravate Chris's condition? Should he be compensated?

Dick P. 38, is a cop's cop. He has worked all the difficult and prestigious assignments, has often been selected for special assignments as a SWAT Team member, an instructor at the acadmeny, and so on. He has been highly respected throughout his career. During this career he had incurred several injuries, one which resulted in a 10% disability in his arm. After each injury he returned to work as soon as possible.

Dick P.'s wife died a year ago of cancer. His daughter has just been arrested for a drug problem. He is also teaching some special classes at the academy dealing with the importance of being quick and alert in the field. One day he starts crying like a baby. He doesn't feel that he can handle the job any longer. He just can't take it. He can't go to the captain because he doesn't think the captain will understand his sudden inability to handle the job. As a result of all of his problems, combined with his disability, he becomes afraid that he won't respond quickly and effectively enough to occurrences in the field. He just doesn't know what to do. He feels inadequate, alone, and wants to quit. He needs out of the job.

Is he a victim of stress? And if so, is he entitled to compensation for his injury and inability to work? Should he be granted disability retirement?

Emily W. 32, has worked a variety of assignments in her 10 years as a cop. She is considered by all a "damned good police woman." She and her husband have tried to have children, but she has had two miscarriages. As a result of dangers to her health, she is forced to have a hysterectomy. After recuperating, Emily is surprised to learn that she is being moved from a job she likes, with a regular day schedule and weekends off, to a job she doesn't like on the early morning shift. This creates difficulties with her husband, which, she believes, is the cause of their eventual separation. With these various pressures, Emily finds it impossible to get out of bed. She becomes subject to fits of uncontrollable tears and depression and stays away from work.

Is she entitled to work related-stress pay? Did the shift change increase a predisposition to depression? Are her real issues with her personal life? Did her work cause or aggravate her condition? And how much must work contribute to the condition? Should it be that compensation is awarded even if work is only a minor contributor?

Some interpreters of the law believe that compensation should be granted whenever work is a factor, no matter how minor its influence.

The issues are not clear-cut. But solutions need to be determined that are benficial to all—employees, managers and the public.

REFERENCES

Cobb, S. and Rose, R. "Hypertension, Peptic Ulcer, and Diabetes in Air Traffic Controllers." *JAMA,* 1973, 224(4), pp. 489-491.

Cooper, G. L. and Marshall, J. "Occupational Sources of Stress: A Review of the Literature Relating to Coronary Heart Disease and Mental Ill Health." *Journal of Occupational Psychology,* 49, (2), 1976.

Levinson, H. *Executive Stress.* New York: Mentor Books, 1975.

Durner, J. A. et al "Divorce: Another Occupational Hazard." *Police Chief,* 42 (11), 1975.

Eisenberg, T. "Labor-Management Relations and Psychological Stress-View From the Bottom." *The Police Chief,* 42(11), 1975.

Ellison, K. W. and J. L. Genz "Police Officer as Burned-Out Samaritan." *FBI Law Enforcement Bulletin,* 47(3), 1978.

French, J. and Caplan, R. *Organization Stress and Individual Strain.* In A. J. Marrow (Ed.) The Failure of Success. New York: Amacom, 1972.

Grencik, J. M., in Pitchess, P. J., *The Psychological Fitness of Deputies Assigned to Patrol Function and its Relationship to the Formulation of Entrance Standards for Law Enforcement Officers.* Law Enforcement Assistance Administration Grant, Final Report, June, 1973.

Guralnick, L. "Mortality by Occupation and Cause of Death Among Men 20-64 Years of Age." 1950, *Vital Statistics-Special Reports,* 1963.

"Coping With Stress." *International Association of Chiefs of Police Training Key No. 257.* Gaithersburg, Maryland, 1978.

Hillgren, J. S., Bond, R. and Jones, S. "Primary Stressors in Police Administration and Law Enforcement." *Journal of Police Science and Administration,* 4(2), 1976.

Horowitz, M. J. *Stress Response Syndromes.* New York: Jason Aronson, 1976.

Jacobi, H. *Reducing Police Stress: A Psychiatrist's Point of View.* In Kroes, W. H. and Hurrel, J. (Eds) Job Stress and the Police Officer. U.S. Department of Health, Education and Welfare. (Niosh) 1975, p. 85.

"Job Stress in Police Work." *International Association of Chiefs of Police Training Key No. 256.* Gaithersburg, Maryland, 1978.

Kroes, W. H., Margolis, B. and Hurrell, J. "Job Stress in Policemen." *Journal of Police Science and Administration,* 2(2), 1974.

Kroes, W. H. and Hurrell, J., (Eds) *Job Stress and the Police Officer.* U.S. Department of Health, Education and Welfare, (Niosh), 1975.

Kroes, W. H. *Society's Victim: The Policeman.* Springfield, Illinois: Charles Thomas, 1976.

Maslach, C. "Burned Out." *Human Behavior,* September, 1974.

Police Federation Newsletter, 4(5), 1963.

Wagoner, C. P. "Police Alienation: Some Sources and Implications." *Journal of Police Science and Administration,* 1976, Vol. 4, pp. 389–403

President's Commission on Law Enforcement and the Administration of Justice: The Police, Washington, D.C., U.S. Government Printing Office, 1967.

Reiser, M. "Stress, Distress and Adaptation in Police Work." *The Police Chief* 1976, 43(1).

Richard, C. and Feld, R. D. *Health Factors in Police Job Stress.* In Kroes, W. H. and Hurrell, J. (Eds.), Job Stress and the Police Officer. U. S. Department of Health, Education and Welfare (Niosh), 1975.

Selye, H. *The Stress of Life.* New York: McGraw Hill, 1956.

Selye, H. *Stress Without Distress.* Philadelphia: J. B. Lippencott, 1974.

6

POLICE MARRIAGES—
DETERMINING THE BALANCE

If being a police officer is difficult, being married to one isn't easy, either. Those in law enforcement have extra roadblocks in their marriages—shift changes, exposure to people in trauma, denial of emotion, other job demands, which affect their families deeply.

Marriage means different things to different people. The rules and behaviors of each couple are different. There are monogamous and open marriages and myriad other living and mating arrangements. Although some officers and their mates have experimented with alternative life styles, most see marriage in the more traditional way.

By comparing people raised in the 1930's and '40's with those raised in the 1960's and '70's we get a sense of what has happened to marital relationships. Marriage in the '30's and '40's generally consisted of a man (breadwinner, husband, father, disciplinarian), a woman (wife, mother, housekeeper and child bearer) and children (to be seen and not heard). In most cases, the wife did not work. Although during World War II many women went to work in factories to help those fighting overseas, but when the war ended, they usually returned home again to clean house and raise children.

Traditionally husbands made the majority of economic and "important" decisions, with wives rarely questioning the decisions or their husband's right to make them. If women did make decisions, they concerned running the household and managing the children. This system was generally accepted by everyone. The wife supported her husband and he in turn provided for and protected her.

During the turbulence and confusion of the '60's and '70's a diversity of life styles developed. Temporary sexual and living arrangements, young working mothers, childless couples and inter-racial and open homosexual relationships became more apparent. Single-parent families, step-parenting, live-in relationships and working wives all became a part of American life. And police officers growing up in the 1960's and '70's, like the rest of us learned these varied ways. They tend to marry later, wait longer to have fewer children, and have more two-income households than those raised in the '30's and '40's. However, many still hold most of the traditional views of men's and women's roles in relationships.

Our society's view of permanence in relationships has evolved from such dramatic changes as this one: there was one divorce for every 1,234 marriages in the 1890's, and one divorce for every 2½ marriages less than 100 years later. With over one million divorces in 1975 and yet more in the '80's; our divorce rates, already the highest in the world, continue to rise.

With the advent of the birth-control pill, legalized abortion and a rising resort to sterilization, couples nowadays have more of a choice about whether to have children and when. More couples wait to have children, allowing the wife a chance to develop her own career.

Over one-fourth of all American women (44 million) work. They make up 42% of the entire work force. Sixty nine percent of women born between 1956 and 1960 work. The typical environment for American females has shifted from home to work place. This change causes a rippling effect influencing attitudes, values and views about male and female roles, marriage, work, etc.

The 1980's couple has one-half the number of children as their parents, on the average, and uses more child-care services. After child-bearing, women continue to work, establishing their careers and building their security.

There is no one way to describe the typical American family any longer. There is no "normal" relationship in America, but rather a multiplicity of ways to live in a marriage and family.

The changing styles of the 1980's are reflected by TV programs that depict a divorced father living with his divorced daughter; two men or women living together; a young daughter who leaves her family to live with her boyfriend; a blended family with children from two prior marriages, and so on.

Where will this lead? Some commentators believe the 1980's will look like "the good old days" compared with times that are coming for society and the family.

Naturally, these upheavals affect police families as well as others. Whether the divorce rate for those in law enforcement is higher than for those in other professions is often debated. But the answer to this debate is not as important as recognizing the strain that law enforcement places on marriage and family life. Conversely, the stability of an officer's home life affects his work. Emotional pressures that result from unhappy relationships or divorce can influence the officer's judgment and lessen his emotional control. It should come as little surprise that the major issues cops present to psychologists or other mental health professionals are relationship problems, marriage problems, the ability of men and women to live together in a compatible, vital, meaningful and growing relationship.

In the beginning of relationships, there are two complete and separate human beings who for a variety of reasons are attracted to each other. After this initial attraction, each person still retains his or her own individuality. However, they begin to share more of themselves and get to know each other better and more intimately through their communication of feelings, and ideas. As their relationship continues and they begin to spend additional time together, discussing in more detail their values, attitudes, and beliefs, the two people start to talk more in terms of "we" or "us." After further communication and time together, they may feel that they know each other totally, understanding each other "as no one else could." Their wants and needs become the same or compatible. They fulfill each other's needs. And when this closeness is achieved they may decide to marry.

A relationship built on honest communication and understanding must be continually cultivated. Sometimes partners assume that each other's values, wants and needs will stay the same forever. They forget that their values, which were once similar, can change. Changes in society's mores, in work and in social life, combined with the influences of each person's daily experiences, make it unlikely that both will *not* change, in fact, these different experiences and changes need to be communicated, or the relationship will be dull, unfulfilling and lifeless. Communication is the key. People get to know one another, love and marry because of understanding developed through communication. Communication makes them closer. Conversely, a lack of it or dishonest communication seems to drive them apart. The causal factor of many problems in all marriages, including those of police officers, is often related to inappropriate, ineffective or dishonest communication between spouses. A *US NEWS AND WORLD REPORT* study involving communication between spouses (not the conversations during television commercials, such as, "Get me a beer") indicated that the average American married couple spends approximately thirty minutes a week in direct communication with each other. Some police officers and their spouses think that this estimate may be too high!

Even more important than the quantity of communication is the quality: What one communicates and how. What in the relationship is open to communicate? Everything? Only positive comments? Thoughts? Feelings? Does each partner have to present a certain image? Can a man have feelings, weaknesses and fears, and be able to express and discuss them with his spouse? Or must she always see him as strong and invincible?

Often in communication individuals get caught up in the content of the message. They feel they must tell each and every detail of every event. Although the events or tragedies that officers experience at work do not have to be communicated in exhausting detail, their reactions to those events, at least, should be communicated. Statements of feelings such as "I'm bushed"; "I'm feeling great"; "I had a good day"; "I had a rough day," tells a great deal.

It is assumed that when a couple decides to marry, they have similar values to begin their venture. But too often as the years pass marriage partners tend not to pay attention to or share their changing experiences, reactions, values, wants and needs.

If you sat down and made a list of values that are important, to you now, and then made a list of what was important to you fifteen, ten or even five years ago, you might be startled by the changes. For example, think of your values in the '60's, your thoughts about the Vietnam war, "hippies," the civil rights movement, busing, college unrest, etc. Today your concerns and attitudes might be totally different, reflecting the tremendous changes we've gone through individually and collectively.

These shifts in values happen to everyone. However, how they affect people's behavior may be different—and of course this is true of husbands and wives. Unless they communicate often and well, it's easy to see how they could drift apart over the years.

Bill and Carol F., were in their late twenties and married for seven years. Their decision to marry developed naturally from a sharing of common values and interests, and their deep love for one another. Everything was easy for them. They considered themselves to be the "perfect match." The young couple could envision their life style for at least the next ten years and they were in perfect accord on what they wanted. Their goal was to keep up with the "Joneses" and possessing all they wanted: the conveniences, flash and splendor of the modern world. To accomplish this, they would both work for at least three years, then have their first baby. Carol would work until the sixth month of her pregnancy to supplement Bill's income in case of emergency.

All went according to plan. After the baby's birth, things seemed fine for a year or so. The funds for "extras" were somewhat limited, but they were financially stable. Although Bill's income steadily increased and his position was secure within the police department, he began to fret about maintaining their style of living. He felt compelled to keep up with his peers who had no children and two incomes. Without consulting Carol, Bill began to work overtime occasionally for additional money. Soon he was working two shifts a day. Because of the long distance between home and work, Bill began to sleep in his camper truck at work, leaving Carol and the baby home alone at night.

Any marital relationship based on the above scenario would be prone to problems. As pressure mounted between the couple, they chose to see a counselor. After the initial introductions and general conversation which enabled the couple to feel more comfortable, Bill was asked to describe his needs and wants in the relationship. He replied, "To provide Carol and the baby with a very comfortable life style."

Carol, when queried, burst out, "I don't give a damn about expensive clothes, a beautiful home, a nice car, a swimming pool, a boat, or anything else that might impress other people. I want to spend more time with you. I want you to hold me, touch me. I want to be with you!"

Barely listening, Bill angrily interrupted, "What's gotten into you? We both knew exactly what we wanted, didn't we?"

Tragedies like this occur to couples when either person presumes there will be no change in their relationship, values, wants and needs. One's assumptions could be exactly the opposite of what the other is feeling or thinking.

When one partner in a relationship begins to change and the other doesn't, there will invariably be problems. As officers change during their occupational passages from their initial application until retirement, so will their spouses. Hopefully in the same direction.

When examining priorities in one's life and marriage, it is interesting to look at the behavior, rather than what is said. It's fine to say: "I love my wife." or "My wife and kids are very important to me." or "I would do anything for my wife and children." All are meaningful and committed statements. Yet, the same men who are saying these things might spend hardly any time with their families.

For most cops, work takes up to 40-plus hours a week. Commuting to and from work takes up another 5 to 10 hours. Changing clothes, washing up and eating away from the house several times might add an additional 10 hours a week. Recreation and exercise could add another 10 hours. Some officers go to school, which might take about 10 hours; and 10 hours could be added for miscellaneous private pursuits. Finally, an average of 7 hours a night for sleep would add 49 hours a week. This totals 137 hours since there are only 168 hours in a week, these hypothetical officers are left with 3 or 4 hours a day to be with the spouse and family, including mealtimes.

Obviously, there are occupational hazards inherent to marriages in certain other professions. Movie-stars' alliances, for instance, are notoriously difficult for obvious reasons. Likewise, law enforcement marriages encounter specific difficulties.

One reason that psychologists report high divorce rates among the police is because the people they counsel or work with are cops having difficulties. If this is the case, we psychologists may be doing what we accuse cops of— judging a whole category of people from the small group we experience. Several studies report high divorce rates, while others report low. Our assumption is that police have about the same amount of divorce as the general population. This could be increased some by the stress of the job or decreased by their conservative and traditional values regarding marriage and family life.

Whatever the divorce rate, spouses do certainly experience the "weight of the badge" throughout the course of their relationship. At various times, it may weigh heavily, while during other periods it is a source of pride and honor. It may be the basis for alternating states of euphoria and depression.

In the beginning of a relationship, the officer's badge is something in which both partners take pride. In many cases the initial character of the relationship is like a knight in shining armor and his lady fair. The officer/knight is treated as the dominant partner; a warrior, protector, provider, hero—the solid rock of the relationship. He fulfills his emotional needs by being all these things. At the same time he serves people on his job and projects a positive image which indicates that he is in control and can handle stress. The lady, on the other hand, is fulfilled in the role of the "woman behind the man." She builds the

knight's ego and keeps his image intact. Fulfillment
stems from his spit-and polish-appearance and the fact
that he is providing a valuable service to the community.
She can sit back with pride and say, "That is my man."
She is also fulfilled by being the one person with whom
the knight can relax and with whom he needn't project all
the strength and power required in his job. At every graduation ceremony there is evidence of the woman's pride,
joy, and satisfaction because her husband became a law
enforcement officer.

While not every relationship starts out this way, many
marital partnerships in law enforcement show this initial
pattern. They did, especially, in previous generations. The
man is often looking for a particular type of woman, one
who is willing to let him be the leader. The woman, too, is
looking for something at this stage of her life; she wants
to be taken care of, to sit quietly on the sidelines and let
her man be the public figure and breadwinner.

Consider the law-enforcement cadet at the academy. He
has to spend many hours on the academic part of his
training. His wife or girl friend spends considerable time
and effort helping him memorize and perhaps even write
papers while at the same time making sure everything on
the home front runs smoothly. She sees to it that he is
immaculately attired. It is not unusual for wives to also be
responsible for cutting lawns, trimming hedges, painting,
home repairs, and so on.

After initial compatibility of wants and needs, the
stresses incumbent to the officer soon become obvious. He
has unusual working hours, scattered weekends, extensive
overtime hours both on duty and in court, and he's always
on call for emergencies.

These alone are enough to cause numerous stresses in
the relationship, and a series of adjustments have to be
made. Most of these obvious pressures are adapted to and
handled rather quickly. However, there are other stresses
that can have long-range effects on the relationship.

These are the unexpected pressures and hazards of the job. In many instances, these stresses take their toll over a period of time, with neither person attending to warning signals or being able to pinpoint reasons for difficulty until finally all that is said by either person is, "I don't know why, but you've changed."

From the beginning of their careers, officers are trained to control their emotions while on the job, often with the result that they learn to deny feelings such as anger, disgust and sadness. Eventually, over months or years, any show of emotion may make them uncomfortable. They begin to build a wall so that whatever emotions still exist will no longer effect them. It becomes impossible to leave the robot image at the station, and so it is carried home. The spouses, meanwhile, are looking forward to being with their mates and may, have lots of feelings and thoughts they'd like to share. But often they won't be able to get through the invisible wall.

> Jeanne D., after attempting to get through to Penn and not arousing much response, finally said, "I give up! When I talk to you I feel like I'm talking to a brick wall! I work hard to get through your wall! I chisel all around the brick! I loosen the mortar! I reach in to take out one brick so I can get through to you, and as soon as I get it out, you push in a replacement!

> Rita G., in discussing her husband John, described the following: "I've also learned first hand that, while dealing with death may be part of John's daily routine, it hardly prepares him for the emotionally devastating experience of cradling the head of a wounded partner or the horror of photographing a fellow officer in the morgue. Most men can switch television channels or turn to the sports section of the newspaper when they've had their fill of violence, but we police wives know that even after a case is solved, the facts often lurk somewhere in an officer's subconscious even when he's trying to relax at home."

Often, when policemen are required to perform difficult tasks, they presume their spouses would be upset if they knew what happened. So the officers choose to remain silent, feeling that the less the wives know, the less they'll worry or make trouble. But as one wife states, "This lets the wife suffer alone in silence."

Because of the trauma and degradation they observed each day, officers tend to become overly protective of their wives and families. The job teaches the officers to be observant and their adoption of a suspicious nature is seen as desirable. Without meaning to however, they can carry this over into the relationship with the family.

At times they are overly concerned about where their spouses or children are, whom they are with, and what they are doing. They attempt to keep them from seeing or learning about the tragic aspects of life. The dependency that results from their desire to shelter their families can often backfire.

Because of their more sheltered existence, spouses may not be as concerned about their own safety as the officers are. During activities such as driving alone at night, traveling to different parts of the city, attending night classes or other activities on their own, the spouses may be comfortable while their mates may not. Officers may be pessimistic about life and spouses optimistic. The reality is probably somewhere in the middle.

Peggy G., an officer's wife, worked as a food waitress in a popular restaurant near their home. She enjoyed her work, although hectic, and liked meeting new people. Her husband, Harry, wasn't thrilled with her working, but understood that financially it was necessary. One evening Peggy's boss asked if she could work just that night as a waitress in the bar. Peggy explained that Harry didn't like her working in a bar. She checked with Harry to see how he felt about it, and although he wasn't too happy, he agreed, but only until midnight. At exactly 12 o'clock Harry arrived to pick his Cinderella up. She was extremely busy, the bar was full, and she was making excellent money in tips. He said he would wait just a few minutes, but that she should get ready to go. While waiting, Harry went into the restroom and encountered a man snorting cocaine. He also thought he saw another person outside smoking marijuana. These two incidents convinced him that his wife should not be working in the bar. He immediately told her that she had to leave. Peggy went to her boss and tried to explain the situation. He was totally unsympathetic, responding, "Tell Harry that *he* can support you from now on!" Peggy lost her job and was upset that Harry couldn't understand her viewpoint. She felt that what he had encountered was not typical of this pleasant restaurant-bar, and she enjoyed her work. And yet, Harry didn't want his wife to work "in such a place."

Both Peggy and Harry's viewpoints were accurate and reflected their own individual needs and values. How they chose to solve their differences was to honor Harry's feelings. Peggy felt left out of the decision and remained angry with him. He, on the other hand, did nothing to understand her anger, and felt his decision was just.

Law enforcement agencies have a basic paramilitary structure, and orders are expected to be accepted without question. When an assignment is given, officers are not expected to question its resonableness, disagree with the instruction, or refuse to carry through. They have to do as instructed. Thus supervisors can be a target of anger at times, but such anger cannot be vented within the structure of the agency.

After restraining themselves around supervisors and controlling themselves all day in dealing with the public, the officer may come through the front door in a highly charged state. Unfortunately, some harmless remark or action on the part of family members often triggers off these pent-up feelings. The family may even be set upon without provocation.

Captain Brock S. left for work a little early to take care of personal things before his nonstop schedule started. He knew that it was going to be a busy day, but that he'd be able to handle it. With about three hours to go before leaving for home and then venturing out again for a dinner function, he was told the sheriff needed to see him. He rushed down for a meeting with the sheriff, which took longer than expected, causing him to run late. After the meeting, he continued to meet all his commitments and then began the long trip home on the freeway. Being under stress and quick to irritate as a result of the day's pressures, he sensed himself becoming angrier and angrier as he traveled on the crowded road. At the end of the bumper to bumper trip, Captain Brock pulled off the freeway two blocks from home. As he turned the corner, the car had a flat tire. He was fuming—and walked the two blocks home. As he got close to his house, his dog ran toward him with the paper in his mouth. Brock reared back and kicked him.

Although the behavior was not the most appropriate, it illustrates how officers can bring their pressures home with them. Rather than displacing the anger on the dog, he might put it on his wife. Both officers and spouses must realize what's going on here. The officers must realize where their anger needs to be directed, and the spouses must understand that this anger is not related to them— and that they don't have to take it.

Many officers view their jobs as *the* important ones. Whatever the spouses' occupations, be it housewife or business executive, the officers believe their jobs are more necessary and significant. Police work involves excitement, danger, drama, life-and-death issues, and as a result they may see everything else as mediocre or boring. If this feeling exists it could lead to indifference and insensitivity at home and a blocking out of communication with spouses.

Barbara T. works as a director and counselor of the educable mentally retarded in an area that has a wide diversity in ethnic population. She is very excited about her job, takes it seriously, and has a personal feeling about each one of her students. She often brings home stories about La Shaun, Damion and other students. Barbara's husband, John, is the SWAT Team leader for a major law enforcement agency. He is involved in all types of crises, from suicide attempts, to hostage negotiations. It is not unusual for Barbara and John to be out at a nice restaurant and hear his "beeper" go off. This can end for them an evening they had planned for weeks. Generally, she takes this in stride, but during one three or four month period things exploded for Barbara and John. She began feeling that John's job took precedence over their relationship. While he felt he was handling all the crises that came with his job, she felt that he wasn't listening to her or even caring what happened in her own career.

Finally, one night after Barbara had tried for hours to talk with him, she said, "I'm going to have to try to commit suicide for you to listen to me! I'll just call your headquarters and tell them Lieutenant John T.'s wife is committing suicide and I'm sure I'll get a very quick response from you!" Finally, he heard her. Now they have a standing joke that when Barbara feels she is being ignored she just says, "I'm going to kill myself!" and John knows that it's time for him to listen to her. And, John has learned that Barbara's career, though different, is interesting and special in its own right.

Jim and Marty T., a police officer and his wife, went to a financial adviser to discuss ways they might better prepare for the future. When they got to the subject of life insurance, Jim said that they wanted life insurance only for him. The adviser asked if they had considered life insurance for Marty. Jim remarked that he didn't really think that was necessary, because he was the main provider for the family. The advisor then asked him how much money he thought he would need to have someone provide the services in the home that Marty performed. Jim was a little taken back. He had never thought about that. He had grown accustomed to expecting those services as a way of life. The adviser pointed out that he would have to consider hiring a babysitter, financial manager, cleaning lady, nutritionist, someone to do the laundry, a gardener, a part-time teacher, a counselor, etc. Jim felt that perhaps $200 a month— $2400 a year—would cover that. Marty was pleased when the financial adviser informed them that her services could not be duplicated for less than $15,000 a year.

Robert and Janet W., have a 1½ year-old baby. Both get up at 5:30 a.m. Janet, in addition to fixing breakfast for Robert, has to feed, clean, change and dress the baby. They leave the house at the same time. Robert has to be at work by 7 a.m. and Janet has to drive about 20 miles to drop the baby off at an all-day babysitter. Although Robert drives right by the babysitter, he refuses to either take or pick up the baby. Janet then drives 15 miles back towards her house to go to work. Robert finishes work at 3 p.m. and takes a nap at home until about 6 p.m. The wife finishes work at 5 p.m., drives the 15 miles back to the babysitter, and then the 20 miles back to her home. She quickly prepares dinner for Robert, they eat and Bob watches television, leaving Janet to do the dishes, clean up the house, and bathe and change the baby. Bob wants nothing to do with the baby and only wants to interact with Janet when she has completed all her duties. She gets her first chance to sit down by 9 p.m.

After a few minutes to unwind, it is time to turn in for the night so that she'll be able too get enough sleep before the early beginning of another busy day.

This is the pattern in this family during the work week. On weekends Robert often goes out and does things with the boys of a recreational nature, while Janet stays home to take care of the week's laundry and attend the baby.

Janet remains angry at Robert, while Robert see it as "her problem." Either things must change for this couple, or Janet may find life much easier without him. Each person must feel the worth and contribution of his/her work to the relationship. If this doesn't happen an imbalance is created, and both people may become dissatisfied.

If officers do not share their concerns with their wives and families, they generally share them with fellow officers—who are available at 2 a.m. when wives and families are not. The isolation of shift work typically results in the tendency of officers to associate exclusively with each other. Clannishness reinforces their reluctance to seek support from "outsiders." The officers' desire to protect their spouses from the seamy side of life, their reluctance to alarm them by disclosing the difficulties they may be facing, and their hesitancy to unveil feelings for fear of appearing weak—all serve to reduce communication between spouses and increase braggardly interaction between officers.

Seeking support and solace from fellow officers, in itself understandable and positive, increases the possibility of drinking problems arising, since alcohol is one of the most socially sanctioned ways of unwinding. After a few drinks, it is more acceptable to admit weaknesses or failings because you're with friends and don't have to wear the protective armor you've worn all day.

Drinking also fits in with the masculine image of strength and power. Statements like, "He can hold his liquor well," or "He can drink anyone under the table," imply that such an ability is positive and manly. This enables officers to enhance their "he-man" image and let their concerns show at the same time.

Although such activity may often even be healthful, facilitative and cathartic, it can also create difficulties. Officers who share their fears and frustrations only with fellow officers will receive feedback and direction only from their peers, who often view things in the same way. People with non-law-enforcement points of view, especially the wives, are often left out of the process and therefore do not see a multi-dimensional person. By admitting fears and problems only to people exactly like themselves, the officers are able to preserve the image they think their spouses and everyone else expects of them.

The police officer's job influences his role in the family.

Doug T., in his early 30's has been a policeman for eight years and worked in his present assignment for the last four. Currently, Doug is experiencing difficulties with his wife, Debbie, difficulties with his sergeant and difficulties with his girl friend. He is also experiencing financial problems. By attending school he suffers more difficulties because of limited time with his two kids. His behavior does not measure up to the view he would like to have of himself as a father. For a while, Doug was able to handle all of these trying and at times competing demands. But it appears he handled some of the stress by being a little too active in the field.

Doug received a physical injury, making it impossible for him to continue working in the field. As a result, he was given an assignment that most cops dread—the complaint desk. Doug was still experiencing problems with his wife, Debbie, his girl friend, and the sergeant (who sat right across the hall from the complaint desk). Doug's initial reason for seeking psychological assistance was the frustration he felt about having to listen to citizens' complaints. When the tension on the job began to rise, Doug would answer the phone by saying, "Don't be such an asshole," or, "Don't be such a turkey," or, "How could you be so stupid"—and then hang up. Doug became concerned that this behavior might get him into trouble, especially since he could be overheard by his sergeant and all phone calls were tape recorded.

After relating the above, Doug became hesitant, quietly reporting, "I don't know how to tell you this,

Doc, but, now I'm having other problems ... difficulty
achieving an erection, or maintaining one." This caused
additional problems of stress between him and his wife
and girl friend. Doug was in quite a fix. Individuals can
handle only so many pressures at any one time. If they
become overburdened—whether it be by extramarital
affairs, financial difficulties, school schedules, whatever—the whole of life can fall out of kilter.

A major problem for police departments and their officers is shift work and its effects on the individual and
family. Shift changes, a necessary part of any law-enforcement organization, force officers to adapt. Biological
changes occur, including adjustments in the our circadian
rhythms which regulate body temperature. When an
officer switches shifts, this "time clock" must adapt, and
doctors estimate that it takes approximately 30 days.

Police officers working nights or early mornings have
little contact with their families. However, during days off
they may switch their sleep schedules in order to spend
more time with them. This causes their circadian rhythms
to constantly be out of balance, with subtle effects on their
entire systems.

If officers face 30-day biological adjustment periods,
many spouses believe it takes the family at least three
months or longer to adjust to shift changes.

Current scheduling practices around the country
include changing shifts as quickly as once a week, to six
months or longer. Some changes are determined strictly
by personnel movement, and officers are allowed to move
or switch shifts according to seniority. Determining the
optimal time for shift changes is difficult, at best. Each
department's functions and needs are different. Three to
six months would appear to be best.

At times, some officers want to work particular shifts
that are undesirable to others. It may be appropriate to let
these individuals work the shift of their choice for a

longer time. This procedure allows them to have a say in their work life, which leads to increased satisfaction, while also allowing other officers to work shifts they prefer.

One important measure of "marital bliss" is the degree of sexual satisfaction felt by each partner. It is a very important way of relieving stress and an invaluable means of communication, as well as being a consummate joy for its own sake.

One night, Lt. Beau S. was called to a hostage situation. It was early in the evening, but as the hours dragged on with no foreseeable end he called his wife, Paz, to tell her he might not make it home. She decided to go to bed. The hostage situation ended more quickly than Beau had thought, so he headed home. He had spent most of the evening drinking coffee, talking with the SWAT Team members, and waiting to see what would occur. He was anxious to get home, to tell Paz what had happened. The fact that it was 3 a.m. didn't enter his mind. He was wide awake and "wired."

As Beau approached the dark house, he realized that Paz was asleep. But he felt sure she wouldn't mind being awakened and informed of the evening's events. She was glad he was home, but having been asleep for 5 hours, was a little groggy. This didn't bother Beau, as he went ahead and told her the night's events. After which, he decided it was a perfect time to make love. Beau wasn't sleepy and Paz though sleepy, was awake.

The next morning they discussed the night before. Paz mentioned that their lovemaking had been different. She said he had been more aggressive and not in tune to her feelings. She wasn't very excited about making love, while he was. He really needed to be with the person he loved. The hostage situation had left him in a keyed up state and he wanted to talk and be close to someone who understood. She had been asleep and concerned about getting enough rest for her work the next day. They had misconnected that evening.

What happened to Beau and Paz happens often to police couples. To alleviate this, some couples plan for occasional weekends together so that they can have time to get back in touch with each other. They feel that their lives are too hectic and confusing during their normal work weeks for them to really hear and communicate with each other. They use their weekends to be together and leave the world of work and home behind.

Some couples experiencing marital problems may seek counseling assistance. At times these couples have not made love in a year or two, or even longer. Making love will not solve problems, but the degree of satisfaction and frequency of sex is an indication of the health of a marriage.

The women's liberation movement is a major influence on many marriages in the United States. Whether one believes in the Equal Rights Amendment or not, the multitude of choices available to women has certainly changed American life. Women know and understand their sexuality more. They may expect more from their husbands. Their husbands, on the other hand, may view this new liberation with some confusion and even anger. In the past, the officer came home to his castle and could expect his "lady" to be ready to serve him and meet his needs. Today, the officer comes home and his wife may not be there. She may be pursuing a career of her own. The household chores which she did exlusively in the past may now be shared. Her sexual expectations may be different. She may want and expect that more attention be paid to her needs in the relationship.

Law-enforcement officers have tended to marry at an early age. By mutual choice the officer may be in charge both on his job and within his family. As years go by, this may change. As the wife grows and learns about herself and the world, she may change her interests and even some of her values. If she goes back to school, she may meet women who have a different view than her own. Or through working or being with other people, she may find herself questioning things she had always taken for granted. This is a natural growth process for everyone. But in a marriage, if these changes aren't discussed or shared, it causes difficulty.

> Tom and Eva C., a couple who were having trouble understanding each other's needs, came to counseling. They were asked to think about their individual wants and needs in their relationship and then share them with each other. Tom spoke first saying, "Sure, that's easy! I want you to do what I tell you to do, when I tell you to do it, without any backtalk!" Eva didn't seem at all surprised as she commented, "So, what's new?" Her wants and needs had changed a great deal, while Tom's has remained the same. He wanted to be in charge.

Change can be either growth producing or destructive. Much depends on how it is shared and discussed between marital partners.

Women in law enforcement who choose to marry face many of the same problems in relationships as men officers: shift changes, nonemotionalism, paramilitaristic structure, etc. But many of these problems are compounded by female stereotypes.

The traditionally "feminine" woman is unaggressive: She is kind, gentle, refined, obedient, courteous and decorative. Successful women officers are anathema to that womanly ideal. They are taught to be aggressive, controlled and independent in action and decision making. Questions may arise in a marital relationship as to "who wears the pants?" While shift changes may be accepted by an officer's wife, a husband may view them as destructive or controlling by his officer wife. He may question his wife's commitment to the marriage and the family. Many men expect their wives to value the marital relationship above the job, while they in turn appear to value the job more than family. Society has taught men that women should derive their sense of self-worth primarily through relations with men rather than through their own achievements. Yet the woman officer feels her own sense of purpose and may appear to put her marriage second.

As the officer learns to control her feelings, her husband may assume that she is no longer in need of his emotional support. This forces her to rely more and more on fellow officers who understand her world. This lessens communication and leaves the husband feeling like an outsider. If he is not an officer, he may become jealous of his wife's relationship with those in law enforcement. He may also feel threatened by the macho image of the male officers.

Often women officers seek marital partners who are also involved in law enforcement. They assume that these men will understand the difficulties of the job and be more accepting. However, this is not always the case. As has been explained, men officers are traditional in their views of women and are often unwilling to compromise in a marital relationship. And if we consider the stressors confronting an officer, we have double this load for the married police couple. If she advances in rank sooner or more often than her husband, the male ego and the relationship may be greatly tested. Because of these concerns, some women choose the more traditional female roles in law enforcement: juvenile, custody, etc. These jobs have more consistent hours and often allow women more flexibility in scheduling. They also are accepted as more "feminine" than riding patrol.

Those women who seek full participation in law enforcement need a life style that is compatible with the job. They, too, must have stability in their lives to be effective officers. However, extremely high divorce rates have been reported among these women. And if there is a divorce generally the woman has custody of the children, which can add more problems for the career oriented woman.

Where does this leave the married female officer? Must she be an authority figure at work and submissive to her husband at home? If both are working, who's responsible for household chores? Even if her police job is more demanding than her husband's, does she end up like many of the women who work, still doing all the cooking and cleaning?

Children of police officers have some unique privileges and problems. There may be difficulties, but being a cop's son or daughter is valued by most. This is evidenced by the large number who follow their father's footsteps into the profession.

Cops' kids, like any other kids, learn and grow by imitating their parents and then their peers. They need protection as well as the responsibility of freedom. They need to be accepted as unique human beings who may have very different attitudes and values from their parents. They are full of curiosity and mischief and quick to respond. And they need the guidance, support and love of both parents.

Police officers view much human corruption in society and tend to believe it results from society's permissiveness. They often believe this permissiveness starts in the home. They guarantee against this in their family by strictness, while at the same time being protective.

Larry C. came for counseling very upset that he had caught his 17-year-old son, Eddie, smoking marijuana with friends. Larry saw this as evidence of his lack of control over Eddie. It also meant that Eddie was on his first step to ruination. Larry knew that marijuana led to other drugs. Larry's perception of the world was different than his son's. Eddie saw smoking marijuana as something that "all my friends do" and a way of expressing his independence. Actually, experimenting with marijuana is common for most teenagers in our society. But for a cop's son it can be disastrous if he gets caught. Larry loved his son and was willing to listen. Eddie felt the same about his father, respecting him a great deal. This situation was worked out so that both were comfortable. Often when parents set down laws with no input from children or acknowledgment of society's changes, problems result. Like with marriages, communication is the key to parent-child relationships.

When officers feel a need to protect and control their children during the teen-age years—at the same time those children are attempting to establish their own identities—it can be a trying time for all involved. Understanding by all concerned can avert a continual bucking of heads and a battle for who is in control.

Officers' shift changes cause additional problems for children. It is possible for them to grow up and rarely see their fathers. A pattern that exists in families is for the mother to raise the children with the father entering the picture only for disciplinary matters and an occasional holiday. The children see the father for either negative reasons (discipline) or very positive ones (holidays). They don't get a chance to share the specialness of everyday living and to see their more human sides. The father misses the opportunity to see his children grow and develop. Balancing the responsiblity of raising children with the burdens of police work takes good communication and some sacrifice.

The difficulty some officers have in expressing emotions to their families affects both the marital and father-child relationship. Betty White, writing in the Saturday Evening Post, recalled: "My dad was chief of police and he was tough as granite. Hugging him would have been like hugging a statue of Abraham Lincoln. You just didn't do it. My whole family was undemonstrative. My mother, my brother and sister and I—we never touched each other or expressed our affection openly."

A positive side to being raised as a cop's child is the opportunity to live with someone who is committed and dedicated to helping people and improving society. This child also probably lives in an environment where traditional values are honored. While society's values may continually change, most police officers' children know their values.

The traditional American family (father as breadwinner, mother as housewife) exists in approximately 10% of American households in the 1980's. No longer is the "average" American family a nuclear unit of husband, wife and two kids. Although there are families like this in our society, there is a growing number of single-parent families and step-families. The structure and values of these new families are different from the traditional family, and so are the joys and sorrows.

The chances of becoming a single parent or a step-parent have soared. There has been much discussion about whether we are currently witnessing the decline of the American family. While there is an inability on the part of an increasing number of couples to achieve satisfaction in marriage the first time around, a second attempt seems worth the effort. The remarriage rate suggests that family ties and all they represent are what we as human beings need for stability, continuity and nonconditional affection (Bane: 1978).

Whether one is a single parent, a visiting parent, a step-parent, or an adult in a live-in situation, life can get sticky unless handled with as much foresight and caring as possible. The divorce of two people can be extremely ugly and emotionally damaging, or it can be seen as a step to a new way of life.

Many people see divorce as a failure on their part and feel ashamed or disgraced. For some it comes unexpectedly; for others it's been a long time in coming. Thoughts of being alone may be terrifying or exciting or both. Whatever the circumstances, much change will take place in a relatively short period of time. For many, divorce places more stress on a system that may already be overburdened. For police, it is imperative that they understand this and find ways to cope with it. Communicating feelings and seeking solutions from someone who is willing to listen—whether it be a partner, family member, friends or a professional counselor—can be very helpful in learning to function anew.

Once a divorce is completed, new problems arise. For those with children, their roles as parents change. On the surface, the children of divorce don't seem any different from kids whose families are still intact. They wear the same tattered jeans, smile with the same metallic braces, spend mindless hours listening to popular musical. But they are different—for divorce, though no longer a stigma, produces a series of emotional and developmental crises that sets these children apart. The problem is formidable in numbers alone. There are currently 12 million children under the age of 18 whose parents are divorced—and approximately 1 million children a year who suffer through the dissolution of their families.

How parents should handle children during the divorce process and after is both complicated and unique to each situation. Often children, especially younger children, believe that they are the reason the marriage has broken up. They may also fantasize that they can get their mother and father back together. Children need to be approached with as much honesty as possible. This doesn't mean going into clinical detail about the reasons for the breakup, but it does mean giving them as much information as possible about both parents' feelings and thoughts about the future. Children need to be constantly reassured about both parents' love for them and the fact that, although mommy or daddy is leaving, they will still be with them in spirit. They need to be encouraged to talk about their fears and feelings, particularly when they are negative. Children may become manipulative with parents, plotting one against the other. Parents need to set guidelines for the children that both parents will keep. Consistency is important.

Financial burdens generally increase with divorce. An officer often seeks to work overtime in order to afford two households. He may resent this, particularly if his ex-wife is not working or has remarried. Socially, the officer will have little time away from work to meet and intermingle with people. Human beings need a balanced life style. If an officer continues to overwork he is quicker to anger, which affects how he interacts with people on the streets, as well as the people he loves. All of us need to examine our finances and find ways to meet our responsibilities without burning out.

If an officer marries again, his financial picture changes along with his interactions with his ex-wife, children, new wife and possibly step-children. His family ties have again been established but with a new set of players and rules. Ideally one enters a second marriage having learned from past mistakes, with new hopes and goals for this relationship. Unfortunately, some reasons for the failure of the first marriage may be inherent in the job and what it does to the officer. The need for guarding one's emotions, the always changing shift work, the fear for and protection of the spouse, and the need for the macho image of the job must be addressed in the second marriage. If a second attempt is to be successful, both partners must find ways to combat these problems.

Currently over a half million adults become step-parents each year in the United States. One of every five children under 18 is a step-child. There are many guidelines for good parenting, but few for step-parenting. Some believe you should be a "friend" to the child while others encourage being a "second father." Some support strict discipline while others suggest lax rules. A common theme among all successful step-families is consistent rules, communication, patience and mutual support by the parents. As Aristotle once said, "Those who educate children well are more to be honored than those who produce them."

Police wives are remarkable women. What appear as terrible stumbling blocks to a relationship, they seem to handle as a matter of course. People mention the "woman behind the badge" and the "supportive" role of the wife. This presents a distorted picture. Police wives stand at least equally with their husbands in keeping their relationships growing, their households happy, and their children healthy. Frequently the importance and difficulty of their role goes unrecognized by law-enforcement administrators, the public, their husbands, and unfortunately sometimes even themselves.

> At a police function Mary Jo D., a police chief's wife who worked with handicapped children and loved it, was engrossed in a conversation with Maureen D., an officer's wife. Later Mary Jo's husband came up, interrupted them and said, "Well, that's enough shop talk, ladies." Both women were disturbed by this particularly since they had been listening to "cop talk" all night.
>
> Later, Maureen cornered the chief's wife. "What does your husband think of your work?" she asked. Mary Jo said: "He doesn't care about it at all. In fact, he really has no idea what I do and doesn't like me talking about it."
>
> Maureen was amazed! Here was a vital woman doing important work and her husband couldn't care less.

For women who work in the home this problem could be compounded. Society has yet to value the difficulty and challenge of being a good homemaker, not to mention being an officer's wife as well.

Many police wives feel their husbnads don't listen to them, particularly if they talk about things at home. If this becomes a pattern in their lives, spouses can try to establish communication by eating out together, taking weekend excursions away from the police world, and exploring other possiblities for mutual pleasure. It is helpful if each partner can spend some time in the other's world so they can both understand the difficulties.

Each of us must value what we do and know that our support of our spouses and their work helps them be more effective. The reverse is also true: Our spouses' support and understanding can give us the confidence to keep growing.

178   *Police Passages*

REFERENCES

Bach, G. R. and Deutsch, R. M. *Pairing*. New York: Avon, 1970

Hageman, M. "Occupational Stress and Marital Relationship." *Journal of Police Science and Administration*, 6(4), (1978).

Jacobson, D.S. "Stepfamilies." *Children Today*. Jan-Feb 1980.

James, P., and Nelson, M. *Police Wife*. Springfield, Illinois: Charles C. Thomas, 1975.

Lotimen, A., with Feldman, P. M. *Remarriage*. Running Press, Penn 1980.

May, R. *Love and Will*. New York: W.W. Norton E. Company, Inc., 1969.

Maslach, C. and Jackson, S. "Burned-Out Cops and Their Families." *Psychology Today*, 13(5) 1979.

Niederhoffer, H. and Niederhoffer, E. *The Police Family*. Lexington, Massachusetts: Lexington Books, 1978.

Reiser, M. "The Problems of Police Officers' Wives." *The Police Chief*, 45(5) 1978.

Ross, J. K. and Halatin, T. "When Family Stress Affects Worker Productivity." *Supervisory Management*, July, 1982.

Schwartz, F. N. "Reducing Stress in Two-Career Families: Expert's Advice." *U.S. News and World Report*, 11/2/81.

Visher, E. B. and Visher, J. S. *Stepfamilies-A Guide to Working with Stepparents and Stepchildren*. NY: Brunner/Mazel, 1979.

"The American Family-Can It Survive Today's Shocks?" *U.S. News World Report*, 79(17), 1975.

"The Children of Divorce." *Newsweek*, 2/11/80.

7

JOINING THE FRATERNITY—WOMEN AND MINORITIES

Minority officers are a special group of people with unique problems beyond those of the average officer. Minority cops, whether they be black, Hispanic, Asian or women, are confronted with added stress from within and from outside the department.

Until recently, most law enforcement departments have been fairly homogeneous—overwhelmingly white males. Even in large departments, the sight of dark-skinned or woman officers was unusual. However, within the last decade the hiring of these minorities has continued to increase. Even so, the attitudes and values of the majority officers and their departments may not change as quickly as new laws or court decisions are made. Negative or prejudicial beliefs about fellow workers can magnify differences between majority and minority officers and create a climate of mutual mistrust—especially in a profession which depends on teamwork and reliance upon one another.

The trend toward ethnic diversity, like most change, can cause stress, misunderstanding and confusion. How the administration and individual officers handle this change will depend on their insight, sensitivity and understanding of one another. For both the majority and minority officers, the extent to which they accept this change can be a matter of life and death.

In 1865 the Civil War almost tore the United States apart. Even today the scars of this strife are still healing as prejudice continues its destructive ways. Yet our country is established on the principle of the equality of all men and women and the recognition of the rights of all individuals regardless of color, creed or sex. The fact that all of us do not abide by these principles is obvious and creates monumental social problems. And law-enforcement officers are right in the middle of this turbulence.

Police attitudes and methods of performing their jobs are shaped within the para-military structure. Just forty years ago, the military of the United States was segregated. During World War II, when our country's future was at stake, segregation came first. There were separate units for Negroes, and women were placed only in such traditional roles as nurses and secretaries. Until recently, many top-ranking law-enforcement officials had been part of the World War II military operation and its influence.

For years, there has been an identification between the police and right-wing extremism. During the 1930's, investigations of the Black Legion, a neo-fascist organization in the industrial Midwest which engaged in terror and vigilante activities, indicated that it appealed to police. Not only did the Black Legion include many patrolmen, but a grand jury reported that the chief of police of one large industrial city was an active member. The Legion engaged in kidnapping, flogging and even murder of suspected communists. Father Coughlin, who was probably the most important pro-fascist leader of the 1930's, also found heavy backing within police ranks. An investigation of his organization, the Christian Front, revealed that 407 of New York's finest belonged to it.

There is an increasing body of evidence which suggests an affinity between police work and support for radical-right politics, particularly when linked to racial unrest. Gunmar Myrdal, in his study of the race problem in the late 1930's and early '40's, *An American Dilemma,* asserted that much of the Ku Klux Klan activity in the South was carried on by law enforcement officers. This finding matched with reports of the membership of the Klan during the early 1920's when it was at the height of its power, controlling politics in many Northern as well as Southern states. Klan leaders took particular pride in emphasizing the large number of law enforcement officers that had joined their order. Typical of Klan propaganda which attracted police support was the plank in the program of the Chicago Klan which called for "supporting officials in all phases of law enforcement." According to Charles Jackson, membership-lists seized in different parts of California indicated that "roughly 10% of the policemen in practically every California city," including the chiefs of some of the largest cities, belonged to the Klan. The home base of the organization in Atlanta reported a very high percentage of police membership. Considerable police backing for the Klan was also reported in analyses of its operation in cities as diverse as Portland, Oregon; Tulsa, Oklahoma; Madison, Wisconsin, and Memphis, Tennessee.

Twenty-five years ago, Gunmar Myrdal noted that police in the South were prone to express deep-seated, "anti-Negro" feelings in brutal actions against blacks and thus undo "much of what Northern philanthropy and Southern state governments are trying to accomplish through education and other means." He believed this phenomenon resulted from the fact that the police generally held the prejudices common to poor whites. "The average Southern policeman is a promoted poor white with a legal sanction to use a weapon." His social heritage and limited education had taught him to despise Negroes, Myrdal wrote. Arthur Niederhoffer's 1967 study of the New York City Police Department found that "for the past fifteen years, during a cycle of prosperity, the bulk of police candidates had been upper lower class with a sprinkling of lower middle-class; about 90% had no college training." In a survey of the occupations of the fathers of 12,000 recruits who graduated from the New York Police Academy, he found that more than three-quarters of them were manual or service workers.

Movements of ethnic intolerance and right-wing radicalism have tended to recruit from the more conservative segments of the poorer and less-educated classes. On the whole, the less education people have, the more likely they are to be intolerant of those who differ from themselves, whether in opinions, modes of behavior, religion, ethnic background, or race. Policemen, like others, simply reflect the background from which they come.

These authoritarian tendencies are only encouraged by the type of work a cop must perform. In general, the policeman's job requires him to be suspicious of people, to prefer conventional behavior and to value toughness. A policeman must be jaded about human behavior. As Niederhoffer points out, "he needs the intuitive ability to sense plots and conspiracies on the basis of embryonic evidence." The political counterpart of such an outlook is a monistic theory which takes a conspiratorial view of the sources of evil, and this basically describes the attitude of extremist groups, whether of the left or right.

As mentioned before, policemen often harbor feelings of resentment against society. They are asked to risk their lives in order to enforce society's laws, but receive relatively little prestige and get a relatively low salary compared with others who have much less authority. Many police look upon themselves as an "oppressed minority" subject to the same kind of prejudices as other minorities.

Often, they become closed and bitter and allow only those with similar views into their ranks and confidence.

Thus, through a long history, those working in law enforcement have developed attitudes and values which are basically conservative, and slow to change; and yet society has demanded that police departments begin integrating their ranks with racial minorities and women. This has caused anger and confusion among some in the profession.

James Baldwin, a renowned black writer, perhaps best expressed the dilemma of the policeman working in the ghetto:

> "The only way to police a ghetto is to be oppressive. None of the police commissioner's men, even with the best will in the world, have any way of understanding the lives led by the people: they swagger about in twos and threes patrolling. Their very presence is an insult, and it would be, even if they spent their entire day feeding gum drops to children. They represent the force of the white world, and that world's criminal profit, and ease, to keep the black man corralled up here in his place. The badge, the gun in the holster, and the swinging club, make vivid what will happen should his rebellion become overt. . .
>
> "It is hard, on the other hand, to blame the policeman, blank, good-natured, thoughtless, and insuperably innocent, for being such a perfect representative of the people he serves. He, too, believes in good intentions and is astounded and offended when they are not taken for the deed. He has never, himself, done anything for which to be hated, which of us has? And yet he is facing, daily and nightly, the people who would gladly see him dead, and he knows it. There is no way for him not to know it. There are few things under heaven more unnerving than the silent accumulating contempt and hatred of a people. He moves through Harlem, therefore, like an occupying soldier in a bitterly hostile country: which is

precisely what, and where he is, and is the reason he walks in two and threes."

If this desciption is basically true, those in law enforcement who try to alter this situation face an incredibly difficult task. Those in society face a task of the same magnitude, to understand what police face daily and to support their efforts. But before offering ways to change the situation, it must be realistically acknowledged.

Although virtually all police departments explicitly subscribe to the principle of the equality of all people and the equal treatment that each ought to be accorded by law enforcement officers, it is not being done. William Westley, who studied police in a midwestern city near Chicago, commented in 1951:

> "For the police, the Negro epitomizes the slum dweller and, in addition, he is culturally and biologically inherently criminal. Individual policemen sometimes deviate sharply from the general definition, but no white policeman with whom the author has had contact failed to mock the Negro, to use some type of stereotyped categorization, and to refer to interaction with the Negro in an exaggerated dialect when the occasion arose."

Although this statement was made in 1951, similar problems still exist. In locker rooms or in a gathering of police, statements such as, "Did you see that nigger run?" or, "Everyone wants to kill a Boon," can be heard. I knew a cop in one large city who played "jungle music" over his loudspeaker every time he received a hot call to enter a minority community.

Some cops, instead of being open about their prejudices, have learned to hide them, at least from some. This can heighten the distrust among officers. One way or another, the minority officer tends to stay on the fringe of the inner circle of the buddy system.

Black officers also have to face up to the fact that some white citizens don't want to deal with them. Stationhouses in certain neighborhoods will often receive phone calls from people who specifically ask for a white officer to be sent. Even in emergencies, people sometimes refuse entry to a black officer.

A call came into the station from a citizen who said, "Send somebody over here quick—there's a nigger in my back yard." So two officers were dispatched to the scene, and as it turned out they were black officers. Ten minutes later the watch commander got another phone call, and it was from the same citizen. This time he complained: "Now I've got *three* niggers in my yard!"

Latin-surnamed police officers face different brands of prejudice from the community. For example, Mexican-American citizens are often annoyed to have to deal with a Chicano patrolman who doesn't speak Spanish. They fail to understand that, with policemen, the only brotherhood is with other policemen.

In another instance, Deputy Jorge encountered a black man on the street, and the man asked him, "Hey, do you speak Spanish?" Jorge, who had heard this question once too often, replied bitingly, "Yeah, as a matter of fact I do. Do you speak African?"

Who are these minority men and women who become officers? What motivates them to enter this profession?

One officer explains, "It was 1965 and I had just gotten out of the service. I was looking for work and policing was one of the few well-paying jobs you could get that didn't require some college training. I grew up in a Chicago ghetto, but I hadn't had any bad personal experiences with the police. O. W. Wilson was the superintendent of police here then, and the department had a pretty good reputation."

Minority officers' reasons for entering the profession are parallel to those of the majority. They see the profession as a place where, with minimal education, they can have a secure job, earn a good salary, possibly get ahead, and help people in the process.

Although they understand the conservative traditional aspects of the profession, they might not be fully aware of the ramifications to them personally until they are totally immersed in it. "But it didn't take me long to find out what was really going on," one minority officer remarked.

Officers soon begin to see exactly what is expected of them. When they watch a suspect being illegally beaten by their fellow officers, they know they are either to join in or keep their mouths shut. When they hear their supervisor tell a racial joke, they know they are expected to laugh. The consequences may be harsh for those who don't follow "the rules." They might receive the worst shifts or have their tires slashed by fellow officers.

Minority officers began appearing in some departments as early as the turn of the twentieth century. Sam Battle, who eventually rose to lieutenant, was hired as New York City's first black police officer in 1911. Other departments were integrated in the years immediately following World War II. But only in the last ten years has the number of minority officers begun to move toward the percentage of blacks and Hispanics in the nation's population. A 1975 study by the Federal Equal Employment Opportunities Commission of 2,303 state and local police forces found that about 10.3% of the reported 281,005 full-time police officers were members of minority groups. Few departments have minority employment figures that equal the populations they serve. But improvements have been made almost everywhere in the last ten years. There are several major cities that now have minority chiefs, sheriffs or public safety directors.

Although there have been statistical changes in the numbers of minorities employed in law enforcement, the changes in attitudes have been much slower. "As a black cop, you're in a mine field," said Officer Paul Allen, president of the all-black Dallas chapter of the Texas Peace

Officers Association. "You're automatically a Tom to a lot of black people, and you don't necessarily have the respect of your white counterparts. You get a dualistic concept of yourself that borders on the schizophrenic." The officer must "make peace with himself that he's not the enemy and then convince the community he's not." One officer recalled the time when he was on the street in uniform and ran into an old high school friend. When his friend recognized him, all he said was "You're chicken shit. I thought you were a nice guy."

Despite employment gains in recent years by minority officers, policing is still far from thoroughly integrated. The 1975 EEOC study of policing found the percentage of minority police adminstrators to be negligible (4.2%) and increasing at a snail's pace. Some minority officers contend that white officers are "tracked"—sent to specific assignments that groom them for administrative jobs—while minority officers are put on patrol or undercover work. Allegedly, schedules are arranged for whites so that attending college is more convenient. By working on choice assignments, white officers are exposed to many situations that can help them as administrators' much the same as a student who goes to an upper class high school has an advantage over one who attends a ghetto school. This type of subtle discrimination leaves the minority officer angry and still lacking in the political power and knowledge he so desperately needs.

Often assignments seem to be distributed on the basis of race. Lee Reynolds of the National Urban League complained that too many minority officers are assigned to undercover narcotics and vice squads. In such units, said Reynolds, a veteran of more than 21 years with the New York City Police Department, "they are more prone to injury and to departmental disciplinary charges, while at the same time they are denied the broad patrol experience most departments look for in candidates for promotion."

Some discrimination is much less subtle.

Officer Allen R. who ranked No. 1 in the promotion exam for sergeant happened to walk by the chief's office just as the secretary handed him the rankings on the examination. The chief's first comment after having examined the list was, "That goddamn nigger made No. 1! That black son of a bitch will never get it while I'm here!" For the next year the chief filled the sergeant's position with "temporaries." Just before the next sergeant's exam was to take place, the chief was called into a neighborhood disturbance and asked to field some questions from concerned community leaders. One of the first questions asked was, "Why don't we have any black officers to relate to black people?" Al was promoted to sergeant on the next exam.

Tokenism has been used in the past by some in law enforcement to appease the community. Today federal and state laws are looking for proof of compliance with civil rights acts, and tokenism isn't enough. But within some departments there is still a sense among minorities that tokenism still prevails, and this creates intense pressures. The highly visible minority officer can feel the need to perform exceptionally well. He understands that, should he fail at any one particular task, it may be looked upon by some as a failure of the minority rather than the individual officer. He might hear people saying behind his back: "I knew Joe couldn't handle the job. He should have never been hired in the first place."

Even with the civil rights acts demanding that law-enforcement departments hire minorities to reflect the minority population, cities have dragged their feet for so long additional problems have arisen. The few jobs in law enforcement that come open, often must be given to minorities. This causes additional white backlash and complaints of reverse discrimination such as those brought up in the Bakke case. It further adds fuel to the fire of seasoned white officers who say that departments are now hiring less qualified people.

At the very crux of discriminatory practices is the admission process used by many law-enforcement agencies. Many aspects of the process have been successfully challenged as discriminatory by the Law Enforcement Assistance Administration (LEAA) and the Federal Office of Revenue Sharing, or by minority officers themselves.

Most departments use some sort of intelligence test, civil service test, or entrance examination as part of the entrance process. Such exams have been judged in court to discriminate against minorities, in violation of the 1965 Civil Rights Acts. According to John Furcon, an industrial psychologist at the University of Chicago, not only do these tests display cultural biases in favor of white middle-class applicants, they have never been validated as to whether they can predict on-the-job performance. Yet in many departments officers are required to pass such tests to be hired.

One of the most subjective, and some feel the most biased, parts of the entrance process is the interview. Although the procedure for interviews might be strictly consistent, with identical questions and interviewers, the interpretation of responses by the interviewee is very subjective. How one is viewed through the interview may be as important as the answers themselves. One's dress, mannerisms, choice of words and race play a critical part in the final outcome. Some feel that race itself is enough to be a determining factor in whether an applicant passes an interview or not.

Background checks of police applicants have also been widely accused of being a means of weeding out minority applicants. "I know of cases in which minority applicants have had points scored against them because they had books like *The Autobiography of Malcolm X* at their homes," said Lee Brown, Houston's chief of police. "This was cited as evidence of their anti-police attitudes," he said, "even though the book is assigned reading in many college-level social science courses." How background officers interpret information such as school records, life style, references, friends and associates is dependent on their own beliefs and attitudes—all of which can be biased against the minority officer.

Once in the department, minority officers face things that often they had not expected. They may experience coolness and some distance from a few white officers, but they didn't expect to have to take sides on race-related issues having to do with department organizations and assignments. In these situations many minorities feel that, whatever side they choose, they lose.

In most major departments there are police associations/organizations formed to support the opinions and complaints of the average street cop. These organizations confer with the administration on issues that are of concern to officers, i.e., wage negotiations, needed training programs, disputes between officers and supervisors, etc. Quite often these police associations are seen as being concerned with majority officers' interests and not representing minorities. They might tolerate minority membership and accept their dues, but still not involve them in the process. Some police organizations in the United States have yet to have one minority on a committee, let alone as one of the elected officers. There may be reasons for this that can be attributed to the small number of minorities in the organization, a lack of interest by minority officers, or a feeling by minority officers that these organizations don't represent their needs. Thus parallel organizations have been formed by minorities to fill the gap.

These minority associations research important issues, evaluate legislation, attempt to sensitize the administration, exchange information and act as a spokeman for members. They also deal with what they see as racism within the department and among individual officers. This causes great anxiety for some departments and may force the minority officers to choose between different police associations. If he chooses the majority organization, he may be seen as an "Uncle Tom" by his friends, and if he selects the minority organization he may be seen as "one of them" by the department.

Some departments, believing that the minority officer relates better to his own people than a white officer does, assign them to the more difficult and dangerous areas. In 1965 when there were major riots in Cleveland, Mayor Carl Stokes pulled all white officers from the area and placed black officers there to calm and control a dangerous situation. The riots were stopped, but there were many questions left unanswered as to the best use of both white and minority officers.

One minority officer who works in a ghetto says he believes that many white officers see blacks as "all bad, particularly in this area," and thus treat them very sternly. Black officers on the other hand, wouldn't tend to see all blacks as "bad" and would approach them as individuals. This may cause black officers to be labeled as indecisive, soft or disloyal. Some white officers even fear that they "won't be backed up" by their minority partners if they are in a jam in a minority community. Minority officers, forced to shoot minority suspects in order to save their white partner, might hear disparaging comments in the community about their loyalties.

There is a great deal of misunderstanding about the different approaches that minority and majority officers take with community members. While white officers may feel that the minority officers are "too soft," minority officers may feel that white officers are "too harsh." Rather than trying to understand the reasons behind each approach, officers may get into behind-the-back name calling, which further polarizes them. The old cliche that "we're not black, brown or white, but blue" may be just wishful thinking in some police departments. But racial unity can replace conflict when initial prejudices and hostilities are overcome.

Some believe that the only way the minority can succeed in the majority world is to adopt the majority behavior. But this creates a difficult dilemma. It asks the
minority officer to forget himself, his background, his way
of life and his essence, and to become white in thinking
and acting—an impossible task. When this happens, the
minority cop risks losing a sense of himself, and the
majority loses the opporutnity to learn and understand
the ways of a different culture. And yet minority officers
are almost forced into this position if they want to be
accepted as "one of the boys." When law-enforcement
leaders realize that they can learn a great deal from their
minority officers, perhaps community resentment and
suspicion of the community for police will begin to ease.

The president of the National Organization of Black
Law Enforcement Executives (NOBLE), Hubert Williams
stated: "People have got to begin looking on black and
Hispanic officers as assets to their communities. I want to
make it clear that we don't want to see any diminution of
standards for hiring or promotion. But if you really want
people who are best qualified to police our cities, then you
must hire minority candidates. You are going to get better
minority communities. And in the absence of that community support, we cannot function as a democracy, and
that's a problem that goes beyond the minority community to the community at large."

Throughout the history of this country, women have
played a marginal role in law enforcement. In particular,
women have rarely been assigned to regular patrol operations. A smattering of women have worked in most major
police departments performing duties limited to clerical
work, matron tasks, and work with special classes of
offenders, i.e. women and children. In 1967 the President's
Commission on Law Enforcement and Administration of
Justice recommended an increasing use of women in the
American police service. The commission stated:

"Policewomen can be invaluable assets to modern law
enforcement and their present role should be broadened.
Women should be utlized in such important service units
as planning and research, training, intelligence, inspec-
tion, public information, community relations, and as
legal advisors. Women could also serve in such units as
computer programming and laboratory analysis, and
communications. Their value should not be considered
as limited to staff functions or police work with juveniles; women should also serve regularly in patrol, vice
and investigative divisions. Finally, as more and more
well qualified women enter the service, they could
assume administrative responsibilities."

In 1971, there were fewer than a dozen police women on
patrol in the United States, and only a few women in
police supervisory positions. In 1974, there were close to a
thousand women on patrol and several hundred women
sergeants, lieutenants, and captains supervising male and
female patrol officers and detectives. Women are now
patrolling the streets in most cities across the United
States. Nationally, the percentage of women in all aspects
of law enforcement is increasing. In September 1974, Gail
Cobb was the first United States policewoman to die in
the line of duty. Her death is dramatic evidence of
women's increased involvement in law enforcement.

Though the integration of women into law enforcement
has begun, studies show serious obstacles. The psychology of women also complicates things. Some women are
not quite comfortable in "male" jobs; they worry about
feeling, or seeming, unfeminine. The psychology of men is
a factor, too, especially when they resent the "intrusion"
of women into a previously super male militaristic world.
Overall, the most troublesome difficulties are attitudinal,
having little to do with what women can actually accomplish and much to do with what others think they can or
should accomplish.

One of the first women police officers said recently, "Other people's attitudes can make life very difficult—when other people would look at me and say, 'We don't want you in our department,' or, 'You're doing a man's job and you don't belong here!' That's the biggest problem that I ever encountered in the department—negative attitudes from other people."

Women in law enforcement face many of the same battles as other minorities. They too have to make a decision on whether to adopt the majority's in approaches and attitudes. Some try to imitate men, with questionable results. And yet many of their more feminine ways are not acceptable. One female detective explained it this way: "Part of the problem is that female detectives are just too new. For example, I like to dress well; I like to wear feminine sandals. But the guys here say things like, 'You're not going to get out on a case, climbing hills *in those*?'" She added, "Suspects, informants and even the families of murder victims also seem surprised at times to discover that their case is assigned to a team of women. They usually say something like, 'You don't look like a policewoman.' It's as if they felt only big, hefty, heavy-duty women are capable of doing the job."

If a woman officer does decide "to join the majority," she may try to imitate the sexual ways of the police world. For some men in this macho world, the more women they take to bed the more esteem they have among fellow officers. Although surely there is more talk than action in this regard, if a woman chooses to imitate what she hears she will make advances toward a great many men. This might result in disillusionment for the woman when she finds that she still isn't considered "one of the boys." And she may also be labeled as a woman who "gets over" by offering sexual favors to escape from demanding tasks. If such a woman advances in the department, she may be accused of "sleeping to get ahead." She may also make it difficult for other women who enter law enforcement with different approaches toward being accepted.

Men are often at a loss on how to treat their new "partners." They tend to fall into one of two categories in their treatment of women: the "Sergeant Daddy Know-It-All" who treats women as children or "Sergeant Sexual Shakedown" who treats women as sex objects.

The "Sergeant Daddy Know-It-All" believes that women can play an important role in law enforcement—the supportive role. According to him, women do their best work with juvenile and women offenders, as secretaries, or in other noncombatant areas. When this sergeant has a woman partner he will tend to protect her since he is convinced that she can't handle it on her own. This puts him in jeopardy and insults women officers who want to prove that they can be competent and effective. As one woman stated: "Instead of giving women a chance to perform their duties to their full potential, some supervisors constantly give them boring and demoralizing tasks."

Many women in law enforcement report that they have been sexually harassed by supervisors and other officers. As one woman stated, "They'll promote you if they can get down with you." Endless sexual comments by coworkers are met with a mixture of anger and amusement, or women simply try their best to ignore them. The "Sergeant Sexual Shakedown" does not understand why women want to be police officers, and his only way of relating to them is through his and her sexuality. If he has a woman partner she is certainly not his equal and he, too, may try to protect her and will constantly point out how she does not equal him in strength, leadership ability, and so on.

In fact, being accepted as "one of the boys' is nearly impossible for women officers. In order to do an effective job as a police officer, one must be part of the group. Trust, understanding and caring must exist between partners. Yet women entering the field, find that this isn't readily given. One said: "My first year as a police officer was spent in constant battle with men who refused to accept women in patrol. This was complete with practical jokes, calling in sick, sexist remarks, and some who just outwardly refused to work with women. There were days when some of the female officers left the precinct cursing, crying but stubbornly returning the next day to face the same harassment they had vowed and sworn they didn't have to take."

There are still very few women in law enforcement. And because of this they remain isolated from the culture around them. Women are strangers to enlisted male culture. Males share folklore, lexicon, and secrets of how to cope successfully. Females must be dependent upon males exclusively for support and training. Because of the continual female turnover, there are few protege networks and senior role models to help orient the female newcomer. As more women join law enforcement and tokenism breaks down, exposure to large numbers of them as peers should help break down stereotypes and foster acceptance.

The most frequently voiced fear by male officers is that a woman "won't be able to back me up when I need her most. She just doesn't have the strength to fight a man." There's some truth to that, and most women will agree, but there's another side to the issue that isn't as frequently heard. Women, due to their very nature, have learned other means of handling confrontations rather than fighting. How many fights have *not* occurred because a woman was present? They don't have a "macho" image to protect and will be more likely to look for means other than fighting to handle a conflict. How they learn to handle these situations will determine whether they are ultimately accepted by male officers as true partners.

An interesting phenomenon discovered by both men and women officers is that some suspects "might fight to the death rather than yield to a woman." During the

Israeli war of independence, women did engage in combat, fighting as well and sometimes better than men. However, before they were permanently withdrawn from the front, the enemy refused to surrender to women. This caused the mixed-sex units to suffer exceptionally heavy casualties. Some officers in the United States have witnessed the same thing happen when women officers have been used in riot patrols. It seems that for a man to surrender to a woman is the worse possible affront to his manhood.

Officer's wives also frequently question the need for women in law enforcement. Many of them fear the closeness that could develop between their husbands and female officers. This fear increases if the wives feel left out of their husbands' worlds. But wives need to understand that women officers, for the most part, are merely looking for professional recognition, not after-hours affairs. A female cop who had established a caring relationship with her partner and had just saved his life said: "After a couple of days, we were alone; we talked and embraced, crying in each other's arms over the fact that we were both alive. The thoughts of his buying a new home he hadn't moved into, his wife and children . . . he was simply glad to be alive and able to enjoy them." In other words, it's possible to care for your partner and have a loving marriage and family too.

One woman officer states it clearly:

> "Does the fact that you carry a gun, have killed a man, make you any less feminine? Or does the fact that you have proven you can protect yourself as well as your male partner make you less of a woman or him less of a man? No!! It proves only one thing; two police officers, two human beings accomplished compassion, friendship, support and understanding, none of which are restricted to only males or females, blacks or whites."

Women officers who in addition are a racial minority

may have even greater feelings of confusion and face even more resentment and harassment. As one officer put it, "I didn't know if it was because I was black or female." These women may carry a double burden as well as have twice as much to offer in furthering understanding between majority officers and minorities. The positive effects of all minorities in law enforcement continues to increase in numerous ways.

The chief passed out "dream sheets" to all of his officers asking them to list, among other things, which particular officers they would prefer to have as partners. Officer Marilyn T. who was mentioned most often was not only black, but was a woman, as well. This illustrates the fact that officers value competence above all else. The black woman in question simply did good work and was extremely reliable. (Plus, it should be added, she was very attractive.)

REFERENCES

Baldwin, J. *Notes of a Native Son.* New York: Beacon Press, 1955

Baldwin, James *Another Country.* New York: Dial Press, 1962.

Baldwin, James *Going To Meet The Man.* New York: Dial Press, 1965.

Blackmore, J. "Incident Report: Detroit: A Case of Cowardice or Sexism?" *Police,* 3(4), 1980.

Clowers, N.L. "Prejudice & Discrimination in Law Enforcement." *Police,* 8(5), 1964.

Dreifus, C. "People Are Always Asking Me What I'm Trying To Prove." *Police,* 3(2), 1980.

Morse, D. & Furst, L.M. *Women Under Stress.* New York: Van Nostrand Reinhold Co., 1982.

Myrdal, Gunnar *An American Dilemma.* New York: Pentheon Books, 1962.

Niederhoffer, Arthur *Behind the Shield: Police in Urban Society.* New York: Doubleday, 1969.

Niederhoffer, Arthur *The Ambivalent Force.* New York: Holt, Reinhart and Winston, 1976.

Niederhoffer, Arthur *New Directions in Police Community Relations.* San Francisco: Reinhardt Press, 1974.

Rafky, D.M. "Police Race Attitudes and Labeling." *Journal of Police Science and Administration,* 1(1), 1973.

Rafky, D.M. "Are Cops Prejudiced?" *Police Chief* 50(3), 1973.

Westley, William *Violence and the Police.* Cambridge MIT Press, 1970.

8

BEING IN COMMAND—
PROMOTION AND
SUPERVISION

Prestige, money, social ties, status and many other advantages come with being a cop and increase as one advances in the profession. The young officer entering law enforcement often hopes to become a sergeant, lieutenant, perhaps a captain, maybe even sheriff or chief. The typical ambitious officer is an achiever with an action orientation, a "hard charger" who wants to do more for society.

Supervising other people is a challenging endeavor. In law enforcement supervision is especially complicated because cops operate independently and rarely are seen by, or spend much time with, sergeants or higher superiors. When things don't go right, the bosses in the organization are criticized. Cops are quick to "bitch" about their supervisors and feel that, if given the chance, they could do a better job.

Being promoted is almost always automatically valued

and usually means more prestige, higher earnings and other benefits in addition to the new title. But not everyone is meant to be a supervisor, and all people should not seek promotion. Law enforcement organizations need competent people at all ranks, and an effective street officer is just as essential as a captain. What is important is that each of us take a good look at our strengths and weaknesses and find the position that is best suited for our skills, which can help build a happy and successful career.

Stories of officers who sought and achieved a higher position but then were dissatisfied are not uncommon.

> Denny S. worked at a busy station as a patrol deputy and performed so well that he was selected to be a training officer. In that position he was so successful that he was assigned to work with the most difficult trainees, which he didn't particularly enjoy. However, soon enough he was promoted again, to the detective bureau. He was such a good detective that he landed a premium job in the homicide division. It was a very satisfying time for him, and again he performed admirably—so well, in fact, that he got promoted to sergeant and assigned to the county jail. Suddenly, instead of handling exciting homicide cases, he found himself worrying about such things as how to prevent prisoners from stealing silverware from the kitchen and sodomizing each other. Instead of being out on the streets working independently, he found himself tied to a desk and punching a time clock. Denny became frustrated and disillusioned and wondered out loud to his fellow officers: "What's the point in being promoted if it takes all the glamour out of police work? What's the sense in doing a good job if they just turn around and take it away from you?"

Promotion should be considered in light of what is best for one's way of life, despite the implied pressure from both peers and administration. Some assume that if individuals don't try for a promotion, or if they turn it down, they lack the initiative which is necessary for a career in law enforcement.

Many common expressions imply the importance of promotion and rank: "I'm *just* a patrolman," or, "My husband's a captain." One's standing in the social order is also affected, since people of the same rank and their spouses usually associate with each other.

In seeking a promotion, some people don't think about the consequences of a new job, which can lead to disillusionment and frustration. By looking ahead and plan-ning, however, there can be more opportunity for personal satisfaction. A few questions to consider are: "Do I fully understand what the new position encompasses? Am I aware of, not only the salary aspects, but also the skills required? Do I believe that I possess these skills or can learn them quickly?"

The cop who might have been a natural leader on patrol may find that he lacks the organizational skill required to be a leader from a desk. An officer could be promoted beyond the level where he really did his best and truly enjoyed himself. He might miss the activities which origi-nally brought him into the profession. When this happens, the officer finds himself in a difficult dilemma, which in turn creates problems for the people under his command, as well as his family. It affects his feelings about the people around him and most importantly about himself.

Officer John G. reflects:
"I've worked for sergeants and lieutenants who felt uncomfortable in their new positions and consequently began mucking around in decisions that should have been made at a much lower level. I've even seen this happen in chiefs. I remember one new lieutenant, in par-ticular—he just worried himself to death about the most piddling decisions—matters that even the sergeants

didn't concern themselves with. This lieutenant got
involved with so many small problems that the rest of
us realized he was doing it because he felt uncomfortable
dealing with the bigger picture. They should have left
him at his old rank, because that's where his head was
still at."

Officers seeking a new position need to discuss it with
their spouses and family, and perhaps their peers. All
may have insight into the officer that can help him make
a good decision.

An officer should consider the position he's now holding. Does he really enjoy it? Or does he feel that he's
achieved all he can in that position and is feeling a bit
bored? Is he satisfied with his life as it is? Does he have a
real sense of himself in his present position? He needs to
look at both the negatives and positives of his present job
and then compare it with what he sees as the negatives
and positives of the position sought. He needs to be realistic in his assessments of himself, his capabilities and his
life goals.

Promotion is not for everyone. To realize this does not
mean admitting incompetence; quite the contrary. It is the
mature, well-functioning individual that realizes how he
can best utilize his talents. The increase in dollars,
although always of concern, must not be the sole motiva-
tor for change of duties; certainly not if it becomes disastrous to the emotional well-being and social relationships
of the new supervisor.

After making the decision to seek a promotion and then
going through the often lenthy process—written exams,
oral interviews, appraisal of promotability, etc.—no one
sits back and hopes he does well. If and when he gets the
word that he's made it, it's time for celebration with fellow
officers, family and friends. It is a moment of excitement,
and the additional money is tallied up and often already
spent.

Now it's time to return to work. Often, in large agencies, there's a different location and shift, with all the encumbrances and inconveniences to the new promotee and the family that follow. Then the officer must adjust to his new assignment. Each level requires certain skills not required of the previous level, and without training (which is sorely lacking for most supervisorial positions), it can become a matter of giving it your best shot and hanging in there. Most people will need a great deal of support at this time as feelings of incompetence are bound to creep in, although these may be shielded by a strong facade.

> Patrolman Bill F. relates this story:
> "Lenny used to work in patrol, but then he went to the vice squad and worked there for 11 years. At that time he got promoted to sergeant and went back to patrol. He liked the idea of being a sergeant, but in the 11 years since he'd left patrol everything has changed, from what the department expected of its officers to the resources that were available to the overall policies. So when he went from vice back to uniform, Lenny felt like he'd been put down on another planet. Consequently, for the first few months as a sergeant he didn't do much except watch what was going on and try to catch up. In other words, he became one of the boys. He just sort of hung around with the officers instead of supervising them, and this didn't sit well with his superiors. Lenny felt incapable in his new job, and he acted that way, and he kept getting called in and given hell about it. He became totally unmotivated, and all in all it was probably the biggest mistake he ever made, to let himself get promoted."

It is no wonder that the person promoted finds it difficult to exercise the proper authority and leadership in supervising the people who were just recently his peers. He is a member of management, perhaps the same management from whom he and his fellow officers felt little support. And from the moment he gets his first promotion he's in the middle. There are some colleagues he is responsible for and others he is accountable to.

Supervision requires organization skills, finesse in social interactions, and an understanding of people. In addition, the new promotee must maintain the trust of his people while developing his own style of motivating them.

Problems are often compounded because of faulty communication between the new supervisor and his charges. This can easily happen if the supervisor had previously been a partner or peer of the underlings and if their expectations are different.

A dozen officers gathered one night to drink beer at the end of a deserted pier. One of the men noticed that their sergeant wasn't drinking, and so he asked, "Hey, Sarge, how come you called the party but you're not joining in?" And the sergeant explained: "I've had these stripes for six months now, and I'm starting to get some heat from upstairs. The problem is this. . . we have had good work reports, but the lieutenant says he's gotten at least a dozen complaints about how loose we are—about how we're lax on radio procedure, and how we take too long on coffee break, and how most of you guys forget to put your caps on when you're out of the cars. Now I'm not going to play nursemaid, but I'll tell you something: Trying to keep the brass happy and you guys happy at the same time is a bitch. I'm not the kind of guy who likes to crack the whip, but let me suggest that we try to look a little sharper on the job, OK?" The other men listened, and then agreed that they'd try to tighten up their procedures. Only then did the sergeant pop open a beer and join in the party. "I'm glad to get my first ass-chewing session out of the way," he told his officers. "Now I hope you guys let this be a lesson. Every time I catch hell, I'm going to give it right to you. Fair enough?"

The partner system, which is so efficient and necessary within its own realm, creates hazards for law-enforcement supervisors. There is a tendency for supervisors to let things slide for an old partner or peer. If a cop's unacceptable behavior is being covered up by fellow officers, the supervisor might act unaware.

The employee's task is to get the work done; the supervisor's responsibility is to see that the work gets done. Although this sounds simple, it is not easily accomplished. The employees sometimes believe they are doing their work very well while the supervisor disagrees.

There are numerous methods devised to supervise, ranging from autocratic to laissez-fair. Ultimately, the supervisor must find his own style, and one that is suitable to the department.

Sgt. Frank D. had screwed up; he knew it and he got caught. It was a relatively minor thing, yet he was called to Captain P. Donnelly's office. Frank was working Vice at the time and Captain Donnelly was one of those guys who enjoyed chewing people out, not because he wanted to make his point, but because it propped his ego up. Donnelly was a scrawny little guy; some suspicioned that when he was a kid he never got to school once with his lunch money. But when he was promoted to captain he could finally tell people what to do and they really couldn't laugh to his face.

Captain Donnelly called Sgt. Frank in and chewed him out. Frank said, "Yeah, you're right, Captain; I'm wrong and it won't happen again." That kind of took the wind out of the Captain's sails, but he ranted and raved anyway. Frank continued to tell him, "Yeah, you're right—I'm wrong. I'm terribly sorry, and it won't happen again." Finally, after this had gone on for quite a while the sergeant said, "Listen, you're beginning to repeat yourself and I'm beginning to get a little tired of hearing it. I don't know what else I can say. But let's put this whole thing in perspective. My wife won't screw you. My dog won't come when you call him. My kids won't mind you. What I did ain't bad enough to get fired over, and you can't kick my ass, so what in the world are you going to do now?" The next day, Frank was transferred to one of the worst assignments in the Department.

Historically, most management decisions were made on the basis of how supervisors handled related issues in the past. "This is the way we've always done it," was the rationale.

In the early 1900's Frederick W. Taylor became concerned with methods of increasing worker output through improved production methods. As an engineer, he began by studying various jobs and the best way to accomplish each one. He set up specific methods for performing different aspects of each task. Taylor's concept of "Scientific Management" was used by many companies throughout the country, and his methods reduced the amount of energy expended and increased production.

Followers of Taylor introduced the concept of time and motion studies. Their goal was to find the one best way to accomplish any given task. Workers over time resented the often inhumane manner in which these scientists treated them and their work. Finding the one best way and using scientific methods to solve all problems became management's goal.

As part of this movement the "Hawthorne" studies of the Hawthorne plant of Western Electric were conducted in the late 1920's and 1930's. The initial studies were designed to see how physical changes would affect the production of assembly workers. Lighting was adjusted to different levels of brightness, temperatures were raised and lowered; noise levels and other factors were altered. Whatever the examiners did to the room, productivity continued to increase because the workers felt that an interest was taken in them and that they were being treated as individuals rather than as automatons on an assembly line. These studies emphasized the importance of the employee—the human being—without whom nothing can be accomplished. Likewise, in law enforcement the supervisor must pay attention to and take an interest in the individual officers who work for him. Supervisors must get to know their people as distinct individuals rather than pieces of equipment.

Now let's look at assumptions that supervisors, managers and departments make about the people who work in the organization. This can be done by examining McGregor's concepts of Theory X and Theory Y.

Theory X assumes that people: 1) do not like to work and will avoid it whenever they can; 2) must be coerced, controlled, directed and threatened with punishment for them to do an appropriate amount of work; 3) prefer to be directed, avoid responsibility, have little ambition, and want security above all; 4) are inherently self-centered, and, 5) are gullible, not very bright, and the ready dupe of the charlatan and the demagogue.

Theory Y assumes that people: 1) like to work just as they enjoy rest and play; 2) are not passive or resistant to organizational needs, but rather will exercise self-direction and self-control to meet objectives they are committed to; 3) are committed to objectives as a function of rewards associated with that achievement; 4) learn, under proper conditions, not only to accept, but to seek responsibility; 5) believe that imagination, ingenuity and creativity in the solution of organizational problems is widely distributed in the work force; 6) are only partially using their intellectual capability at work, and, 7) believe the essential task of management is to arrange organizational conditions and methods of operations so that people can achieve their own goals best by directing their own efforts toward organizational objectives.

Even though many police officers possess Theory Y charactistics, there is rarely any input or involvement from them in the decison-making process.

Bittner's, 1970, statement, "The police is the only large scale institution in our society that has not benefited from advances in management science," reflects the fact that law-enforcement organizations usually rely on Theory X approaches to the problems they face.

Law enforcement is generally structured in a para-military fashion. As a result, communication is often one-directional, i.e., downward. In that situation, the employee may be reluctant to express any opinions, doubts or, cer-tainly, disagreement. Those attitudes could be viewed as an attack on administration, and the employee also fears that if something negative is said to a superior there will be retributions, such as assignment to unpopular shifts. If this climate exists, officers may find it hard to make inde-pendent decisions for fear it will be interpreted as insub-ordination. Thus, they may choose to keep their mouths shut, even though their familiarity with the situation may give them greater insight into a proper course of action.

Consider the assumptions made about employees by supervisors or departments when they require that all officers who are sick stay home or call the station to let them know where they're going if they leave the house. Is the message, "We care," or, "We don't trust you?" What about the officer who is recovering from a broken arm or leg, surgery or an emotional problem. Is he trying to dupe the department and take advantage of his "good" misfor-tune? Or is he trying to rehabilitate himself more quickly by exercising or getting away for a day to fish (or what-ever) at his doctor's advice?

Even hospitalized patients are encouraged whenever possible to take walks, to interact with visitors, to main-tain as normal a life as possible. Forcing police officers to remain home when sick could cause them to feel isolated and to dwell on their sicknesses rather than to set out on the road to recovery.

There is no question that in law enforcement there are certain situations when all personnel must follow orders and do exactly as told. When riots, hostage situations, raids or other dangerous field actions occur, all law-enforcement personnel must follow orders to the maximum.

Although "crisis management" would often describe both field and organizational approaches to problems, this does not have to be the case. Often forgotten is that most law-enforcement decisions are not made in highly dangerous situations. Rather, in most instances personnel can be questioned at leisure about their ideas and views on solutions to problems confronting the department, station or unit. The more say that a person has in a situation, the more he is committed to the action. Just to know that the administration or the boss is interested in what you say can make a difference in your attitude toward him, the department, and the way you perform your job.

There are many ways for small departments and units to be involved in particpatory management, simply by getting employees together, discussing problems, and finding possible solutions. In large departments it is not always possible to have direct participation. However, various forms of involvement can be gained through the use of employee representatives, quality circles and suggestion boxes.

One way of examining the quality and type of communication between supervisors and employees is to apply the principles of transactional analysis. This is a model which, as the words imply, analyzes the transactions between people. Accordingly, both supervisors or employees may be functioning as either parents, adults or children in relation to each other. If the communication is functioning effectively according to this model, both supervisor and employee behavior would be adult in manner. An adult employee would be carrying out his assignment and the supervisor would be seeing that the work is being done properly or assisting the employee to do it more effectively. However, there are many instances when the boss acts as a parent toward his employees. He wants them to know that he wants to help them with all their needs and difficulties. When this occurs, employees often start acting like children. They exhibit their personal problems by getting to work late, taking long lunches, leaving work early, turning in inaccurate reports, and so on. They presume the fatherly supervisor will understand their problems and will gloss over or not notice the inappropriate behavior.

> Officer Gary F. was stopped and brought to the station for being under the influence while driving. I visited him at the station at 6 a.m., and asked, "What time are you supposed to be at work?" "Seven a.m.," he said. I told him, "You're never going to be able to make it today," and he answered: "Yeah, I know. They know at the station I have problems. They know my wife left me and I have to raise my two kids. They just know things have been rough for me. In fact, they've been great. It's nothing for me to get in late or leave early. Or if I'm really having problems to miss a day or two. They'll cover."

This approach wasn't helpful to this 30-year old officer, and after this incident he realized he needed to put his life in order. As a result, Gary started assessing his life and got professional counseling. Since then he has not missed a day of work, and two years later he received an outstanding evaluation. This is quite a change, considering that all of his previous evaluations were competent to marginally competent. It's possible that Gary's problems could have been overcome sooner if someone had held him accountable for his life and what he was doing, rather than letting him slide. While we all have to take care of our own problems, if people confront us supportively about our improper behavior we may get through the destructive and unhealthy aspects of that behavior much quicker.

Officer Tim G., who is working a desk job, gets up in the morning, drinks a large, glass of vodka, brushes his teeth, and goes to work. Upon returning home at night, he and his wife drink vodka until they fall asleep. The next morning he drinks the same, full glass of vodka, brushes his teeth, and goes to work. This pattern continues throughout the week until the weekend. And on the weekend he begins the day in his usual manner, and then he and his wife proceed to consume as many as nine bottles of vodka before Monday morning dawns. When I learned about this excess I asked Tim how he made it through the day at work. His response was, "It's pretty f---ing difficult, but if I get a couple of stiff ones at lunch I can usually make it. But what's really good is when I can go with my lieutenant, because then I can have four or five."

Here's a man in his middle forties who, unless he changes his behavior, will not make it to 50. And what about the lieutenant? Is he helping out? Or, does he have a similar problem? It's similar to the "nice guy" supervisor who says, "Hey, Joe, let's go have a few drinks and talk about your drinking problem."

These two examples highlight a method of "killing with kindness" rather than having the officers face their problems and be responsible for their actions. Too often people who have been problem employees wish their supervisor had "pulled them up short" rather than allowing them to dig a deeper hole for themselves.

Supervision can place the supervisor in ambivalent situations. While deficiencies are recognized, the problematic officer may be a nice guy, perhaps an old buddy, or maybe he used to be a good cop. None of the supervisor's alternatives are pleasant. However, there are several ways such situations have been traditionally handled in law enforcement.

The issues of honesty and giving feedback are often nonexistent. In a profession where one's life is dependent

on the support of another and where one's life is risked for
another it's surprising how seldom difficult issues pertain-
ing to inappropriate behavior are discussed. What should
be done with an officer who has a drinking problem?
Everyone knows he has the problem, but no one is willing
to talk to him about it or tell him to shape up. A quick
perusal of employee evaluation forms demonstrates there
is little if any difference between the rating of a good
employee and that of a poor employee—as if there were an
unwritten code of never writing anything negative about
another officer.

> Officer Howard H. called me and said: "I have a real
> problem and I don't know what to do. My partner
> drinks—before work and throughout the shift." I then
> asked him what he had done before calling me. He re-
> plied, "Nothing, I just don't know what to do. I can't tell
> the sergeant because then I'll be seen as a fink and no
> one will want to ride with me. It would be like telling on
> my brother."

When this situation is widespread within a unit, the
supervisor is not doing his job effectively and it is detrimental for everyone—the officer, the department, and the
supervisor.

The following are ineffective supervisory techniques
often used to handle problem situations.

A. **Ignoring the Officer:** At almost every station there
tends to be an officer or two who are experiencing problems and are not coping with the demands of the job. Too
often supervisors ignore the obvious difficulties and hope
in vain that the problems will correct themselves, which
might occasionally happen when the officer is injured or
finally retires. The tendency to ignore problems is serious,
because the problem officer could be a danger to himself
and others.

Too often personnel files are devoid of any mention of

deficiencies, even though such problems are well known not only to supervisors, but to other members of the law enforcement community, as well.

One day a supervisor called me asking for advice. He began, "We've had this officer at our station for the past nine years and he has never performed well. But now we have to do something because he caused damage to three officers' cars when he left last night." Definitely the supervisor had to do something. But why didn't he do something sooner? Probably he hoped the problem officer would retire early, or he thought that holding people accountable would cause other officers to dislike him. Or perhaps the "buddy system" was in effect. Whatever the reason, procrastination can cause simple problems to become complicated.

There was an officer who was boisterous, threatening and trying to impress everyone in the bar with his peace officer status while drinking off-duty. He received a letter of reprimand and was given several days off. Subsequently he was involved in a second off-duty incident and again received a letter of reprimand and a few more days off. A third incident occurred when the officer became very inebriated in a bar, got into an altercation, and held a weapon to another patron's head in the parking lot. As a result of this last altercation the officer was terminated.

The issue is not whether this officer should have been terminated. The issue is: why didn't anybody ever sit this person down and talk to him about his problem. Sure, he got a couple of letters of reprimand, but no one confronted him personally. It is not the supervisor's right to interfere with or worry about the personal behavior of an employee. But it is the supervisor's job to focus on job performance and behavior, and to address those personal issues which affect the employee's work.

B. **Hiding or Transferring the Officer:** Many times, especially in large organizations, when an officer is performing poorly there is a tendency to place him or her in a less demanding or unimportant function. Smaller agencies cannot hide their problems as easily. Again, as when the problem is ignored, the officer usually has never had the problem discussed, nor is he told the specifics behind the transfer other than it is being done for the good of the organization.

Sometimes, a cop will be denied a transfer because of problems that are, once again, not brought out into the open.

Officer Tom C. was a good employee with the same organization for 22 years. He had worked several different assignments throughout his career and his record of performance was well above average. Tom had been working a patrol assignment for a number of years and decided he would like to transfer to a prestigious detective assignment such as homicide, narcotics or vice. He went for an interview for one of these assignments, and the interview ended with the good possibility that he would be joining the detective unit within a few weeks. Then nothing happened. So Tom went through the same process with another unit and the same results followed. As it turned out, the supervisors in both cases had called Tom's present working unit and heard some informal derogatory statements which had abruptly stopped his transfer chances. But Tom wasn't told a thing and never had a chance to face his accusers. After 22 years it seems this officer deserved some direct feedback about what was stopping his move. He should have been told what he was doing that wasn't liked and what could be done to correct the inefficiency. Not telling him was unfair and dishonest.

C. Firing the Officer: If either of the first two approaches is utilized, problems will never be confronted and can end with the eventual termination of the officer. Rather than recognizing, discussing and dealing with the employee's difficulties, a supervisor may allow the negative behavior to build up and reaffirm itself. Eventually a sufficient case is built for the employee's incompetence and he is asked to resign or is fired.

D. **Disability Retirement:** Throughout the country law-enforcement officers are receiving disability retirement as a result of what have been perceived as work related injuries or illnesses. Some officers, especially those an agency regards as problem employees, have even been encouraged to file for workmen's compensation or disability retirement even though the loss ranges from $1 million to over $2 million per officer considering benefits and replacement costs. The local government will have to cover the expense, but the organization won't have to cope with the problems presented by that employee any longer.

SUPPORT SERVICES

Support services for police save money, and, even more important, the humanness of the approach results in better performances all around. Having support services available is a clear message that supervisors, administrators—all of management are concerned about the health and welfare of their employees.

These services could include confidential counseling for employee and family; peer counseling for alcoholics, widows and those involved in traumatic incidents; management consultation for problem employees; a spouse's program, and a counselor available for emergency situations. Additionally, it is essential to have an overall organizational attitude—officers are entitled to have problems and can still perform on the job. Whatever support programs are designed, they have to be viewed as tools to assist individuals, with full knowledge that by aiding the individual the department will also benefit. After all the department is the sum total of all of its employees.

Throughout one's law-enforcement career an officer

may see all of the ineffective supervisory methods
employed. A tragic example is that of Karl Hettinger, as
described in Wambaugh's *Onion Field*. This officer was
involved in a traumatic incident during which his partner
was killed and he, luckily, escaped. After the incident Mr.
Hettinger was ostracized except by the detectives investigating the homicide. Their major concern, however, was
the obtaining of facts with little apparent concern for the
officer's well being. Fellow officers isolated him, and his
mistakes were used by training officers in a manner derogatory to Hettinger. The officer's work performance
progressively deteriorated to a point where he was
assigned less demanding duties ranging from desk jobs to
being chauffeur to the chief. With his physical and emotional health continually deteriorating, he filed for a
workmen's compensation and a disability claim, which
were denied, and he was finally dismissed from the force
as a result of petty-theft charges against him. Subsequent
employment was difficult to secure because of his background, and he eventually found work as a gardener and
farmhand.

It is regrettable that at the time of this incident few, if
any, support services were available to officers. If they
had been, it is possible that Hettinger could have dealt
more effectively with his feelings of guilt, anxiety and
responsibility. It is even possible that with effective support services he could have completed his career as a dedicated and competent police officer. At the very minimum,
if this event had happened in the 1980's officer Hettinger
would have been granted Worker's Compensation and
possibly a disability retirement.

Initially Hettinger was *ignored,* then he was *hidden* and
transferred to a variety of assignments, then he applied
for *disability retirement,* which was denied, and finally he
was *fired.* As a result of Hettinger's experience and other
similar incidents, the concept of providing *support services* was established to provide programs that would be

effective to help an officer through the variety of experiences and problems he may face throughout his career.

In the area of effective supervision there is a "vicarious" liability" legal issue concerning negligent retention. The law states that if a supervisor has information that would lead him to believe an employee may perform inappropriately and the supervisor takes no action, the supervisor can be held civilly liable for the improper actions of the employee. If Lieutenant Jones has information that Officer Smith could be too aggressive while on patrol and does not take any action (take him out of patrol, watch him more closely in the field, talk to him about accepted standards), and if Officer Smith commits an injurious act on a third party, Lieutenant Jones can be held personally liable, as can the department, plus the city or county.

Allen vs. Los Angeles City illustrates this well. Allen was the roommate of a police officer for the city. There was information available to the supervisor and the department that the police officer could act inappropriately. No action was taken, and subsequently the officer shot Mr. Allen in the back. Later, Allen sued the city of Los Angeles and was awarded a large sum for negligent supervision.

Thus inaction by supervisors, as well as endangering problem officers and citizens of the community, can also cause a tremendous drain on governmental finances.

There is a specific approach to problem employees that can be effective. Most important is that the employee is respected. Even if he must be firm, the supervisor must not lose his concern for the employee.

This approach involves:

1. Documenting specific instances of deteriorating work performance.

2. Having a frank and firm discussion with the employee regarding poor performance.
3. Explaining to the employee that, unless he or she voluntarily decides to seek help, his or her job will be in jeopardy.
4. Suggesting that the employee consider contacting the department psychologist's office for confidential counseling and/or getting involved in some other helping program.
5. Ensuring the employee that the psychologist will not discuss this meeting with his employer, even if the supervisor has made the appointment for the employee. (The only information that will be given is whether the employee keep his appointment or not.)

If needed, the department psychologist's office can provide supervisors with consultation on methods of working with problem employees.

The following are recommendations of appropriate and inappropriate behavior for supervisors in working with problem employees.

DO

- Make it clear that the supervisor is concerned only with job performance. Unless performance improves, the employee's job is in jeopardy.
- Explain that the employee must decide for himself/herself whether or not to accept assistance.
- Emphasize that all aspects of the department psychologist's office and all programs are completely confidential and anonymous.

DON'T

- Try to diagnose the problem.
- Discuss the problem unless it occurs on the job.

- Moralize.
- Be misled by sympathy-evoking tactics, at which the problem employee becomes an expert.
- Pin a label (alcoholic, neurotic, addict) on anyone who has not first labeled himself/herself.
- Cover up for a friend. Misguided kindness can lead to a serious delay in real help reaching him/her.

Supervisors must keep in mind that the sooner the problem is identified and dealt with, the more likely a satisfactory solution will be reached—a solution that will benefit the department, the supervisor, the employee, and the community which they serve.

Participative or group management enables workers to have a voice in organizational decisions and issues. In an organization of 50 or 100 workers it might be difficult to get direct input from all employees. However, there is an approach that is working in the Los Angeles County Sheriff's Department, which has over 6000 employees. A sworn advisory panel representing the sworn personnel from all divisions and a civilian advisory panel representing all of the civilians have been established. These panels meet once a month with the top administration of the department to recommend suggestions and solutions to problems confronting their respective groups. Many beneficial things have happened. A major problem confronting all levels in the department—promotional procedures—has been addressed, and changes and improvements mainly suggested by these advisory boards have been implemented. Employees are more aware that the administration is interested in solutions to problems confronting all members of the department.

Another important concept is that supervisors take active personal interest in the employees under their direct supervision. It is recommended that supervisors spend 15 minutes a week talking to their employees on a personal basis, getting to know them, their values, beliefs, ideas, etc. If this is done the employees will feel respected as human beings and probably will perform more effectively.

Studies have shown that workers do better when:

1. They are singled out for personal attention.
2. Communication is open and candid-up, down and sideways in the organization.
3. There is prompt feedback and fair performance evaluations.
4. They feel they are being treated fairly.
5. They work for employee-oriented supervisors.
6. Social needs as well as monetary needs are recognized.
7. They have pride in their work and a sense of satisfaction in doing a good job.
8. They are able to get along with co-workers.
9. Work conditions are paid attention to.
10. Their perceptions of the effectiveness and quality of the organization are high.

The performance of supervisors is extremely important, since employees work better if they're given good leadership and if they have a high regard for their superiors.

Conversely, it could be that employee performance problems are a result of ineffective supervisors. Accidents are associated with low morale, and accident-prone individuals often have complaints about employees being treated unfairly. Consider what the supervision and approach to employees must be like in an organization where:

- 18% of the employees felt it was dangerous for them to express an honest opinion;
- 70% felt bosses did little or nothing to make them a part of the organization;
- 40% said they had no chance to talk over work or anything else with their supervisors, and

- 30% believed they are guilty of any accusations until proven innocent.

One problem officer from such an organization lamented out loud: "I want you to know that if I ever get out of this jam—if I ever get back on the streets again—I will never treat people as poorly and derogatorily as those assholes have treated me. They are just trying to f--- with me. I've worked here 12 years and all of a sudden I'm treated like an asshole. Everything I get is in writing ... sergeants look the other way when they see me. I know I didn't do anything wrong, and if I have to keep dealing with them I may start believing I'm a terrible person. It's also effecting my home. They call a couple of times a day to check if I'm there. There have been a couple of officers go by my house several times. What the f--- did I do?"

The major issue that supervisors and the administration need to address is the message and attitude they communicate to their employees. Effectiveness of employees is related to how supervisors approach and interact with them—especially, when some cops feel they are not treated as fairly as they treat people on the street.

REFERENCES

Cooper, C. L. *Developing Social Skills in Managers.* MacMillian, 1976.

George, C., Jr. *The History of Management Thought.* Englewood Cliffs, New Jersey: Prectice-Hall, Inc., 1972.

Iannone, N. F. *Supervision of Police Personnel.* Englewood Cliffs, New Jersey: Prentice-Hall, Inc., 1978.

Likert, R. *New Patterns of Management.* New York: McGraw-Hill, 1961.

McGregor, D. *The Human Side of Enterprise.* New York: McGraw-Hill, 1960.

Taylor, F. *Scientific Management: Compromising Shop Management.* New York: Harper Press, 1947.

Teten, H. D. and Minderman, J. W. "Police Personal Problems—Practical Consideration for Administrators." *FBI Law Enforcement Bulletin,* January 1977.

Whisenand, Paul *Police Supervision.* Englewood Cliffs, New Jersey: Prentice-Hall, Inc., 1976.

9

THE BIG ONES— TRAUMATIC INCIDENTS

Every officer involved in a traumatic incident does not experience problems. Approximately one-third have minimal, if any, problems; one-third have moderate problems; and another third have severe difficulties that affect their families and sometimes lead to separation and divorce. No two police officers are the same, and so the experiences of officers involved in shootings are often different. Even though there are some commonalities to such incidents, the reactions are as varied and unique as the individuals involved.

If unprepared for these incidents or possible reactions to them, officers may easily doubt their courage, strength, or fitness for duty. Ultimately, they may start to fear that they are losing their sanity. The more they try to avoid the issues, the more haunted they can become.

Trauma and upheaval are part and parcel of a police officers' job. They might witness a partner being killed or a critically injured officer narrowly escaping death; they might accidentally shoot a fellow officer or shoot and kill a suspect; they might see a child killed or abused; they will often be on the scene of fatal traffic accidents, plane crashes and bizzare criminal cases. Though these events are traumatic, the severity of the reaction is dependent upon the officer's individual personality, current life situation, prior history and support systems.

Academy training often emphasizes the violent and/or dangerous. Tragedies are part of the job, what you get paid for, and a non-emotional response is a necessity. Police training and peer conversations stressing strength, manliness and power give some officers the idea that shootings and other violent events are the best and most rewarding part of the job. Officers' expectations may include being praised and admired for courageous acts and receiving commendations and awards for heroism.

A detailed survey of 60 Los Angeles County Deputy sheriffs involved in shootings from 1980 through 1982, conducted by the Psychological Services Unit of the department, determined that the majority of the shootings occurred during the officers' first few years in patrol. Seventy three percent of the shootings involved other police officers, as well; 91% of the incidents occurred on duty, and 45% were fatal. Particular psychological reactions noted were time distortion, sleep difficulties, fear of legal consequences and various emotional reactions such as anger, elation or crying. Thirty percent of the respondents felt that the shooting incident affected them greatly, or a lot; about 33% only moderately, and about 35%, not at all.

Several other studies have come up with similar results. Typical reactions reported were time distortion, emotional numbing, a feeling of isolation, the use of denial in dealing with post-shooting stress, flashbacks, sleep disturbances, legal problems and guilt. Anxiety and specific fears, as well as a loss of interest in work and a difficulty in returning to it, also appeared to be important components.

Nielson discussed in a more structured way some of the psychological responses of police officers to shootings. He reported data on the relative frequency of perceptual distortions, including slow motion, tunnel vision and auditory blocking. The prevalent experience was the slowing of time, followed by physical symptoms. The predominant physical problems were nausea and stomach upset, headache and general fatigue. Emotional symptoms included thought intrusions, depression, anxiety, sleep disturbances, fatigue and the inability to focus thoughts. Changes following the shooting incident included increased cautiousness, apathy, interest in family and an equal experience of support and curiosity from fellow officers. A small percentage of the officers were aggravated by the voyeuristic reactions of their peers.

In our study, 63% reported a range of emotional reactions including anger, elation, confusion, anxiety, depression and mixed feelings. During the incident 80% experienced time slowing down, as if in slow motion. Twenty six percent also reported time speeding up. The senses are keenly attuned to such an incident. Every sense is heightened to indelibly record the impact of the event. At first, it seems like a movie appearing in slow motion. Then it becomes even slower, like viewing one frame of a picture after another. Senses are highly charged to perceive any movement or change.

Officers reported seeing such things as the bullet leaving the gun and entering the body, seeing the blood coming out of the suspect's body, and the body bending and breaking as it slowly fell to the ground. They saw the grimaces on the face, and the final body movements whether they be trembling, jerking or gasping for a last breath. In addition, they heard the anguished screams or blood-curdling yells, as well as the multitude of other sounds that go along with such destructive violence. These vivid experiences are recorded in the officers' minds, as if on tape, to be kept forever, always ready to be played back.

Policemen's macho images, their need for non-emotional responses and their penchant for seeking out the most life-threatening and violent assignments can lead to an inability to express feelings of inadequacy or pain. If affected by trauma, they must continue to keep up a brave front so that it appears as if they were unaffected by the incident.

Jim S. shot and killed an armed-robbery suspect who was leaving a store. The shooting was necessary, and the officer did his job. A few days later, Jim reported no difficulties. The suspect had to be shot; he wasn't affected. Reactions that other officers had were categorically denied for himself. He was fine; no problems. He saw little, if any, value for an emotional debriefing session. He didn't need it.

On a hostage call, we met again. He told me: "I saw you three years ago after a shooting. Many of the things we discussed have happened. I lost 20 pounds. I'm divorced. I've screamed in the middle of the night and have been startled out of nightmares. I don't have the same drive, and my interest in work is lost."

Billy G. was involved in two shootings in two months. When we met, he was quick to state that he wasn't bothered by the two shootings. However, Billy G. reported experiencing some minor difficulties at home. He was sleeping only two hours a night, losing weight, and he appeared anxious and irritable, and moved nervously in his chair. These reactions were attributed to his minor home problems, not the shootings. Even though Billy G. was waking up in the middle of the night screaming profanities and yelling for people to die, he adamantly insisted the shootings didn't effect him.

Officers can't have emotional releases or breakdowns over every incident. They must be in control. However, many behavioral scientists believe that emotional releases are better for individuals than keeping feelings bottled up. The emotional release is seen as a step in the process of avoiding stress-related diseases. An emotional release is normal, yet law enforcement is an occupation which demands that people be objective, unemotionally involved, and not affected.

Police applicants are often asked if they could shoot and kill another person. Invariably, their response is the same. "I wouldn't like it, but if someone else's life or my life was in jeopardy, I could shoot and kill someone. There are tragedies that occur and that I'll be expected to handle, but that's part of the job and if you have to do it, it has to be done. I would be able to do it."

> Peter D., a two-year patrolman, got between a group of people and a man approaching with a long knife. The only thing Peter could do was to shoot the suspect. In discussing the shooting he said, "Two years ago when I interviewed for the job, I was asked if I could shoot someone and I answered 'yes.' My expectations then and the realities now are totally different. It really bothered me. I can't quit the department because of financial reasons. But I don't want to work assignments where there is the possibility of killing someone—which is almost impossible in police work. I want to work places where my chances of shooting someone are minimal and hopefully I'll leave law enforcement in a few years. Killing someone is a bummer, even if he's crazy, criminal or a bum."

Emotional release, if and when it occurs, is usually after the fact and away from the police environment. If there are strong emotional reactions at the scene, they usually occur when no one is present. Consider an officer who, after shooting a suspect, runs up to him, gives him mouth-to-mouth resuscitation, and yells, "Live man, live!," because he doesn't want to be responsible for this person losing his life. It would be considered just as inappropriate as if an officer stood over a person he had just shot and screamed, "Die man, die!," because he couldn't handle seeing the body wiggle and writhe on the ground.

> Matt S. was in an incident where he had to shoot a suspect. Matt, a religious man, entered police work to help people. He never envisioned himself shooting anyone. When he had to shoot, he went blank. He remembered nothing from the time he unholstered his gun till the time the gun was returned to his holster. He was unable to see himself fire a weapon and shoot someone.

Recurring thoughts or flashbacks occur without exception, and anniversary dates of the incident or holidays close to it are often reminders of the event. When officers drive by a location where a shooting occurred, they tend to be reminded again of the incident and may even have the same bodily and emotional responses they did at the time of the shooting. Whenever anyone experiences a significant emotional event—whether it be something tragic, like a shooting, or something joyful, like the birth of a child—those impacted do not forget the details or the emotional experiences. Officers have refused to work anniversary dates of traumatic incidents because of the feelings they generate.

A common type of flashback occurs in dreams or nightmares. Dreams can be seen as a way for feelings and thoughts to surface that we can't acknowledge in our awake state, but need to be addressed. Issues we cannot handle consciously such as fear, weakness, anger or depression may only be dealt with in our sleep. Officers have been awakened by their spouses because of thrashing movements, sitting straight up in bed, or yelling profanities and shaking. Others have broken out in sweats, like "having buckets of cold water" thrown on them, and have awoken to find their beds soaked.

Officer Gary F. was involved in a shooting with a suspect who was high on Phencyclidine (PCP). Gary's police car was parallel to the suspect's car. When the suspect fired several shots, Gary returned fire, hitting the suspect three times. The suspect, although hit, got out of the car and began to walk toward the officer. As the suspect approached the officer, he formed a fist and went for Gary's face. At this point, the officer shot the suspect twice more. Gary frequently woke up in the middle of the night, and saw the suspect's fist coming towards him, shots being fired in the man's face, and then the body falling away.

Another officer, retelling a shooting incident he was involved in eight years earlier, mentioned that he didn't dream or have nightmares every night as before, but thought or dreamed about the incident "only three or four times a year." He still remembers the suspect's name, can easily identify his face out of a mug book, and whenever he drives by the location of the incident he relives the entire tragedy once again.

On a Monday night at 8:30, four police officers prepared to serve a warrant to a suspect in a house. Four additional officers were used as backup and cover for the four officers preparing to enter the house and serve the warrant. Inside the house, the warrant was served, when suddenly from a doorway in the hall another suspect shot and killed one of the officers. The suspect ran down the hall and leaped out a bedroom window. One of the officers drew down as the suspect came out the window, but the officer was unable to shoot. The suspect ran around the house, and an officer from inside came out and shot and killed him.

The seven surviving officers and I met as a group two

weeks after the incident. I made short presentations on stress and officer-involved shootings, and suggested that they share some of their feelings, reactions and thoughts. After a period of silence, one of the officers in this close knit and prestigious unit began to talk about his reactions then others followed. Each officer in the room had a somewhat different reaction. Each officer cried when expressing his feelings. One frustrated officer, sitting on the floor, was slamming his fist into the carpet. There were concerns about the dead officer's widow and her children. The officer who had been unable to shoot wondered if he would be able to shoot the next time. Another officer wondered how he would act when he returned to the streets. Many of the officers were concerned about the welfare of the officer who shot and killed the suspect.

At one point during this Tuesday meeting, an officer mentioned that at 8:30 p.m. the previous night (precisely two weeks after the incident) he was having dinner with a friend. When he said this, all of the other officers in the room joined in to say that they also knew exactly where they were and what they were doing on Monday at 8:30 p.m. It was as if each of them checked his watch at 8:30 and said to himself: "This is the time that our fellow officer Bill was killed."

Just knowing that everyone had the same reaction made it easier to accept what could be seen as strange thoughts. Because of sensory distortions and flashbacks, officers in such situations can begin to wonder if they are keeping themselves "together," or if they are close to the edge of craziness. Knowing that these reactions are typical is often a big relief after a traumatic event.

Forty-seven percent of the 60 officers we surveyed experienced new fears related mostly to legal entanglements or to job security, with about 14% concerned about the department's reaction to them. As our society relies more and more on the courts to settle disputes, the possibility increases of the district attorney filing criminal charges against officers. Officers' decisions in the field have to be made in seconds while examinations by the district attorney or courts can take months, and every possible alternative is examined before a decision is made.

Officers who have had charges filed against them are fearful of a repeat performance. Several officers have reported that when they had to shoot they saw things they owned—house, boat, their entire security—being lost. These officers are more cautious and hesitant because they don't want to re-experience their ordeal.

> Officer Bobby D. as a result of actions he took while working patrol, had manslaughter charges filed on him by the district attorney. This process took a year and a half and cost Bobby over $20,000. After selling his house for defense funds and enduring a divorce and severe emotional problems, Bobby was acquitted. Subsequently, back on patrol, Bobby saw a suspect walking with a long object under a blanket. As he got closer he saw it was a shotgun. As the suspect reached and aimed the shotgun towards the officer, Bobby unholstered his gun. He then remembered his previous experience, threw the gun down and instead ran after and jumped on the suspect holding the shotgun. Bobby justified his behavior by saying he would rather be dead than go through the emotional and financial trauma caused by being involved in a shooting and having criminal charges filed against him.

When our lives are threatened or we're nearly killed or seriously injured, we may question the way we are leading our lives and the choices we make. When we narrowly escape death, we are confronted with our lives and must determine if we want to do things differently with our "second" chance.

> Officer Dave P., often bitter and depressed, was expe-

riencing marital problems and facing financial and career decisions, with many loose ends. He received a "hot" call and, while taking appropriate measures, opened a door and was hit in the stomach by a blast from a sawed-off shotgun. The initial days were critical; Dave was in intensive care and only a heartbeat from death. As he began to recover, his problems were seen in a different perspective, and he made promises to himself that have been consistently kept. Priorities were rearranged, and Dave began to lead his life with more direction and control than he had ever experienced before.

If an officer has been in a tense situation where he was expected to shoot someone and was unable to, returning to work is difficult, if not impossible.

Officer Harry S. drew his gun on a suspect and yelled, "Drop the gun! Please drop the gun!" Although the suspect's gun was pointed directly at him, Harry was unable to pull the trigger. Instead, he fell behind the car as he was fired upon, leaving his partner to shoot and kill the suspect. Harry, after much self-flagellation, quit law enforcement and took up another profession in a different state.

Officers involved in shootings and other traumatic events often re-examine the meaning of life. The sheer shock of killing a person, even when seemingly justified, has often led to intense consideration of anyone's right to take another human life. Sometimes officers want to know more about the dead suspect's family, his siblings and other aspects of his life, and sometimes they feel an increasing sense of guilt depending upon what these private investigations turn up.

Being involved in situations where people are alive one minute and dead the next confronts the officers directly with the finiteness of life. Dealing with death has caused significant changes in officers' behavior, thoughts and ideas regarding life and death.

As soon as possible after an incident, other units and a supervisor are notified. The officer reports enough preliminary highlights of the event to give the supervisor basic information so that he can leave the scene and return to the station to wait for the detectives assigned to handle the case. At the station the officer may be isolated so that recollection of the incident is not influenced. Even though conversation about the incident should be kept to a minimum, isolation could cause the officer to have feelings of guilt, believing he did something wrong like a troublesome child in school. It is helpful to have an officer not involved in the specific incident lend personal assistance or support to the involved officer, to be his buddy throughout the initial hours after the shooting until the detectives have concluded their investigation.

Waiting for the detectives' interview seems to take forever, especially when the officer is not allowed to talk with anyone. Often the detectives are delayed because they must first check the crime scene; they need a clear understanding of what has occurred from their direct observation and interviews with all witnesses. For the affected officer, time is of the essence. Although a quick response to the waiting officer's needs may not be possible, it should be kept in mind.

When the detectives arrive, the officer begins telling what happened repeatedly. After the initial lengthy interview, which examines every aspect of the incident in detail, the officer is sent home to rest. But he will need to go over the story many times. High-ranking department officials must know about the incident, and others may just be curious.

After the first day or two, the officer is allowed to go home or to an administrative assignment for a few days. He is told to call if he remembers more. At this point, it is almost impossible for the officer to get the incident out of his mind. Added to this are the other calls he often gets from fellow officers who want a full description of the incident from beginning to end. With all the attention given to them by fellow cops, many officers begin to feel that they are being looked to as heroes. Often their feelings are the exact opposite. They wish they could totally forget the incident.

However, their actions are reviewed by the media, the district attorney, the training staff, and others, the process seems to drag on forever.

With the officer's life disrupted, so too, is his family's. The lengthier the process, the more pressure added to the family unit and the relationships within.

While the officer is required to repeat his story to many people, he is not allowed to tell it to the media. Even though headlines blare, "Police Shoot Unarmed Man," the officer cannot tell his side.

At 2:00 a.m., deputies received a man-with-a-gun call. On responding, they saw the possible suspect, and asked him to stop and raise his hands. Instead, the suspect reached in his waistband and from 20 feet away pulled out what appeared to be a gun. The officers responded quickly and shot and killed the suspect. Unfortunately, the suspect's "gun" ended up being a toy. The media grabbed the story. Every newspaper, television and radio station was reporting, "Officers shoot man with toy gun." The stories continued for the next several days, clearly emphasizing that the officers should not have shot. Finally, Sheriff P.J.P. called a news conference. On his desk were three weapons: two real ones, and the suspect's toy. The Sheriff then invited various members of the media to pick out the toy gun. Three different reporters walked up to the desk and identified the weapon they thought was the toy—and all three picked the wrong weapon. That night on the three major networks, the shooting story was carried in much the same way, emphasizing that the suspect had a toy gun. Only one network showed the film of the three indistinguishable guns and reporters being unable to determine the difference. (The reporters' scrutiny, by the way, was under appropriate lighting and from less than a foot away, while the deputies were in the dark and more than 20 feet away.)

Some wonder how officers who have been in wars and killed men in combat with minimal reaction can have such strong reactions to police shootings. The two situations are different. In war, the enemy is known, his weapons are as good, if not better, and he is as skilled in combat. The objective is to destroy the enemy. The person you are shooting at doesn't live in your town. He is the enemy—the bad guy. Everyone is shooting. Everyone accepts the role and what has to be done. In the service, the fighting is clear-cut. The enemy soldiers usually wear uniforms, look different and may speak a different language.

Although some refer to police officers working the streets as being at war, there is a vast difference. While crime exists, not everyone is committing it. Not everyone is the enemy, It is a much more subtle battleground, in all respects.

Often the strongest guilt reactions occur when an officer's partner has been shot, and especially if he has been killed. The surviving officer often feels responsible, believing that if he had taken a different action, been more careful, or said something different, the entire misfortune could have been avoided. Officers risk their lives, to protect and cover for one another, and when one dies it is presumed by the partner to be his fault. Everyone else knows the surviving officer did his best for his partner, and yet he refuses to relinquish responsiblity.

Generally, officers whose partners are killed experience more guilt than from other types of police tragedies. Even worse can be the accidental shooting of one's partner, a fellow officer, or an innocent victim. Constant reconstruction of the incident—looking at ways it could have been handled differently—only adds to the guilt and frustration.

When one's partner has been killed, the surviving officer may try to help with some of his partner's responsibilities. He might try to help out the widow and children and take care of things that were important to his partner.

> Carl Hettinger in Wambaugh's "Onion Field" illustrates well this guilt-reaction phenomena. Carl felt terrible that his partner, Ian Campbell, had been killed. His efforts to return to work were mainly ineffective as Carl's thoughts and feelings of guilt remained. His guilt increased as he blamed himself for not doing more or taking other action. As his work deteriorated, he continued to feel guilty. He felt he should have been reprimanded or punished. He wasn't, and, as a result, finally ended up being arrested for shoplifting. Consequently, he chose to resign from the department in lieu of disciplinary action. Carl felt responsible for taking his partner away from his wife and family. He frequently visited them and tried to assist whenever possible. As is often the case, even though he performed effectively, he felt responsible for his partner's death. Since no one would punish him, he brought about punishment himself by acting inappropriately or doing something bizarre or illegal which caused him trouble.

The circumstances surrounding serious accidents cause trauma for everyone—victims, witnesses and law enforcement personnel. The aftermaths of car and plane crashes, where lives are taken and bodies are mangled, present the officers with formidable tasks which can impact them deeply. Officers who arrive at the scene of a severe incident are confronted with mutilated and distorted bodies: the gore of human tragedy. In some cases, they may find an arm on one side of a car and a leg on the other; or see a head in one place and another part of the body somewhere else. They are expected to handle this human carnage routinely, providing as much help and assistance as possible. To perform their functions, they suppress their feelings. However, the emotional onslaught may stay with them much longer.

Officers working in these incidents have had nightmares and flashbacks. The senses are keenly affected; they see destruction, smell pungent odors, touch dead bodies, and hear the screams of injured victims. They recall all the gruesome destruction of human bodies they experienced during the incident. All these sensations and experiences are not quickly, if ever, forgotten.

Officers who investigate or witness the bizarre and revolting acts that man has committed upon others don't always forget these at the end of the day, either. They are constantly reviewing or examining human destruction and horror: throats of girls slashed in a particular way, nipples ripped off with pliers, vaginal areas ripped open, or bodies cut in pieces and left in trash bags. Officers must face and live with these experiences. When they have to frequently look at the result of mutilation and torture, they are bound to be affected or to shut off their feelings. They might question their values, the purpose of their work, and the direction society is headed.

> Officer Ralph W. was expected to dig for bones of young girls who had been sexually molested. Their bodies had been dismembered and buried. Earlier that year Ralph's 13-year-old daughter had disappeared. Imagine the feelings and reactions he could have had if he had to approach this task.

Officers experience particular difficulty in incidents related to children. Viewing bruised or abused children or seeing young children injured or killed in traffic accidents often causes officers serious problems. These situations can be particularly hard when officers have children about the same age as the injured, abused or dead child they see at work. These events can cause officers to question their parental behavior. They may overprotect their children and be fearful of everything the children do away from home or when the officer is away.

Some reactions are similar to those of officers involved in shootings. Other responses are particular to the specific truamatic event, the officer's life situation, his psychological makeup, and his prior experiences. The bottom line is, there are a variety of experiences officers may be exposed to which can cause them and their families severe distress and problems. Awareness of possible reactions and assistance through difficult times can aid greatly in reducing trauma for the officers.

A traumatic incident can bring about a life crisis for some police officers. Crisis theory states that people, at whatever level of psychological health, are for the majority of their existence in a period of equilibrium or homeostasis. When a significant emotional event occurs which has the potential to upset homeostasis or equilibrium, stress and tension are placed on the individual. Coping mechanisms are then brought to bear. If these mechanisms are unable to meet the situation, upheaval occurs and there is often a painful period of disequilibrium and disorganization. The person can only exist with the stressful situation for a short period of time and must develop some method of coping and adjusting to the crisis. The period of adjustment involves a reintegration by the individual.

This reintegration process usually begins immediately or within four to six weeks after the event. The re-establishment of equilibrium may be at the same level or at a higher or lower level of psychological functioning, depending on the method the individual uses to handle his predicament. In other words, he gets better, he gets worse or he remains the same. The emphasis in crisis theory is that the level of equilibrium finally achieved by the person in crisis is dependent upon the immediacy of treatment as well as the effectiveness and ability of the people who are intervening.

The effects of a traumatic incident and the subsequent re-adjustment by the officer are described in Figure 4. This diagram represents an officer in good mental health. When a traumatic event happens, he may start to spin into a period of disruption where he is out of control and incapable of handling many aspects of his life with which he had previously coped. At some point, he will have to return to equilibrium. Anyone with whom he comes in contact—including homicide detectives, department officials, psychologists and peer counselors—will have an effect on the level of equilibrium reached. The goal in working with the officer should be to at least help him maintain the equilibrium he had before the crisis and hopefully to aid him to a healthier level.

Examining the wide range of results that may ensue from the various methods for resolving a crisis, the entire process can be seen in the two characters which make up the Chinese symbol for crisis: danger and opportunity. There is the danger of less healthy psychological and social adjustment, and there is the opportunity for growth in effectively handling a very disruptive life experience.

Departments can establish reliable methods to deal with traumatic incidents for officers. But first these departments must recognize that officers can have emotional reactions to various aspects of their jobs. Some of this can be accomplished through training at the academy and through the attitudes that supervisors and management take toward their officers. This approach would encourage officers to seek assistance if bothered by some incident or aspect of their work. Such assistance could come from psychologists familiar with traumatic reactions, or from an officer or a group of officers who have experienced similar traumas.

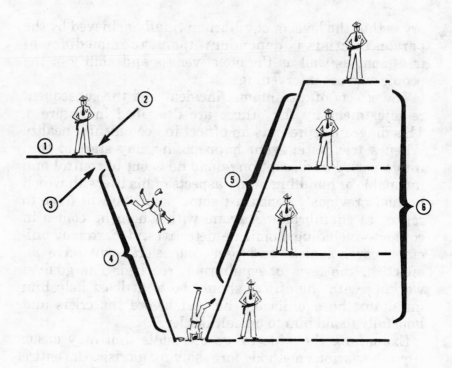

Figure 4

Levels of Psychological Well-Being

1. Officer in equilibrium at present psychological level.
2. Taumatic incident.
3. Crisis created by the traumatic incident.
4. Period of disorganization.
5. Period of reorganization—reestablishment of equilibrium.
6. Post-crisis equilibrium at possible psychological levels of reintegration is affected by treatment of all who interact with officer.

The emotional debriefing session must remain confidential between the officer seeking assistance and those assisting. Sometimes departments and officers have regarded a consultation with a psychologist after a traumatic incident as an evaluation. In an evaluation process the pscyhologist is making a determination whether the officer is psychologically fit to work, if he should be given another assignment, or if he should be asked to retire. However, in an emotional debriefing session the officer is seeking help because he has experienced a significant emotional event, not because he did anything wrong or because his psychological fitness is questioned.

Answers to some of the following questions may provide direction and ideas for responses to officers involved in shootings.

What is the policy for use of deadly force for your department? Is this the policy that is followed in the streets or is it the policy of the sergeant or field training officer? Do the chief's or officers' actions (both word and behavior) show support for such a policy? Is the philosophy of the chief being used in the training of your officers in the use of deadly force?

When the incident occurs, does the officer have his gun taken from him? Is he isolated in a room to wait for the detective interview? Does he feel like a suspect because of the approach used by investigators or superiors? Are some of the methods used for officer-involved shootings similar to those used for those who have done something wrong or violated policy?

What do all the inquiries and phone calls from fellow officers signify? What do commendations and awards received signify? Are officers treated as heroes even when they feel differently and may want to forget about the incident?

When does the officer return to work in the field? Is there a policy or rationale for when an officer should return? Is he kept out of the field so long that he becomes fearful of getting "back on the horse" and handling the job? Should all of this be determined on an individual basis? If so, who makes this decision?

Mike W. was happily married and the father of two children. Late one night, in an unlighted area, Mike pulled up behind two suspicious people. Getting out of his patrol car, he ordered the suspects to stop. They were requested to turn around, at which time they fired weapons at the officer, hitting him four times. One suspect ran away, while the other came up to the officer at point blank range and began to fire again. However, there were no more bullets. The suspect then took the butt of his gun and began hitting Mike on the head, fracturing his skull and causing it to bleed profusely. Out of desperation and with all his strength, the officer reached for a weapon and shot and killed the suspect. Mike at this point did not believe he would live. However, he called the station for assistance. His request for help was barely audible. When he talked, blood spewed out of his mouth like water rushing out of a spigot. Mike expected to die, especially when he heard sirens all around and no one seemed able to find him. He tried the car radio again to direct them. Finally, after what seemed an eternity, officers arrived and rushed him to the hospital.

Three years later, Mike decided to seek psychological assistance. The first words out of his mouth were, "I feel a little strange seeing a psychologist, but I'm having problems and need to talk to someone. I don't know what to do. I work in a very macho department. We see ourselves as impervious to pain and believe we can handle everything. I probably should have seen you right after the incident or not gone back to work in the same station, but I couldn't let the people know I was bothered or wasn't sure I could handle it. Now, I know I can't handle it. I've taken myself out of the field. I still have a bullet lodged in my face, which is painful as hell. It hurts constantly and continually reminds me of that terrible day."

Initially, upon returning to work, Mike drank a six pack of beer a day to alleviate the pain in his cheek. He progressively increased the amount of beer until by the third year he was drinking two six packs of beer a day and taking several pain killers. His pain was almost unbearable. He had headaches and his stomach always bothered him. Mike had gone to specialists to see if the bullet could be removed from his face, but due to the sensitivity of the area, removal was seen as extremely dangerous. Mike saw himself as, "No good for my wife. No good for my kids. I'm just a puke."

For the three years that Mike worked, the pain and fear continued to increase. Even though he killed the suspect to save his own life, he did not feel he could shoot or kill another human being. Mike would shake when he went to work and often vomited in the parking lot before entering the station. Finally he took himself out of the field. But he could not stop the pain and the constant reminders of the incident.

Mike was referred to a lawyer for increased compensation and possible disability benefits. Because of a mistake by the lawyer, Mike did not receive any money for several months. Mike was contacted about a possible job that would not require any regular police duties. The job entailed assisting civilian employees with some personnel work.

Mike's response to the offer: "I really don't like the fact that I don't have much money. I don't like my wife working, supporting me and the children. But I can't take the job." He further stated that he liked the department and his fellow workers, but did not believe he could be around black-and-white cars, uniforms, or anything that reminded him of law enforcement any longer. It seemed to cause him physical and emotional pain.

Officer Frank S., a 15-year veteran, worked for a small city department. Frank was considered one of the best, if not the best, officer in the department. Often he was able to resolve situations peacefully, without force. He was assigned to train all new officers because of the high regard everyone had for his work. Very early in his career, Frank had been involved in a shooting where he shot and killed a man. Frank could have been killed,

except that the man's gun misfired. After 14 years on
the job, Frank experienced another shooting. The subject died and Frank lost the first digit of the ring finger
on his left hand. A third incident occurred within a few
weeks of the second. Two young boys (12 and 9) broke
into a store and, when exiting saw Frank and drew
down to shoot at him. Frank didn't have it in him to
shoot kids, so he shot above them intentionally. Fortunately, the boy's weapon malfunctioned and Frank was
not killed or injured.

Upon seeing a psychologist, Frank said, "You only get
so many chances in life. I can't take it anymore. I can't
handle it." He related how he was afraid to go out of the
house because people in the community knew who he
was and might try to "get him." Additionally, everywhere he went in the city, he was reminded of the shootings whenever he passed or went near the three
locations where the shootings occurred.

He couldn't live in the city anymore and moved fifty
miles away. This helped. However, if he had to go to the
city for prescriptions or checks, he began to shake and
sweat profusely. Because of these difficulties, he would
have his wife go to the city for him. He has not been in
the city for more than two years. Like others experiencing strong reactions to work-related traumas, Frank's
marriage ended in divorce.

Tragedies like those suffered by Mike W. and Frank S.
might be inevitable in police work. However, it is possible
that they could have been avoided if the officers had
allowed themselves to seek emotional help. Police officers
risk their lives to save others and yet find it difficult to
talk with someone in order to save themselves.

REFERENCES

Brooks, P. R. *Officer Down, Code Three.* Schiller Park, Illinois: Motorola Teleprograms, Inc., 1975.

Fyfe, J. *Shots fired: An Examination of New York City Police Firearms Discharges.* Ann Arbor, MI: University Microfilms International, 1978.

Matulia, K. "A Balance of Forces." International Association of Chiefs of Police, 1982.

Milton, C., Halleck, J. W., Lardner, J., Albrecht, G. L. *Police Use of Deadly Force.* Washington, DC: The Police Foundation, 1977.

Nielsen, E. *Salt Lake City Police Department: Deadly Force Policy— Shooting and Post-shooting Reactions.* Salt Lake City, Salt Lake City Police Department, December, 1980.

Seligman, M. E. P. and Maier, S. F. "Failure to Escape Traumatic Shock." *Journal of Experimental Psychology,* 1967, 74, pp. 1-9.

Wambaugh, J. *The Onion Field.* New York: Dell Publishing Company, 1974.

Wilson, J. P. *Conflict, Stress and Growth: The Effects of the Vietnam War on Psychosocial Development among Vietnam Veterans.* In C. R. Figley and S. Leventman (Eds.), *Strangers At Home: Vietnam Veterans Since The War.* Praeger, 1980.

Wilson, J. Q. "Police Use of Deadly Force." *FBI Law Enforcement Bulletin.* 49(8), 1980.

10

ONE DAY AT A TIME—
ALCOHOLISM

Alcoholism is a disease that affects Americans in every walk of life. Approximately 75 to 80% of all Americans drink alcohol at least occasionally. Ten percent are known to regularly have the equivalent of three drinks or more a day. Nine million Americans are known alcoholics.

Many alcoholics are able to hold jobs, and some of these, naturally are in law enforcement. The impact of alcoholism on those in police work is ably explained by the following story of an alcoholic cop, as told by his former partner:

"Damn, but my ex-partner is looking great! His complexion is good and he's lost all that bloat. Most of all he isn't so uptight anymore. He's more calm and relaxed. For a guy who was packing around the worries of the world, he seems to be doing pretty well. I understand he and Old What's Her Name and the house apes have even found some common ground.

"It's funny, but when I told him that since he went on the wagon things seemed to have turned around for him, he just looked straight at me, and smiled. The S.O.B. was looking right through me and with that grin still on his kisser. Then he told me what he'd been through.

He began. "Things started turning sour for me about four years ago, but I couldn't put my finger on what was happening. Work was OK, but the old "can't-wait-to-get-to-work" attitude was sort of drying up. Oh, I was still having a good time. It's just that the good times didn't seem to start until after the shift was over and I was with my partner and the rest of the guys having a few shooters in the parking lot or at the local watering hole. But I handled it all right until two years ago. That's when Old What's Her Name started to nag me about spending more time with the guys than I was with her and the family. Well, after a while, I figured if she was going to nag, I'd give her just cause. I put a little more time and effort into my conversations with a foxy little squeeze who'd been coming on pretty strong lately. She seemed to understand the stress and pressure of my job and she didn't throw up my failure as a husband and father to me. That's kind of funny, because I thought I was a pretty good husband. Hell, I'd spent a lot of time and effort instructing Old What's Her Name in the area of home economics. I taught her how to mow the lawn, how to fix the plumbing, how to paint the window sills and even how to use the battery jumper cables. But was she grateful? No—she was an incurable nag. That was another thing I liked about the little squeeze. She didn't harp on my drinking. In fact, she was a pretty good two-fisted drinker herself. Unfortunately, I overdid the boozing a couple of times and passed out on the squeeze's couch. I was able to keep from being caught dirty by telling the old lady I was with the boys and we just drank a little too much and I'd stayed over with one of my buddies.

"But you know, my friend, I wasn't raised to be a liar, and after a while I began to get these damn guilt feelings. Of course, the more guilty I felt, the more I drank.

Then the depression and anxiety started to set in. I became confused and even called into work sick. You guessed it, more guilt and depression. By this time, I was convinced it was the wife, or the job, or both, that were the causes of all my problems. I reactivated an old back injury and took some "I" time. I even kicked around the idea of putting in for a service connected disability retirement. But most of all, I just continued to drink.

"You got the picture? I'm hurting real bad and I'm home. I'm drinking heavy and still stuck with this wife, who I believe is the cause of my problems in the first place. So I split and go live with a buddy. I suppose you think I now recover and find my place in the sun. I've gotten rid of Old What's Her Name and I've removed myself from the stress of work. Along with these products of my massive intellect, I've begun retirement proceedings. But that sun had quit shining and I was ready to do a number on myself. Then one morning I wake up with a terrible hangover and have that moment of clarity: Hell, I'm probably just a drunk. My family is gone, the cute little squeeze has dumped me, and I'm getting ready to dump the one thing I have left, my job. All because I have a love affair with the bottle. I've lied, conned and cheated everyone and everything that was ever important to me. Worst of all, I've been lying to myself. I've lost my self respect and I don't know what self-esteem is. That's when I quit drinking and started getting my life in order at home and at work. Things are going good for me now. I plan to work for a few more years and look forward to a long and happy retirement with the wife."

Alcoholism may start out simply as a beer or wine with dinner and develop into a very complex illness. If not treated, (and it can be) alcoholism can result in permanent mental damage, physical incapacity, or early death. Treatment begins with a basic awareness of one's alcohol consumption. Alcoholism can be stopped at any stage if the alcoholic truly wants to end his addiction. But the most important factor is an awareness of what drinking can lead to if we're not careful.

Alcoholism affects the whole person. Perhaps the most evident impact is in the physical area. Even non-intoxicating doses of alcohol produce a slight increase in heart rate and cardiac output, with some rise in blood pressure. Studies agree that blood pressure can *double* in people with high alcohol consumption. In two independent studies in Glasgow, Scotland, researchers concluded that alcohol was involved in hypertension and liver abnormalities. Up to 30% of hypertension in affluent countries can be attributed to the use of alcohol. And with hypertension comes an increase in the the number of heart attacks.

Socially, many people feel that alcohol increases their ability to communicate with others. It is extremely rare for a police officer to attend a function—whether it be a wedding, a retirement dinner or a party—and not have alcohol served. In fact, it is commonly accepted that without alcohol one would have a dull time. But for alcoholics an increase in drinking only narrows their social contacts. They may become hostile, depressed, aggressive or even suicidal, and their friends become fewer. Their emotions may become both confusing and erratic. When they know they should feel "up," instead they may be depressed. A mild, sensitive, alcoholic can turn into an aggressive, hostile drunk. This leaves both friends and family concerned, but in time they will probably move farther and farther away from him.

Spiritually, alcoholics can abandon all their beliefs in lieu of their never ending search for ways and means to obtain more alcohol. And intellectually their thoughts become confused and at times non-existent. They may not remember where they've been or with whom as their blackouts become longer and more frequent. The financial impact of alcoholism on government and industry is incredible. Although many people associate alcoholism with people on skid row, they account for only 3% of alcoholics. Millions of alcoholics are employed in all occupations, and loss of productivity as a result of alcoholism in the U.S. has been computed at over $10 billion annually, and it increases yearly. The total cost to the nation and human loss to individuals, families and communities is incalculable. Alcoholics are absent from work on the average 2½ times as often as other employees. They receive up to three times as much in sickness payments. Fifty percent of all male admissions to state mental institutions suffer from alcoholism. This disease accounts, directly or indirectly, for 40% of the problems brought before domestic relations courts. Thirty percent of all suicides in the United States are alcoholics, and the suicide rate for alcoholics is 58 times more than that of non-alcoholics.

> A memo on the Detectives Bulletin Board read:
> "It has come to the attention of the Station Commander that more and more martinis are being consumed at lunch time. It has also come to the attention of management that vodka is being ordered because of less alcoholic odor. From this date forward, it will be a firm rule of this station that gin must be used in martinis. We would rather have our afternoon interviewees know that our detectives are drunk than to have them think they are just stupid!"

Whether alcoholism is greater among those in law enforcement has not been proven. But there are many who feel that the pressures of the job can encourage heavy drinking. Many of the same factors that lead to the high amount of stress for officers are similar to those that lead to alcoholism: shift work, needing to suppress emotions, having to always be ready for action, a lack of support by both the public and the department, and the militaristic impact in a "man's world."

One of the socially acceptable ways to relax after a hard day is to have a drink. For most Americans this means coming home and having a drink before dinner, or perhaps stopping in a bar for a few minutes before heading home. But the drinking world could be different for the cop who gets off at 2 a.m. When he leaves work, the only people available to talk with might be fellow officers who have also just finished work. Thus, he will share his drinking with individuals who, like him, believe in the masculine image of strength and power. One of the values that fits well with this is the ability to "hold your liquor well." After handling all the pressures of the day, the officer now faces this challenge to his masculinity. Very rarely will an officer feel accepted in these "let-down" sessions unless he is drinking. These times of release, of course, can be healthful, facilitative and cathartic for officers. It's the drinking that can create the problems, particularly if it becomes excessive.

Whether an officer drinks with fellow officers or at home with his family, he can fall into a trap of using alcohol as a means to wipe out the pressures and even horrors of the day. When he leaves the court after having seen a criminal let go on a technicality, or discovers his superiors are unwilling to support him on what he sees as a "clean shooting," he may believe he can erase the feelings of anger and frustration with a drink. Instead of finding ways to solve the problem or handle it, the officer may add another problem—drinking.

There is a tendency for society, the department and officers to somehow overlook the fact that the person in uniform is an individual with the same frailties and weaknesses as others. When this is not understood, the officer must maintain an invincible superman image and often he uses alcohol to help overcome any uncomfortable feelings. Although alcohol may initially help, inevitably it can overcome and destroy.

Alcoholism, as I've said, is a progressive disease. As

time goes on, the signs become clearer and the disease more deadly.

During the *early phase,* alcoholism is almost indistinguishable from social drinking. A person drinks to relieve tension, may want a drink during a certain time of day, and generally drinks with friends. Soon, though, the alcohol tolerance increases and the person may suffer from blackouts (memory blanks). He may begin lying about his drinking habits. The more visible work-related signs will be an increase in the amount of sick days used, being late for work (especially after lunch), and leaving the job early. There is a general decrease in efficiency, with fellow officers complaining about this person's overreaction on the streets, lying, poor judgment, or general moodiness. It is usually toward the end of the first phase when a supervisor or good friend should get involved but rarely does.

The behavior of the alcoholic during *the middle phase* includes surreptitious drinking accompanied with guilt, tremors during hangovers, and a loss of interest. At work, the officer's behavior continues to deteriorate. He is seen as undependable, hostile, unreasonable, and a loner. He begins to take more and more time off, is hospitalized more than average, and has repeated injuries on and off the job. His work pace is spasmodic, at best, and his attention wanders. The officer in the middle phase of alcoholism will begin to experience more crises. He may have family problems, lose out on job promotions, suffer financial reverses, find his wages garnished, and increasingly gets into trouble with supervisors.

During *the late middle phase,* the officer totally avoids any discussion of the problem. This forces him to drink alone, and to avoid people. At this point, he fails in all efforts at control and doesn't even bother trying. Food becomes unimportant. His performance at work is far below expected levels. In fact, he may be considered a danger to his partners. His behavior is overly aggressive, belligerent, and he may begin to talk about very grandiose, unrealistic ideas. The crises in his life continue to mount with separation or divorce and punitive disciplinary action on the job.

By *the late phase,* the officer believes that all other activities interfere with his drinking. He drinks before work "to get started," during work "to maintain," and ends his day in the local drinking hole. By this stage the officer is generally considered incompetent and his termination is inevitable. There is a visible physical deterioration and perhaps eventual hospitalization.

Obviously these stages are not clear cut. Some alcoholics are remarkable in their ability to hide their drinking. But eventually, over a period of time, it finally becomes more evident to co-workers and family that a problem exists. Even with crises mounting, some alcoholics will continue to deny their disease. This makes it almost impossible for family and friends to communicate their feelings and fears, and the alcoholic is forced into a more isolated life.

The time when the denial stops is different for each person. For some it's when their spouses leave. For others it's when their jobs come into jeopardy. And for others it's a minor incident but "the straw that broke the camel's back." The following personal account by an alcoholic officer shows both his denial and then his beginning awareness of his disease:

"Well, the wife and I had another fight last night. Funny, but I can't even remember what it was about. All that seemed important was that I get out of the house. I do remember her shouting that we never did anything as a family anymore and that I thought more of my shift partners than I did of her and the kids. It's funny, but the only place I seem to have any peace anymore is at the station. Anyway, when I left the house I drove straight to the station watering hole and only planned on having a few shooters.

"Well, I met some of the guys and we started drinking and telling war stories. About 0130 hours we decided someone should make a run to the liquor store and pickup some booze since the bar would be closing in half an hour and some of us wanted to continue talking and drinking. I offered to make the run. When I returned, we all decided to adjourn to the local park for some serious R & R. Damn, the next thing I know, it's 0930 hours and the sun is boiling down on my face and I feel like a freight train has run over me and left me shaking like a plucked guitar string. There's vomit all down the front of me and a putrid cascade of the stuff on the car seat and floor. Hell, I'll have to clean up last night's dinner and booze before I can go home. I get out of the car and stumble to the corner so I can pickup a location from the street sign. I'm fifteen miles from home and don't even remember how I got there. Just goes to show you, you can't mix beer with hard stuff. I'll have to remember that.

"First I better call home and tell the wife we did a little partying last night and not to worry. That should go over like a lead balloon. She'll probably remind me I did the same thing five days ago and tell me I'm some kind of an alcoholic. Before I do anything I'd better stop and pick up a couple of beers just to clear my head.

"How the hell can I have a drinking problem? Sure I may have a few drinks in the morning, but I'm getting off "earlies" and it's just like the guy that has a few shooters when he gets home at five in the evening. Besides I never miss work and don't drink on the job. Not only that, but my last two evaluations have been outstanding. Sure I may cut a few corners, but you have to look out for number one. It's a cinch no one else will, and the way this damn world is going nothing is going to get any better. Screw the world, it's not going to beat me.

"God, but I'm scared. Where the hell is it all going? If I just wasn't so damn depressed. If I just didn't feel like I was by myself all the time. If my wife would just get off my back. How the hell am I expected to pay the bills when this crazy inflation is chewing me up?

"You know, I think I picked that stupid fight with the old lady last night just so I could get out and drink. Jeez, if I keep on like this, I'll probably lose the job, too. Somehow I've got to pull myself together. Everytime I've gone on the wagon before I've always felt better, at least for a few weeks. What is it they say . . . alcoholism is a progressive disease? It's funny, but I don't even like to go anywhere unless a few drinks are available."

Another officer's story also shows a pattern of denying and then understanding:

"Twenty years ago I came into this department with a bright future and a lot of potential. I got along well with people and did a pretty good job. Granted, I had a reputation of being a heavy drinker, but it was OK because I could handle it better than most, then. After four years in the trenches I got my transfer to Narco and I'd found my spot, the place I wanted to be. Except, by then, I didn't do such a good job unless I was sober, and that wasn't all that often. They put up with me for three years until, in 1967, I showed up to take the sergeants' exam so drunk that I didn't have sense enough to keep my mouth shut when a couple of lieutenants told me I couldn't take a six pack of beer into the exam. (Dick, if you are reading this, please accept my apology. You used admirable restraint by not punching my light out—which I so richly deserved.) That little episode got me a fifteen day suspension and a transfer to the early morning shift. What I didn't get was the point. Oh sure, I cleaned up my act at work, but I didn't do anything about my drinking, except be a little more sneaky about it.

"The Department thought I had learned my lesson, but the people that I was close to knew better. My kids were terrified of me, what friends I had left figured I didn't have both oars in the water, and my wife got to the point where she was less unhappy when I didn't come home than when I came home drunk. Again, I was where I wanted to be, doing what I do best, but I couldn't stop drinking.

"In the next three years, what little control I had slipped away and I became an everyday drunk. When I should have been out handling my case load, I was sitting in a bar. In the meantime, I managed to total two cars and walk away unscratched. I had long ago lost the respect of my family and now I was losing the respect of my peers. But, more important, I was losing my self-respect. I didn't seem to care how I looked or how I acted or what happened as long as I could drink. Predictably enough things got worse. I got a letter of reprimand and had to transfer to another unit because I had used up all my "free passes." It didn't work out. An old drinking beef that had been under investigation caught up with me and I got another suspension and another transfer. One morning, after a five-day bender that I don't even remember, I woke up in the hospital with critically high blood pressure.

"The doctor didn't waste any words. He told me that if I didn't stop drinking I was going to die. That kept me stone cold sober—for almost six months. Then, despite logic, reason and sanity to the contrary, I just had to have an occasional drink. And every time I took a drink I proceeded to get drunk. After eleven months I was able to pass a physical and come back to work. I still had a job but I found that there wasn't a unit in the department that wanted me, even as a free item, because I was a hopeless drunk. At this point I was fortunate enough to be introduced to an officer who has had considerable experience in these matters. He offered to show me a way to restore my health, happiness, self-respect and sanity, if I wanted them bad enough.

"That was four years ago and I haven't had to take a drink since. You see, that's the key for me: don't drink. It hasn't always been easy but it works. My family and I are back together, I have an excellent position in the department and, best of all, I can look at myself in the mirror without being repulsed. Don't get me wrong, I haven't joined a crusade. I'm still loud and opinionated, but now I can remember who I was loud and opinionated to—and why. The only difference is I don't drink and don't want to. If you can drink without it turning your life into a nightmare, like mine was, go ahead—but be careful!"

Private industry, government and law enforcement have attempted various approaches to deal with problem employees. However, administrators and supervisors have little, if any, background in understanding alcoholism. In the past, the victim suffered the bitter evaluation by his supervisor and peers as an employee lacking in fortitude or will power—a moral weakling. The American Medical Association, however, recognizes alcoholism for what it is: a chronic disease like any other.

The partner system in law enforcement allows for camaraderie, compassion, and understanding by fellow officers. Often there exists an unwritten code which precludes informing on a fellow officer with problems. To report the inappropriate behavior to a supervisor would be seen as a betrayal, and this habit of "looking the other way" can extend to supervisors. Some are ex-partners who have the best intentions and yet are unable to confront officers regarding their inappropriate behavior. Instead they choose to ignore the problem, hoping it will pass or the individual will eventually retire or resign.

Alcoholism afflicts officers at different ages and career levels. It is generally complicated by a variety of other difficulties, often leaving the victim and the employer confused and frustrated as to the nature of and solution to the problem.

Officers are usually quite dedicated to their profession and don't want to lose their jobs. The respectability that comes with the job provides a necessary rationale to deny their alcoholism. They may relinquish their property, even friends and family, but their jobs are the last things that working alcoholics want to give up.

This disease of alcohlism also strikes retired officers. They left a career that was tension-provoking and active, and upon retirement they may find themselves inactive and concerned about their purpose in life. They may have been subjected early in their careers to the idea that alcohol was the panacea for discouragement, boredom or other difficulties. In retirement they may be left with the time, the incliniation and the funds necessary to drink themselves into insanity or death.

It is impossible to provide resources aimed at helping the alcoholic resolve family, financial, emotional, work and/or retirement problems on a lasting basis if the officer isn't first directed into some type of alcohol recovery program. Likewise, an officer suffering from alcoholism will be unable to solve his various related problems if he is unable or unwilling to first deal with his problem with alcohol.

Denial appears in all the stages of the disease. Denial and alcoholism are inseparable. However, without recognition of the problem, recovery is impossible.

One *myth* of alcohlism is that the alcoholic must hit bottom before he can accept help. If society accepts that myth, the alcoholic will surely lose family, friends, job and quite likely his health or life. The truth of alcoholism is that there is almost no chance that the alcoholic will stop drinking as long as other people remove all painful consequences for him.

Generally, the alcoholic cop does not come to the attention of his supervisor until he is between the ages of 30 and 50. In an environment where heavy drinking is often condoned and even promoted as manly, the alcoholic will not be noticed until some of the crises in his life begin affecting his work. His wife probably suspects, and his close friends have questions, but quite often the alcoholic cop is intelligent, skillful and accomplished in his assignments and social interactions. Until the crises that accompany alcoholism catch up with him, denial of problems often continues.

The alcoholic street cop, detective or chief, almost always sets goals that are unrealistic. His failure to reach these goals is eased with temporarily increased consumption of alcohol. He may feel that alcohol provides a necessary relief from his tensions and anxieties. Alcohol brings him peace and calm, provides a feeling of well-being and self-sufficiency. However, the alcoholic's illusions are no more than coping mechanisms developed to combat a very real disease that could be genetic.

Denial, as practiced by the alcoholic, is self-delusional. A faulty memory system lets the alcoholic protect his conscious memory from ugly realities. Blackouts induced by alcohol cause total loss of recall, and afterward the person is left with feelings of fear, confusion and depression. The cure for these feelings is more alcohol—which completes or begins another cycle for the alcoholic.

Euphoric recall prevents the alcoholic from remembering any unpleasant behavior which resulted from drinking. He could imagine that people are lying to him and thus place the blame on others—on anyone or anything but himself. He knows he is a caring, good person and would not do what some say he has done. His distrust continues, and his world narrows.

Recognizing the many complicated problems of alcoholism, programs have been established to combat the disease. Their goal—to stop alcoholics from drinking—is the same, although their approaches may vary. All have as their initial step the need for the alcoholic to admit he has a drinking problem.

Private industries were among the first to establish assistance programs for alcoholics. They report great success in the rehabilitation of problem employees. Most claim a 70% to 85% success rate. While these programs are humanitarian, there are monetary benefits to rehabilitating alcoholic workers. The money saved in sick pay, time lost and retraining certainly makes these programs economically sound, and recovered alcoholics contribute more completely to their jobs, families and society.

The National Council of Alcohol and Drug Abuse estimates one out of ten people in our society has a drinking problem. This 10% cuts across all social, occupational and economic levels. There are no valid statistics on the number of alcoholics employed as police officers. But, whatever the percentage, alcoholic cops are a problem and must be dealt with.

Alcohol programs in law-enforcement agencies generally follow the lead of those in private industry. The first step involves educating the administration about the disease.

The supervisor's role in the program is to evaluate the effectiveness of the officer's performance. When a supervisor lets an ineffective employee "slide," that employee can have even more difficulties. Helping employees face their problems enables them to seek assistance from appropriate professioinals, perform more effectively, and feel better about themselves and their jobs.

Effective alcoholism programs in law enforcement are based on:

> Confidentiality or anonymity for anyone seeking assistance,
> Supervisory training, and
> Administrative support.

Recognition of the problem is the first step. Once an officer recognizes his potential problems with alcohol, he can get help. Los Angeles County's deputy sheriffs developed a successful program called the Peace Officer Fellowship. This provides a strong supportive group willing to help fellow officers with drinking problems. The program is open to all police officers, regardless of department, whether active or retired. Although everything is done on a voluntary basis, all officers are willing to extend a helping hand to a fellow officer in need.

Employees can be made aware of such a recovery program through pamphlets; department and association newspapers; posters; station meetings, training academies, and in-service training sessions for personnel at various levels. (For pamphlet example see pages 266–267).

The Peace Officer Fellowship is anonymous, keeps no records, and is controlled by the officers involved. Meetings are held four nights and one day a week at central locations. All expenses including rental fees and refreshments are handled by the group. Other meetings are held at the same time for the alcoholics' families and friends, who can easily get caught in the cycle of denial. They need to be aware of problems related to alcohol and to offer support, encouragement and understanding as their problem drinkers change their life patterns.

Each month the fellowship publishes information to share with fellow officers in the department paper and police-officer-association publications. Lists of officers unconcerned about their anonymity are also published, including home and work phone numbers. A monthly newsletter written by officers is mailed to all members of the group. (For newsletter example see pages 268–271). Jack's Story, published in the fellowship's monthly column, describes the impact of such a program.

"MY NAME IS JACK.

"I'm a recovering alcoholic...

"In 1976, after having found a way to live sober for almost three years, I found, and joined, a group of policemen who suffered from the same disease I have—alcoholism. We call ourselves the Peace Officers Fellowship, have several evening meetings a week, and have about 200 Alumni. All of us are cops—presently, retired or fired from agencies throughout the county.

"We are not a religious outreach group, an institution of teaching, an EST group, a temperance movement or

miracle workers—we are men and women who are learning from each other how to live sober—one day at a
time.

"A lot of us choose to remain anonymous, but some
people have chosen to relinquish their anonymity in
order to provide whatever service may be needed at
whatever time by any guy or gal who is 'sick and tired of
being sick and tired.' We're available 24 hours a day not
only to the person who is suffering but also to the non-
drinking spouse.

"I'm not telling you all this to recruit 'up and coming
drunks' into a chic society of non-drinkers, nor am I
some kind of 'Guru' promising an instant cure—all I am
is an alcoholic—a recovering, sober alcoholic.

"The program that I use, and share with others, is a
program for those who want it—not for those who need
it.

"The only requirement for membership is the desire to
stop drinking. In looking back over my 'accomplish-
ment' over the last 20 years, no reward has ever been
nor will ever be greater than to see a sick, cynical, jaded,
physically debilitated copper begin to get well.

"There are a hell of a lot of things that I did to my
wife and family that I wish had never happened, but let
me tell you this—if I had a chance to live my life over, I
wouldn't change one day—because I wouldn't be the
man I am today if I had not had to go through what I
did to get here. In a word, I am grateful—grateful to be
an alcoholic—grateful that I know that I suffer from a
disease—grateful that the disease, although incurable, is
arrestable and treatable—grateful that it is treatable by
others like me—alcoholic coppers, working the streets or
shuffling papers or supervising people and vitally concerned with staying alive and well—one day at a time!"

There are few who understand the torment an officer
experiences day in and day out. For those suffering from
alcoholism, the disease is an extra heavy burden. It is like
a cat stalking its prey—it takes the victim unawares.

ALCOHOLISM and the LAW ENFORCEMENT *Profession*

LOS ANGELES COUNTY SHERIFF'S DEPARTMENT

Sherman Block, Sheriff

THE BADGE AND THE BOTTLE

How many of us in law enforcement have had close friends lose their families, their jobs, and eventually their lives because of problems directly related to alcohol?

One will often hear fellow officers advise their peers that the consumption of alcohol will relieve their tensions and provide an atmosphere of conviviality. In most instances this may not be such bad advice. However, 10%-15% of those in law enforcement are potential alcoholics.

All too often problem drinkers are willing to admit they seem to experience difficulties when drinking. However, they believe that if they would limit the amount consumed and be selective as to what they drink, things would not get out of control.

After all, don't most of our fellow officers drink? What will become of us if we are no longer able to reduce our tensions and frustrations by having a few drinks with our friends?

Suppose we are diabetic and after the shift is over it is customary to join our friends in the parking lot or the local candy store and consume 7 or 8 candy bars. Everyone would think we were crazy if we attempted to explain we were only going to have "just a couple" or we planned on limiting ourselves to candy without peanuts.

When any one of us is obsessed with alcohol, it enables us to continue to deny that a very real and tragic disease has entered our lives and the lives of our families.

Perhaps some of us will *finally* get the message. Our first step might be to try and handle the problem on our own. After all, aren't we peace officers capable of handling a myriad of problems for others? What would our fellow officers think? What would our supervisors think? Many of us would rationalize that to seek help would prevent us from advancing our careers.

This simply is not the case. Most of our peers and supervisors were praying we would come to our senses before we ruined our lives or jeopardized the lives or careers of others. Remember, we are attempting to deal with a disease. Without help it can overwhelm us. Would the diabetic try to handle it himself?

THE PEACE OFFICER'S FELLOWSHIP CAN HELP

The Los Angeles County Sheriff's Department created the Peace Officer's Fellowship with the hope of assisting the law enforcement community in the area of alcoholism treatment.

The Fellowship is free of charge and completely independent of the Department. Since alcoholism affects friends and relatives, a special recovery program has been created for them.

The Fellowship maintains no records of its members nor is attendance ever taken at the meetings. It is the sincere desire of the Department that anyone seeking help with a possible drinking problem feel free to contact the Fellowship.

Hiding or ignoring the problem will not make it disappear. For those willing to come to grips with the problem, we can provide a program that offers freedom, growth, and happiness in a true atmosphere of fellowship.

For specific information contact:

ALCOHOLISM DEPUTY–974-5075
PSYCHOLOGICAL SERVICES–974-5075
HEALTH & WELFARE–974-4291
A.L.A.D.S.–986-0144
P.P.O.A.–413-3650
SHERIFF'S RELIEF/RETIRED MEMBERS–974-4176

FLYR 001 - 2-83 - PS 2-83

ALCOHOLISM... A PROGRESSIVE DISEASE

The alcoholic is a person suffering from a progressive disease for which there is no known cure. The alcoholic combines a physical compulsion with a mental obsession to drink. Fundamentally, alcoholism is a health problem rather than a question of will power or morality. Although the disease cannot be cured, it may be arrested by involving oneself in a simple program of recovery.

The thought that we might be victims of a progressive illness is the last idea with which we are willing to come to grips. Many of us believe the alcoholic is the poor fellow on skid row doomed to a life of misery and nonproductivity. Actually this concept only applies to very few alcoholics. The rest of us work, rear families, and get by the best we can.

The alcoholic will continue to proclaim the problem lies with the 5th or 6th drink. He may even convince himself things would change if he switched from hard liquor to beer or wine. It is this same line of reasoning that drives the alcoholic officer to believe his problems and tensions would end if only he could get a transfer, work for a different supervisor, get promoted, get rid of his wife, get a more understanding wife, get back into shape, spend more time resting or quit his job and find something in the great outdoors.

The list could continue ad infinitum. The frightening reality is that even after we have tried some of the above solutions we still find our lives unmanageable and full of problems.

ARE YOU AN ALCOHOLIC?

To answer this question ask yourself the following questions and answer them as honestly as you can.

	Yes	No
1 Do you lose time from work due to drinking?	☐	☐
2 Is drinking making your home life unhappy?	☐	☐
3 Do you drink because you are shy with other people?	☐	☐
4 Is drinking affecting your reputation?	☐	☐
5 Have you ever felt remorse after drinking?	☐	☐
6 Have you gotten into financial difficulties as a result of drinking?	☐	☐
7 Do you turn to lower companions and an inferior environment when drinking?	☐	☐
8 Does your drinking make you careless of your family's welfare?	☐	☐
9 Has your ambition decreased since drinking?	☐	☐
10 Do you crave a drink at a definite time daily?	☐	☐
11 Do you want a drink the next morning?	☐	☐
12 Does drinking cause you to have difficulty in sleeping?	☐	☐
13 Has your efficiency decreased since drinking?	☐	☐
14 Is drinking jeopardizing your job or business?	☐	☐
15 Do you drink to escape from worries or trouble?	☐	☐
16 Do you drink alone?	☐	☐
17 Have you ever had a complete loss of memory as a result of drinking?	☐	☐
18 Has your physician ever treated you for drinking?	☐	☐
19 Do you drink to build up your self-confidence?	☐	☐
20 Have you ever been to a hospital or institution on account of drinking?	☐	☐

If you have answered YES to any one of the questions, there is a definite warning that You may be alcoholic.

If you have answered YES to any two, the chances are that you are an alcoholic.

If you have answered YES to three or more, you are definitely an alcoholic.

(The above Test Questions are used by Johns Hopkins University Hospital, Baltimore, Md., in deciding whether or not a patient is alcoholic.)

PEACE   APRIL

                              OFFICERS'

                                                  FELLOWSHIP
_____

MEETING REMINDER:

WHEN: Monday Night - 2000 Hours

WHERE: Arcadia Christian Reform Church
                1735 S. Baldwin, Arcadia
                A.A. & Alanon held same night and time
_____
WHEN: Tuesday Night - 1930 Hours

WHERE: DOCTOR'S HOSPITAL OF LAKEWOOD
                Candlewood and Clark, Lakewood
                Room 307
_____
WHEN: Wednesday Night - 1930 Hours

WHERE: CARE MANOR HOSPITAL
                401 S. Tustin Avenue, Orange
                Alanon cancelled until further notice
_____
WHEN: Thursday Night - 1930 Hours

WHERE: LOS ANGELES CORONER'S OFFICE
                1104 N. Mission Road, Los Angeles
                Alanon cancelled until further notice
_____
WHEN: Friday - Noon

WHERE: Federal Building (Room 7210)
                Corner of Temple and Los Angeles Streets
_____

ANNOUNCEMENTS·························ANNOUNCEMENTS

BIRTHDAYS: To some, Birthdays are just another day of growing
older and sometimes wiser. But these display a celebration of
growth and continuous happiness in a life of Sobriety. Let's show
up to honor the happiness that they are willing to share with us.
HAPPY BIRTHDAY! AND GOD BLESS.

ORANGE COUNTY: Ken R. 3 yrs; Jim Mc. 4 yrs and Dave J. 3 yrs.

LOS ANGELES COUNTY: Cecilia K. 7 yrs; Norm M. 8 yrs; Larry
L. 5 yrs; Jim G. 6 yrs; Mary Lou P. 5 yrs; Bill M. 5 yrs and Jim S.
6 yrs.

Boy, that's a lot of years! Remember - Arcadia Nites and Los
Angeles Nites are also Speaker Nites. Some of those speakers have

come a long way. I know you'll all be excited to hear
Mr. Lou Sanman (I've been allowed to break his anonymity) of
ABC TV will speak on April 26 at the Coroner's office. He
told me, "Thank GOD I'm just speaking there".

. . . .

Saddest Announcement of my life: With the greatest of sorrow,
I have to share the passing of LES Z. on March 3. LES was
to celebrate 3 years of Sobriety on the 5th of April. LES
passed away sober, and with Honor. GOD rest his soul; he will
be deeply missed by us all. Think of him in your prayers.

. . . .

April 1984 - The fourth month of the year, and we all know
what that means: The Seven Deadly Sins: PRIDE, GREED, LUST,
ANGER, GLUTTONY, ENVY and SLOTH. The Fourth is not as bad as
it seems.

STEP FOUR - "Made a searching and fearless moral inventory of
ourselves". How instincts can exceed their proper function.
Step Four is an effort to discover our liabilities. Basic problem of extremes in instinctive drives. Misguided moral inventory can result in guilt, grandiosity or blaming others. Assets
can be noted with liabilities. Self-justification is dangerous. Willingness to take inventory brings light and new
confidence. Step Four is beginning of lifetime practice.
Common symptoms of emotional insecurity are worry, anger,
self-pity and depression. Inventory reviews relationships.
Importance of thoroughness.

TRADITION FOUR - "Each group should be autonomous except in
matters affecting other groups of A.A. as a whole." Every
group manages its affairs as it pleases, except when A.A. as
a whole is threatened. Is such liberty dangerous? The group,
like the individual, must eventually conform to principles
that guarantee survival. Two storm signals - a group ought
not do anything which would injure A.A. as a whole, nor
affiliate itself with outside interests. An example: the
"A.A. Center" that didn't work.

. . . .

TIDBIT FILE: EXPERIENCE

          Good judgment
          Comes from experience.
          Experience!
          Comes from BAD judgment.

SELF-ESTEEM
You're Worth It!

Don't build your self-esteem or self-image on others' opinions, but learn to seriously look at what they are telling you. Take an honest look at yourself in the mirror every morning. Tell yourself that you are worthwhile and valuable.

Realize that loving yourself and feeling great about yourself is not egotistical. You know that more than any other positive trait, your self-esteem holds the door open to your happiness and high achievement. You are a winner.

-------- ACCEPT YOURSELF!!--------

From the file of BRIAN W.:

HOW TO CHANGE AN ATTITUDE!
1. Good thought.
2. Good thought for the betterment of the individual.
3. Action taken on a good thought.

From the L. M. BOYD file:

The "Whistling Can"

In Japan now, you can buy a can of beer that whistles when you pour it. That's right, the can whistles! Not every drinker chooses to call attention to himself as he pours another. But some do, evidently. This one's for them!

(I wonder if Al-Anon had a hand in this? --Could be!!)

Can you identify this Deputy?

Hear about the drunken Mounted Policeman who was heard to say, as he attempted to mount the horse, and the horse put his rear hoof in the stirrup, "If you're going to get on, then I'm going to get off."

* * * * * * * * * * * * * *

GOLF HIGHLITES: Heard around the 19TH hole!!!
BEHOLD THE GOLFER, for he riseth up early in the morning and disturbeth the whole household. Mighty is his preparation. He goeth forth full of hope and when the day is spent - he returneth, smelling of strong drink and the Truth is not in him.

* * * * * * * * * * * * * *

"I'm almost 66 years old," he confided to his golfing buddy, "I'm worth about a half million and I've fallen madly in love with a gorgeous, voluptuous 28 year old gal. Do you think I'd have a better chance of marrying her if I told her I'm only fifty?" Said his pal, "Frankly, I think you would have a better chance if you told her you were 85."

* * * * * * * * * * * * * *

You're a good loser. . . if you can grip the winner's hand without wishing it was his throat.

* * * * * * * * * * * * * *

And that's thirty for this month — THE EDITOR!!

Many have fallen down the road of alcoholism and many have struggled back with the help and support of a caring department and supportive friends and family. The rewards of sobriety are expressed well by this *street cop:*

STREET COP

A year ago
you killed a man.
Now live with that
as best you can.
    Street cop

Your wife and child
six months ago
packed up and left.
You loved them so.
    Street cop

You're a hero.
You're so brave.
Your pride will put
you in your grave.
    Street cop

And then one day,
bottle in hand,
you take a drink,
then you drink again.
Drink the bottle
til it's dry.
Because tomorrow
you may die.
    Street cop

Am I afraid?
Hell, I don't know,
it doesn't matter,
can't let it show.
      Street cop

Then after years of
fear and pain,
directing traffic
in pouring rain.
And seeing tons, of
guts and brains.
Controlling people
who are insane.
You drink yourself
to sleep at night.
You're sick and tired
of the fight.
      Street cop

And so with years
of death and pain,
maybe it's you
who is insane.
      Street cop

But then tomorrow
the same old shit.
Forget that you're
a part of it.
      Street cop

Forget that now!
Don't try to think!
Things are better
when you drink.
      Street cop

And now you drink
yourself to sleep.
But tomorrow you
won't be on the street
      As A Street cop

The captain has
your gun and badge,
and you have nothing
that you had.
      Street cop

And so that bottle
that relieved your
fear, is the bottle
that put you here.
      Street cop

And no matter
what you say.
Your only hope
is in A.A.
You've got to get
back on your feet.
And maybe back out
on the street.

*And if I can whip
this alcohol,
I know there is hope
after all.
If I can become
a sober man.
And I know
that I can.*

*I won't be a
drunken sot.
Instead I'll be,
a damn street cop.*

R.M.

REFERENCES

Alcoholic's Anonymous. New York: Alcoholic's Anonymous World Services, Inc., 1976.

Alcoholic's Anonymous Comes of Age. New York: Alcoholic's Anonymous World Services, Inc., 1979.

Howard, J. and Howard N. "A Family Approach to Problem Drinking." Family Training Center, Columbia, Mo.: 1976.

Johnson Institute, "Alcoholism: A Treatable Disease." Johnston Institute, Minn., Minn.: 1972.

Stratton, J. G. and Wroe, B. "Alcoholism and the Policeman—Identifying and Dealing with the Problem." *FBI Law Enforcement Bulletin,* 1979, 48(3) pp. 20-23.

Unkovic, C. and Brown, W. "The Drunken Cop." *The Police Chief,* April, 1978, pp. 18-21.

Van Raalte, R. "Alcohol as a Problem Among Officers." *The Police Chief,* February, 1979, pp. 38-39.

Wambaugh, J. *The Choirboys.* New York: Dell Publishing Co., 1977.

11

LETTING GO— RETIREMENT

Retirement should be the pot of gold at the end of the police officer's rainbow in terms of monetary security and personal fulfillment. Retirees have worked long and hard, shouldered their responsibilities, and look forward to a well-earned respite. They should be able to view retirement as the reward which their labors have brought.

Yet, when the time comes, it's rarely that simple. As many have discovered, retirement is not necessarily an unalloyed joy. If not planned for well in advance, the chances for ease and happiness in retirement are even slimmer.

Retirement is often a forgotten step in the officer's career cycle. Police officers tend to have close ties to the department; they are active with many friends among their colleagues. Upon retirement, which in many cases seems sudden, they are unprepared and may end up without friends and feeling isolated from the department.

We have many reasons for pushing aside thoughts of retirement. We believe it is too far off to think about, or we think it will be predetermined by our employers and there isn't anything we can do about it. Most of us are somewhat ambivalent about retirement, even those who have been successful. For most, it means a lowered standard of living and a loss of valued social contacts. For some, it is the end of their central purpose in life, a loss of power and prestige. For those who have been failures, it destroys any lingering hope or fantasy of a late-blooming success.

Whatever the reasons for not wanting to face retirement, not planning for the future is a mistake. Half of those currently retired say they did so unexpectedly. Whether you plan to retire or have selected some given age for it, by 40 you should begin to think about a retirement program as a bulwark against the 50-50 chance that you will need it before expected.

When we retire we leave that activity which, since school days, has determined the answer to the question, "What do you do?" Now the question becomes: "What are you going to retire to?" Some envision sleeping late, spending golden afternoons—nothing concrete, but certainly a new freedom. For others, the question stirs a faint dread, because everything seems so blank beyond that unthinkable day. Others have never even considered the question.

Unless our plans are based on reality, they will flounder among other unrealizable dreams. Most obvious is income. Unless a person is among the nation's wealthiest 2%, his income will be less than it was during his working life. So, of course, will expenses, but not usually to the same extent. The Bureau of Labor has estimated that people need roughly 70% to 80% of their working income level to maintain the same standard of living after retirement.

Most of us feel twinges of aging in our 30's and 40's. Yet despite a sign here or a creak there—our back may ache a little sooner while gardening, or our eyes get scratchy after a lot of close work—our physical and mental conditions remain at more or less the same level for the next 15 to 20 years. Then incredibly, it's the last day at the job. We've been retired.

In some societies this is a form of graduation; you are deemed fit to seek wisdom, no longer having to immerse yourself in the daily trivia of earning a living. But we have a society in which youth, particularly the appearance of youth, is second only to money in desirability. It is a culture in which teenagers are consulted about world affairs and older people are told to go out and play (but haven't enough money to get to the playground); in which change has been so rapid over the whole of your lifetime that the experience of your own youth seems like that of another world—a society in which your opinions and advice are likely to be judged to be out-of-date.

You stand a 50-50 chance of being forced to retire. You stand a 98-2 chance of a considerable drop in income. Your emotions at this graduation to freedom are therefore apt to go beyond pure delight that you don't have to get up tomorrow morning.

You begin, perhaps, to think that society could be right. After all, haven't you looked at retired people and felt a twinge of pity for their failing capacities? Not that you have actually observed them failing, of course, but what else could human capacities be doing under the joint circumstances of retirement and growing older?

Retirement does not come at an old age for most police officers. In most cases, after 20 to 25 years of service a large portion of officers are eligible for retirement. Thus, some officers are in their 40's or early 50's, an age which is considered prime by most working Americans. But after 20-30 years of various aspects of the job, many officers feel it is best to retire and let the kids take over for awhile.

Our achievement-oriented society often defines us by what we do. Our job can define our friends, where we live, and the amount of time we can devote to those we love. In this respect, the feelings that officers have about retirement are probably more complex than for those leaving other professions.

In law enforcement the family-type interdependence that exists within a department provides a model to follow. From the time a cadet enters the academy, "esprit de corps" has been promoted and expected of all officers. They have had partners with whom they share not only the daily drudgery of the job, but their lives. The closeness of partners goes beyond family ties; through the years they come to rely on one another's judgment, skill and common sense in mutual matters of life and death. Oftentimes, this closeness extends beyond the eight-hour shift. Also, officers rely and depend on the department. This type of interdependence is the core of a strong and vital police force.

This network is much like a military structure which gives a set organizational pattern to follow. Officers know exactly to whom and in what way they should report. They carefully guide their career with the help of supervisors and the department. There is a code of honor respected by officers and the department which binds them in ways not often understood by an outsider. The department represents a family that its members have chosen. Their vocational success has hinged on the department. But now in retirement, without the department, they must begin anew. They are forced to redefine their vocational goals, their ideas of success and who they are and why they are on this earth. If no consideration is given for some type of retirement program, they may feel abandoned and/or bitter.

Some officers will die not too many years after going into retirement. The average officer came into his career much healthier and more fit than the average person. That death that comes so soon after retirement could mean the officer's career was difficult, or that not having a career has left him little reason to live. Some of these deaths are tragic, as in the case of the retired officer who drinks most of the day, loses all respect for himself, and eventually dies in pain and loneliness. As Wambaugh relates one officer explaining to another; "It's your friend Andy Kilvinsky, Gus. Your wife said that she was called tonight by a lawyer up in Oregon. Kilvinsky left you a few thousand dollars. He's dead, Gus. He shot himself."

A lack of retirement preparation leaves the officer in a poor position and makes the department appear as if its only concern is for the organization and not the individual officer. An unplanned retirement can make you a ho-hummer—one of those fellows who gets up in the morning and says, "Ho-hum, what am I going to do today?"

The concept of the good of the department has begun to change in recent years. Most organizations are beginning to understand that by having officers who are emotionally and physically healthy the organization can be stronger and more successful. This is evidenced by the increased use of psychological services in law enforcement. The one area which has been left untouched until recently, though, is that of retirement counseling. As this changes, departments will begin to take some responsibility for aiding in the successful retirement of employees who have given more than their eight hours a day to a job for twenty-plus years.

Society also reaps the benefits from successfully retired police officers. These men and women are highly trained professionals in the prime of their lives. They have much to contribute to private industry, other governmental agencies and to society in general.

But let's focus on the individual. Suddenly, the retired officer finds himself with no career and no children. The role of police officer is gone along with that of father. The predominant role of protector of the society and the family must be left behind, or other ways to enact them must be found. For a police officer who has found his meaning in life in these roles, this may be difficult.

Retirement can leave officers feeling "dethroned." They no longer have a powerful position. If status is a source of self-esteem and a vital part of our self-image, then losing it is going to have a big effect. This needs to be accepted or somehow replaced.

Personality and needs are the same after retirement. It's just that new ways of meeting these needs must be found. Problems in this area can arise if we are used to being authoritarian and controlling at work and relaxed at home. When we retire and can no longer be authoritarian at work, we might bring the role into our homes and cause our spouses and families all kinds of havoc.

The deaths of those close to us—mates and friends—is also stressing and disturbing as we grow older. For retired cops who see their cohorts die after retirement, this can become a major life crisis since they are apt to identify with them.

Realizing that the body is wearing out and just can't do what it used to is distressing but needs to be accepted as a life process. For police officers who pride themselves on their physical fitness and agility, the realization that they can't do all that they think they should can be disturbing. Special care should be given to maintain the best health possible, since it affects all aspects of our life. If we feel good physically we'll probably be able to handle the psychological aspects of retiring better.

There are other changes, as well. Women sometimes become more interested in sex after menopause because they no longer have to worry about pregnancy. For the police officer who has generally been the aggressor sexually, this can upset the sexual balance of the relationship. Also, the changing of roles and even time schedules may bring about a change in sexual activity.

All in all, the need to accept change is vital when we retire. We must adjust to a new life style, new roles and new financial arrangements. This can be especially difficult if we have just left a highly structured environment.

There are a great many feelings officers may experience as a result of retirement. Most anticipate a greater sense of freedom and certainly more leisure time. Often they don't expect the isolationism, loneliness and despair that can also be a part of retirement. Whether a retirement is successful or not depends a great deal on the foresight that has gone into it. Without it, retirement may be a step to an early death rather than a time of joy and excitement.

A general guideline for the impending retiree is to start thinking about retirement goals at least five years prior to the date of retirement. This amount of time allows officers the opportunity to explore all avenues open to them, select specific training goals if needed, and emotionally prepare themselves and their families for this separation from the organization. It allows officers to face their retirement as a developmental process rather than a crisis.

Officers might want to attend programs that the department and/or community provide for those retiring. With more and more of the American population reaching the age of 50 and older, communities are beginning to develop extensive programs for the older adult. The programs are varied and appeal to a broad spectrum of interests.

Department programs addressing retirement will vary depending on the size and resources of the organization. The department can issue periodic reminders for its officers to plan for retirement and list some initial steps to take. Information can be distributed listing supportive agencies, recreational activities, occupational opportunities, legislative changes, etc., that retirees should be aware of. On a regional basis, programs can be developed by police employees or management associations to address retirement in a formalized way.

In large organizations, group meetings for future retirees can provide an opportunity for officers to discuss problems, concerns and future plans. Individual counseling could focus on specific conerns whether they be financial, legal, educational or personal, and referrals could be made.

Officers with twenty-plus years possess a wealth of knowledge and experience which can be beneficial to future retirees and the organization. Asking retirees to share their ideas and suggestions enables officers to provide valuable information and feel important to the organization. If interested, they could volunteer and be trained to discuss retirement issues with officers planning to retire.

Even though a formalized retirement program may not be possible, one-day informational seminars are relatively easy to develop and have proven beneficial to participants. Within almost any community, there are agencies and experts with knowledge of legal, financial and psychological factors who will donate their time to make a presentation.

As the years progress toward retirement, officers should become more directed in their exploration, training and goal setting. Retiring officers should evaluate their skills, get training for new skills and set realistic goals for the future. They should ask questions, attend programs, seek assistance and do other things which might stimulate further thinking.

Any type of departmental retirement program, of course, should include the spouse, because retirement is a shared experience for couples. It can be a time of friction or a time to rediscover each other and explore the world together. Good communication will aid in a successful retirement for both officers and their spouses.

When asked how it felt to have her husband home, one wife answered, "Great, I went out and got a job." Another said, "I took him for better or worse, but not for lunch." As a new experience, retirement causes changes in our *feelings, thoughts* and *behavior,* which, if shared, can enhance our communication and relationships.

Not only are there male law-enforcement officers who retire, but there is a relatively new group of career women who are now beginning to retire. These women will be unique in retirement, just as they were unique when they entered their careers, and some of the things they'll face in retirement will be different than they will be for their male counterparts.

Women, like men who have chosen a career in law enforcement, often define themselves by their jobs. Being home may not offer them the opportunities of fulfillment that their jobs once did. Cooking, cleaning, laundry and homemaking duties often won't be enough for the career woman. She may find herself in an alien world—one which has long ago been rejected.

Outside activities and ways to become involved in the world are essential for the retired woman. These activities can be varied, but most of all they should be enjoyed. Developing such activities can cause specific problems for women, since it is still uncomfortable and more expensive for women to do some things alone. It is helpful too, for prospective retirees to establish, social networks that can be continued in retirement. Some retirees may consider moving to apartments or communities that have facilities and activities developed for their age or social group.

Women law-enforcement officers were pioneers as career women. They are now the first policewomen who will be retiring after twenty or thirty years. When they started their careers, it was not acceptable for them to work outside of the the home. They challenged that and proved that women were competent. Now they will again be pioneers, this time in retirement.

REFERENCES

Adler, J. *The Retirement Book*. New York: William Morrow & Co., 1975.

Butler, R. & Lewis, M. *Sex After Sixty*. Harper & Row, N.Y., 1976.

KALISH, R.A. (E.D.) *The Later Years: Social Applications of Gerentology*. Monterey, CA. Brooks-Cole, 1977.

Levinson, D. J. *Seasons of a Man's Life*. New York: Knopf, 1978.

Sheehy, G. *Passages*. New York: E. P. Dutton, 1974.

Solnick, R. *Sexuality and Aging*. Los Angeles, CA: University of Southern California Press, 1978.

U. S. News & World Report Books *Plan Your Retirement Now So You Won't Be Sorry Later*. Washington, D.C.: 1974.

Weininger, B. & Menkin, E.L. *Aging is a Lifelong Affair*, Los Angeles, CA: Guild of Tutors Press, 1978.

Wambaugh, J. *The New Centurion*. Boston: Little Brown & Co. 1970.

Weinstein, G. W. *Life Plans, Looking Forward to Retirement*. New York: Holt, Rinehart & Winston, 1979.

12

KEEPING IT TOGETHER— MANAGING STRESS

In advanced nations chronic stress is believed to be responsible for many of today's health disorders. It's as if this new "disease," stress, came along automatically with modern society and is something that we automatically have to live with. But this isn't true. We are moving from an initial awareness of stress to ways to combat it. It is an uphill race for some, but one worth winning!

When we turn our attention to combating stress, the old adage "an ounce of prevention is worth a pound of cure" is most appropriate. The first step of prevention is awareness—acknowledgment of feelings, thoughts and actions that bring stress into our lives. This sounds simple but it requires a great deal of courage and self-confidence to admit you are afraid, overworked, or just not handling your life well—especially when, as a policeman, you are required by job definition to fearlessly deny emotions.

Self-awareness is not a quick or easy process. It is the basis for acknowledging conflict or problems. It requires checking on yourself, taking readings on your emotional thermometer, important relationships, and physical health.

We have received minimal, if any, education about understanding our emotions or knowing ourselves. Too often, we will suppress emotions to such an extent that they build up like a pressure cooker and explode in some type of inappropriate behavior: pulling the phone off the wall, driving erratically, abusing a suspect, our wives or kids, or attempting suicide.

Self-awareness is essential to any stress reduction program. Our basic security is based on self knowledge and self acceptance. Although the opinions of loved ones, friends and associates are valued, the only real hope for security lies in frank self-evaluation.

Warning signs of stress can help us identify conditions which might lead to additional problems. Reactions to stress should be handled rather than ignored, as avoidance can create further tensions.

Karl Menninger described common methods used to cope with stress which are considered normal and can reduce tension and help the human system operate without malfunction. These regulation devices include self-discipline, laughing, crying, cursing, boasting, over-activity, daydreaming, eating and taking medications. However, when tensions are not reduced by one of these regulatory devices, stress continues to build. In *the first level,* the individual is nervous, experiences increased tension, and the emotions betray the arousal of aggressive impulses. There is an overabundance of emotionalism, and worry is often accompanied by minor bodily and sexual dysfunction. If the conflicts are resolved this state can be quickly reversed; however, if ignored, it can deteriorate.

At *the second level,* the individual experiences growing discomfort, anxiety and feelings of uselessness, with guilt and fears intensifying. There is a steadily increasing inability to perform work or relate with others, which may be covered up at great inner cost to the individual, even to the extent that others might see the performance as superior. The individual often copes by displaying bravado and recklessness or utilizing defense mechanisms such as blocks or fantasies. The stress agent is not attacked, rather the aggression is diverted to more socially accepted forms of activity such as gambling, reckless driving, physical violence or becoming overly generous, friendly or enthusiastic, but with frequent mood changes.

At *the third level* of dysfunction, aggression is no longer inward but directed outward even more noticeably. There may be violent acts toward animals, and a need to destroy "evil" in whatever form evil is perceived by the individual. There will be suspiciousness, hypersensitivity and overactivity. Responses will be speeded up—too much activity, talking too fast, sleeping too little. Impaired judgment becomes apparent to everyone, including the individual.

In *the fourth level,* controls are no longer effective. This level is characterized by severe blow-ups and temper tantrums, and no longer is any attempt made to live up to expectations. The individual may become manic, depressed, schizophrenic or paranoid. The facade disintegrates, and suicide may be the result.

The following warning signs should be heeded because they indicate the possibility of too much stress.

1. Changes from usual behavior patterns and normal routines.
2. Anxiety and irritability. In law enforcement this may be inevitable, but if these feelings are fairly constant something may be wrong.
3. Excessive use of alcohol or any drug. Your problems remain and get worse.
4. Excessive nervous habits.

5. Physical complaints—many doctors believe that 70 to 90 percent of all illness is caused by stress.
6. Accident proneness—too many things on our mind can cause inattention. This can culminate in accidents.
7. Depression/withdrawal—these depressions can become so severe that an individual has difficulty functioning or has suicidal thoughts. Depression in many instances is the way our body and mind tells us we feel overloaded and need to slow down. We become lethargic, fatigued and feel defeated.
8. Taking of unnecessary chances, ranging from not wearing a bullet proof vest to putting oneself in dangerous situations.
9. Home problems.
10. Decrease in the amount, enthusiasm, interest and confidence in work performed.
11. Too many sick days.
12. Inability to get along with others.
13. Extreme defensiveness—blaming others, being argumentative, feeling persecuted, picked on and misunderstood.
14. Over suspiciousness—questioning the wife and children about their activities, their money spent, their friends, etc.; not trusting anyone.
15. Overt hostility.
16. Excessive altercations.
17. Excessive violence.
18. The need to eliminate evil at whatever costs.

Run down the check list of signs of stress in Figure 5. Three or more checks indicate possible concern about stress. The more checks there are, the more one should be alerted to stress problems.

Figure 5

SIGNS OF STRESS

1. ____ Pervasive feelings of anxiety.
2. ____ Chronic fatigue.
3. ____ Constant preoccupation with one's health.
4. ____ Frequent spells of depression.
5. ____ Nervous tension and panic feelings.
6. ____ Physical tremors—"the shakes."
7. ____ Fear of being alone.
8. ____ Inability to sleep well.
9. ____ Occasional thoughts of suicide.
10. ____ Fear of an emotional breakdown.
11. ____ Lack of self-confidence.
12. ____ Wide mood swings.
13. ____ Excessive irritability accompanied by emotional outbursts.
14. ____ Feelings of hopelessness and despair.
15. ____ Negative thinking as a dominant pattern.
16. ____ A sense of unreality—out of touch.
17. ____ Unreasonable complaining.
18. ____ Excessive worrying.
19. ____ Inability to work or perform everyday chores adequately.
20. ____ Continuous unhappiness.
21. ____ Paralysis in decision making.
22. ____ Excessive fear of making a mistake.
23. ____ Dread of supervisory personnel.
24. ____ Inordinate desire to please others.
25. ____ Chronic pains, especially, in the head and abdomen.
26. ____ Poor health in general.
27. ____ Early aging signs.
28. ____ Extravagant spending.
29. ____ Fear of the unknown future.
30. ____ Excessive suspicion and/or fear of others.

There are several ways people can assess their stress levels and how they are handling it. These methods will indicate where one stands, in general, but must be adapted to one's life style and individual differences. They are guidelines to ways of looking at self.

One way to look at yourself in relation to stress is to examine Friedman's Type A personality traits. Those with the "Hurry Up" sickness, who lead shorter lives, possess some, if not all, of the following descriptive qualities:

Vocally explosive

Moves, walks, and eats rapidly

Impatient at the speed of events

Habitual pattern of gestures and nervous tics

Polyphasic or multiphasis in thought and/or performance

Self-engrossed conversation

Preoccupied with action-oriented activities

A chronic sense of time urgency

Feels vaguely guilty when relaxing

Doesn't observe the interesting and lovely in the world

Feels competitive with another Type A personality

Believes success is related to doing things faster than others

Translates life into the "Numbers Game"

Knowing he is a Type A, believes he will have a long life even if he doesn't change

"HURRY SICKNESS"

Please indicate how often each of the following applies to you in daily life.

5-always   4-usually   3-sometimes   2-seldom 1-never

1. ____ Do you find yourself rushing your speech?
2. ____ Do you hurry other people's speech by interrupting them with "Um—hm, um—hm" or by completing their sentences for them?
3. ____ Do you hate to wait in line?
4. ____ Do you seem to be short of time to get everything done?
5. ____ Do you detest wasting time?
6. ____ Do you eat fast?
7. ____ Do you drive over the speed limit?
8. ____ Do you try to do more than one thing at a time?
9. ____ Do you become impatient if others do something too slowly?
10. ____ Do you seem to have little time to relax and enjoy the time of day?
11. ____ Do you find yourself overcommitted?
12. ____ Do you jiggle your knees or tap your fingers?
13. ____ Do you think about other things during conversations?
14. ____ Do you walk fast?
15. ____ Do you hate dawdling after a meal?
16. ____ Do you become irritated if kept waiting?
17. ____ Do you detest losing in sports or games?
18. ____ Do you find yourself with clenched fists or tight neck or jaw muscles?
19. ____ Does your concentration sometimes wander while you think about what's coming up later?
20. ____ Are you a competitive person?

A score of 50 or more indicates a proneness toward Type A behavior, and alerts you to behavior patterns that are detrimental to your health.

People run the gamut of being 100% Type A personality to 100% Type B personality. The higher the Type A behavior, the less likely the chances for a long life. Type B is described as the opposite of Type A. To reduce risks attributed to Type A, the individual needs to reduce the behavior, slowing down and moving toward Type B behavior.

Reflecting on your life style and the amount of change you experience is another way of looking at yourself. The number of changes we go through in any given period of time is the focus of The Life Stress Chart developed by Holmes and Rahe. Their thesis is that, rather than "bugs" or viruses causing illness or the need for medical attention, illness may well be the result of the number of life changes the person experiences. Their finding showed that the higher the number of Life Stress Points (LSP), the more susceptibility to illness; and as the LSP increase in number, the illness tends to become more serious.

LIFE STRESS CHART

LIFE EVENT	MEAN VALUE
1. Death of a spouse	100
2. Divorce	73
3. Marital Separation	65
4. Jail term	63
5. Death of close family member	63
6. Personal injury or illness	53
7. Marriage	50
8. Fired at work	47
9. Marital reconciliation	45
10. Retirement	45
11. Change in health of family member	44
12. Pregnancy	40

13. Sex difficulties   39
14. Gain of new family member   39
15. Business readjustment   39
16. Change in financial state   38
17. Death of close friend   37
18. Change to different line of work   36
19. Change in number of arguments with spouse   35
20. Mortgage over $10,000   31
21. Foreclosure of mortgage or loan   30
22. Change in responsibilities at work   29
23. Son or daughter leaving home   29
24. Trouble with in-laws   29
25. Outstanding personal achievement   28
26. Wife beginning or stopping work   26
27. Begin or end of school   26
28. Change in living conditions   25
29. Revision of personal habits   24
30. Trouble with boss   23
31. Change in work hours or conditions   20
32. Change in residence   20
33. Change in schools   20
34. Change in recreation   19
35. Change in church activities   19
36. Change in social activities   18
37. Mortgage or loan less than $10,000   17
38. Change in sleeping habits   16
39. Change in number of family get-togethers   15
40. Change in eating habits   15
41. Vacation   13
42. Christmas   12
43. Minor violations of the law   11

If you score between:

        0   — 150   your susceptibility to illness is 33%
    150 — 300   your susceptibility to illness is 50%
    over 300   your susceptibility to illness is 90%

Whether one be a "turtle" (one who likes a peaceful and quiet environment) or a "race horse" (one who likes a constant set of challenges and deadlines), all people have their own makeup in relationship to changes they experience. Some people operate very well in the world with LSP over 300, while others progress better with LSP scores of below 150. Each person must determine his or her own individual effective working level. In order to ascertain this it is important that the person establish his or her own goals, not those imposed by another individual, family or group.

In examining The Life Stress Chart, one notices that many of the events listed are negative in nature. However, there also are positive changes. The issue being examined is the amount of change in a person's life in a year, not the number of negative or positive changes.

A third way of looking at yourself is to measure your risk for heart attack by using the **RISKO CHART** developed by the Michigan State Heart Association.

The chart is played by making squares which—from left to right—respresent an increase in your Risk Factors. These are medical conditions and habits associated with an increased danger of heart attack. Not all risk factors are measurable enough to be included in this game.

RULES: Study each Risk Factor and its row. Find the box applicable to you and circle the large number in it. For example, under "Age" if you are 37, circle the number in the box labeled 31-40.

After checking out all the rows, add the circled numbers. This total—your score—is an estimate of your risk.

RISKO CHART

AGE	**1** 10 to 20	**2** 21 to 30	**3** 31 to 40	**4** 41 to 50	**6** 51 to 60	**8** 61 to 70 and over
HEREDITY	**1** No known history of heart disease	**2** 1 relative with cardiovascular disease Over 60	**3** 2 relatives with cardiovascular disease Over 60	**4** 1 relative with cardiovascular disease Under 60	**6** 2 relatives with cardiovascular disease Under 60	**7** 3 relatives with cardiovascular disease Under 60
WEIGHT	**0** Less than 5 lbs. below standard weight	**1** 5 to 15 lbs. below standard weight	**2** 6–20 lbs. over weight	**3** 21–35 lbs. over weight	**5** 36–50 lbs. over weight	**7** 51–65 lbs. over weight
TOBACCO SMOKING	**0** Non-user	**1** Cigar and/or pipe	**2** 10 cigarettes or less a day	**4** 20 cigarettes a day	**6** 30 cigarettes a day	**10** 40 cigarettes a day or more
EXERCISE	**1** Intensive occupational and recreational exertion	**2** Moderate occupational and recreational exertion	**3** Sedentary work and intense recreational exertion	**5** Sedentary occupational and moderate recreational exertion	**6** Sedentary work and light recreational exertion	**8** Complete lack of all exercise
CHOLESTEROL OR FAT % IN DIET	**1** below 180 mg % Diet contains no animal or solid fats	**2** 181–205 mg % Diet contains 10% animal or solid fats	**3** 206–230 mg % Diet contains 20% animal or solid fats	**4** 231–255 mg % Diet contains 30% animal or solid fats	**5** 256–280 mg % Diet contains 40% animal or solid fats	**7** 281–308 mg % Diet contains 50% animal or solid fats
BLOOD PRESSURE	**1** 100 upper reading	**2** 120 upper reading	**3** 140 upper reading	**4** 160 upper reading	**6** 180 upper reading	**8** 200 or over upper reading
SEX	**1** Female under 40	**2** Female 40–50	**3** Female over 50	**5** Male	**6** Stocky male	**7** Bald stocky male

HEREDITY: Count parents, grandparents, brothers, and sisters who have had heart attack and/or stroke.

TOBACCO SMOKING: If you inhale deeply and smoke a cigarette way down, add one to your classification. Do not subtract because you think you do not inhale or smoke only a half-inch on a cigarette.

EXERCISE: Lower your score one point if you exercise regularly and frequently.

CHOLESTEROL OR SATURATED FAT IN- TAKE LEVEL: A cholesterol blood level is best. If you can't get one from your doctor, then estimate honestly the percentage of solid fats you eat. These are usually of animal origin—lard, cream, butter, and beef and lamb fat. If you eat much of this, your cholesterol level probably will be high. The US. average, 40 percent, is too high for good health.

BLOOD PRESSURE: If you have no recent reading but have passed an insurance or industrial examination, chances are you are 140 or less.

SEX: This line takes into account the fact that men have from 6 to 10 times more heart attacks than women of childbearing age.

IF YOUR SCORE is:

  6–11—Risk well below average
  12–17—Risk below average
  18–24—Risk generally average
  25–31—Risk moderate
  32–40—Risk at a dangerous level
  41–62—Danger urgent
      See your Doctor immediately

The Longevity game developed by Northwestern Mutual Life Insurance Company alerts players to important aspects of a healthy life.

LONGEVITY GAME

To play, start at 74, which is the average length of life for Americans today. Moves are made according to the

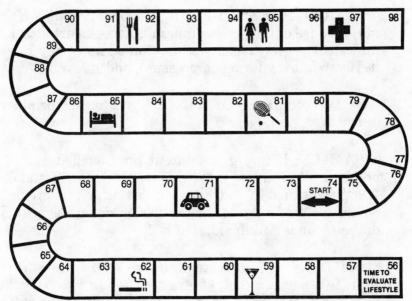

responses to the Longevity Game's eleven areas. If a question doesn't apply skip it. The final score is your projected life age.

EXERCISE: If your work requires regular, vigorous activity or you "work out" each day, add 3 years. If you don't get much exercise at home, work or play, subtract 3 years.

RELAXATION: If you have a relaxed approach to life (you roll with the punches) add 3 years. If you're aggressive, ambitious or nervous (you have sleepless nights, you bite your fingernails), subtract 3 years (and if you consider yourself unhappy, subtract another year).

DRIVING: Younger drivers who have had traffic tickets in the last year or been involved in an accident, subtract 4 years. Other violations, 1. (If you always wear seatbelts, add 1.)

BLOOD PRESSURE: High blood pressure is a major cause of the most common killers—heart attacks and strokes—but most victims don't know they have it. If you know your blood pressure, add 1 year.

Sixty-five and WORKING: If you are 65 or older and still working, add 3.

FAMILY: If any grandparent has reached age 85, add 2 (if all grandparents have reached age 80, add 6). If a parent died of a stroke or heart attack before age 50, minus 4. If a parent or brother or sister has or had diabetes since childhood, minus 3.

SMOKING: Cigarette smokers who finish more than two packs a day, subtract 8: one to two packs a day, subtract 6; one half to one pack a day, subtract 3.

DRINKING: If you drink two cocktails (or beers or glasses of wine) a day, subtract 1 year. For each additional daily libation, subtract 2.

SEX: Women live longer than men. Females add 3, males subtract 3.

WEIGHT: If you avoid eating fatty foods and you don't add salt to your meals your heart will be healthier (and you're entitled to add 2 years). Now, weigh in: Overweight by 50 pounds or more, subtract 8; 30 to 40 pounds, subtract 4, 10 to 30 pounds, subtract 2.

AGE: How long you have already lived can help predict how much longer you'll last. If you're under 30, the jury is still out. But, if your age is: 30 to 40, add 1; 40 to 50, add 2; 50 to 60, add 3; 60 to 70, add 4; over 70, add 5.

1. Work Out ____
2. Relaxed Life ____
3. Drivers ____
4. Blood Pressure ____
5. 65 & working ____
6. Family ____
7. Smoking ____
8. Drinking ____
9. Male vs. Female ____
10. Weigh In ____
11. Your Age ____

Rating yourself according to Type A behavior, the Life Stress chart, the Risko Chart and the Longevity Game should give you some idea of the amount of stress in your life and steps for reducing it.

There are numerous approaches to stress reduction based on various disciplines and philosophical points of view that have been devised by psychologists, physicians, gurus, nutritionists and physical fitness experts. Each of these individuals attempts to sell his method or product as the cure-all for stress and the impetus for longevity. There is no single method that is successful for everyone. For each individual, stresses are different, as are their effects. We all need to find a way to reduce stress that is best suited to our life styles. The more one understands self, the easier it is to develop an effective, individualized stress-reduction program that will enable him/her to feel better, work more effectively, avoid illness and live longer.

Unfortunately, in our society the use of pills, other medications and alcohol are widely accepted ways of dealing with tension. It is certainly not unusual for someone to take a pill to avoid a sleepless night or have a drink after a rough day. Somehow our culture has taught us that that's a good way to reduce tension, when it may be appropriate only in rare instances.

The foremost killers of modern man—heart disease,

cancer, stroke and accidents—are often related to life styles that abuse and neglect our bodies. We have come to expect too much of our doctors and their pills and too little of ourselves. To progress in our health, we must first understand that we do have the ability to avoid illness and enormous control over how healthy we are and how long we live.

The public appears to have the general view that we are basically ill and made well by medical intervention. It would be nearer the truth to say that we are basically well and make ourselves ill. Health depends essentially on taking control of stress, rather than letting stress dictate the quality of our lives. The contribution of health professions is undisputed, and yet their ability to fight chronic diseases is limited compared to what we can do ourselves.

Our attitudes about self and life are extremely important in stress reduction. Do we value ourselves? Do we see ourselves as important and valuable rather than unimportant and worthless? Does our behavior say that we are important? Do we do things to enable us to live a long life? Or are we indifferent about our lives and how long we live?

There are no loved ones, individuals, agencies or organizations that are able to place a higher value on our lives than we do ourselves. If we care about ourselves, we will make an attempt to take care of ourselves, so that we feel good, work effectively and handle stress appropriately.

Individuals who have a commitment to life, positive attitudes toward problems, and meaningful values, goals, and priorities suffer significantly less from stress related disorders than those who do not possess these qualities. Individuals who suffer the most from stress disorders feel worthless, overwhelmed and powerless to reduce tension in their lives, and have an aversion to change.

Equally as important as a positive attitude is an approach to stress that accepts philosophically what you cannot change or have no control over. This means having the strength to change what you can and to endure what you must—and the wisdom to know the difference. Being stressed and bothered by events over which you have no control is a wasted endeavor, and depressing at best.

Physical exercise is one of the most effective stress reducers. It involves dedication and may be uncomfortable; however, the results are rewarding in handling stress. From the holistic view, if your body is in good running order and performing effectively, you will feel better emotionally, socially, intellectually and spiritually. Exercise acts as a release of built-up tensions and lowers blood presssure, pulse rate and cholesterol levels. While all exercises are valuable, the most effective are aerobics, those activities that involve the sustained exchange of oxygen in the cardiovascular system, such as running, swimming, bicycling, tennis, etc. Nonaerobic exercises such as weightlifting or isometrics are good for muscle tone and strength, but provide limited cardiovascular benefit.

If you can visualize a 20-year-old kitchen pipe that has been cut in half, you would see minerals that have built up on the interior wall of the pipe, causing the water to trickle rather than flow freely. Similarly, cholesterol, a fatty acid in the blood stream, builds on the interior walls of arteries and veins to the heart. Years of cholesterol buildup can restrict the necessary flow of blood to the heart, causing a heart attack. Aerobic exercises dispel cholesterol. So when stressful events cause your heart to demand a large flow of blood, the arteries and veins will be cleaner and the blood will be able to flow smoothly.

Secondly, with regular aerobic exercises, the body is capable of building new tissue to bypass the blockage or blood restriction in a vein or corollary.

Thirdly, exercise produces chemicals that aid in relieving depression. In effect, when we exercise, we produce a natural anti-depressent enabling us to feel up and energetic.

> Officer Evelyn G., a six-mile-a-day jogger, quit exercising. After three months of not exercising she gained weight, didn't feel as good emotionally, and thought that her intellectual and physical responses were slower. Getting up in the morning became more and more difficult. When a friend of hers asked if she was pregnant her response was, "No, but I sure feel like it! I'm tired a lot and can't stop gaining weight."

In addition, physical outlets provide a motoric outlet for feelings when they aren't being expressed in other ways. Physical exercises that allow you to hit, swing or kick may aid in venting pent up emotions or frustrations.

Aerobic exercise programs have caused people to feel less fatigue and more energy, to lose weight, and to reduce or stop smoking. Additional reports indicate improved self-esteem, confidence, mental energy, concentration and will power. Aerobic exercise provides extra energy during times of fatigue, and works as an antidote for anxiety, depression and other negative emotional states.

Police officers and firemen who exercise regularly have shown improved working capacity, cardiovascular functioning, muscular endurance and strength, a reduction in the number of sick days used and a lowered incidence of injury.

There is an estimated six-year difference between the life spans of those who have regular vigorous activity compared to those who have minimal activity. Depending on your weight, estimates range from a loss of 2 to 8 years of life from being sedentary.

If a decision is made to enter a stressful profession, concurrently a decision should be made to stay in good physical condition. Just as we wouldn't consider racing an old untuned car in the Indianapolis 500, we shouldn't consider being unfit in police work.

The total benefits of a physical exercise program cannot be overemphasized. Physical fitness improves one's personal appearance, muscle strength, endurance, body efficiency and athletic proficiency. Psychologically, exercise improves mental health, relieves tension, promotes positive personality changes, and can aid in one's socialization process. Improved heart strength, circulation, joint mobility, flexibility, digestion and sleep are added benefits. When we are made aware that the physical fitness of criminal offenders and the general population is better than that of law-enforcement officers, the importance of exercise is most apparent. Due to the primarily sedentary nature of their jobs, many officers often fail to stretch their muscles. Exercises that improve flexibility lessen the chances for back problems, dislocated limbs and soreness due to poor muscle conditioning.

Though exercise is beneficial, if you are out of shape or have been negligent for a long period of time, you should consult a doctor or at the very least start slowly in developing any type of personalized exercise program.

Eating nutritious, well-balanced food helps us to deal with stress. Officers, because of shift work, and the necessity of catching meals on the run, often end up with poor dietary habits. Meals tend to be weight producing and nutritionally deficient. Snack foods, donuts, soft drinks, coffee, alcohol and burgers can become the norm. Necessary vitamins and minerals may be lacking or undue chemicals added. Eating the proper amount and type of food aids health, reduces stress, and promotes effective performance.

Few of us know what makes up the basics of a proper diet. A national survey conducted to determine how much we know about the affects of food and nutrition elicited wrong answers 90% of the time.

On the most basic level, three general rules to remember are:

1. Eat natural foods (vegetables, whole grains, fruits, berries, etc.),
2. Eat fish, poultry and lean meats for protein.
3. Decrease the use of fatty foods, salt and sugar.

A simple daily food guide developed by the United States Department of Agriculture suggests planning your basic diet around four food groups:

Food Group	No. of Servings Per Day
MILK GROUP Includes cheese, ice cream and other milk products.	2 or more
MEAT GROUP Meats, fish, poultry, eggs or cheese—with dry beans, peas, nuts as alternates.	2 or more
VEGETABLES & FRUITS Dark green or yellow vegetables; citrus fruit or tomatoes.	4 or more
BREAD & CEREALS Enriched or whole grains. Milk added to cereal provides nutritional values.	4 or more

This is a foundation for a good diet. Unfortunately, the following example is not at all unusual:

Officer Ron N. rides motorcycles at work and restores them as a hobby. Ron became protective of and attached to an all chrome motorcycle. He spent one or two hours a day polishing it. The motorcycle required a special blend of gases that Ron would spend hours mixing. However, Ron treated himself poorly. He was a diabetic and started the day with cigarettes and cokes. His normal meal consisted of items from vending machines and fast food vendors. He treated the motorcycle with much more care than he treated himself.

If we consider the RISKO Chart used to determine one's risk for heart attack, there are three areas that we have no control over: our heredity, age and gender. However, there are five areas we can control: our weight, cholesterol or percent of fat in our diet, blood pressure, exercise and whether we smoke or not.

The damaging effects of smoking are well known, with warnings of hazards to our health appearing on every package. Your longevity is estimated to be shortened by eight years if you smoke two or more packs of cigarettes a day. The millions of smokers who have quit offer proof that it can be done. There are many ways to stop this difficult habit, from "cold turkey" to hypnosis to aversion therapy. However, the most essential ingredient is the motivation to quit. Will power and the commitment to a longer and healthier life are necessary to stop. By doing so a heavy smoker can reduce his risk for heart trouble by 10 points on the chart.

Other methods of stress reduction include various relaxation techniques such as transcendental meditation, self-hypnosis, autogenic training, yoga and zen. These approaches produce similar results: decreased blood pressure, heart and respiratory rates, oxygen consumption and muscle tension.

Whatever methods one chooses for a relaxation response the following developed by Benson is helpful:

1. Choose a quiet environment, a place with few distractions.
2. Focus on a mental device—a sound, word or phrase

repeated silently or aloud; or an object to gaze at. The repetition of the word helps minimize distracting thoughts. Usually eyes are closed unless gazing. Attention to normal breathing rhythm enhances repetition of word or phrase.

3. Deeply relax all your muscles beginning at your feet and progressing up to your face. Keep them relaxed.

4. Breathe through your nose. Be aware of your breathing. As you breathe out, say the word "ONE," silently to yourself. Breathe in ... out ... "ONE"; in ... out ... "ONE"; etc. Breathe easily and naturally.

5. Continue for 10 to 20 minutes. You may open your eyes to check the time, but do not use an alarm. When you finish, sit quietly for several minutes; at first with your eyes closed and later with your eyes open. Do not stand up for a few minutes.

6. Do not worry about whether you are successful in achieving a deep level of relaxation. Maintain a passive attitude and permit relaxation to occur at its own pace. When distracting thoughts occur during this meditation, try to ignore them by not dwelling on them and return to repeating "ONE."

Another approach is a technique which consists of closing the eyes and deeply relaxing the muscles, beginning at the head and progressing downward to the feet. Notice your breathing, and when a pattern is established you can picture any pleasant and peaceful scene or event that you wish and experience it as if you were there.

In explaining the relaxation response to a group one day, I mentioned that executives who practiced a method of relaxation for twenty minutes in the morning and evening lowered their blood pressure ten points. A police chief queried, "What if you don't have the forty minutes it takes to practice a relaxation method every day? And I told him: "If we don't have an hour a day to take care of ourselves, something is wrong." There are many dedicated officers who work extremely hard to keep criminals off the street. Yet they can find no time to take care of themselves. People are like oil wells, and when the oil is depleted the well is dead. We have the choice of using the oil quickly like a gusher or spreading it over a long period of time.

When police officers die, crime continues to exist and departments still function. At a scheduled 10 a.m. meeting with the chief and his three assistant chiefs, the secretary informed the administrators that Assistant Chief Robert T. had died the previous night. There was silence for about a minute. Then someone said, "He had the western division, why don't you take that Al," and so on. In about 15 minutes Robert T.'s supervisory area had been divided and talk began concerning who would be the new assistant chief.

Robert T., a hard working dedicated officer, liked by many, had a large funeral service. But, in periodic checks with various members of his department, it was discovered that Robert's name, work, or accomplishments were never mentioned after the funeral. Perhaps this is reality. Those alive deal with the living, and when you die, you are gone.

Police officers have a choice to put all of their energy into work and limit their life span, or to work with less haste and live longer. Our health and longevity are up to each one of us. The life insurance industry and public health organizations estimate a difference of 6 years of longevity between a relaxed approach to life vs. an aggressive, ambitious or nervous approach.

In addition to the general stress management approaches, there are many individualized ways to reduce stress. Not all methods work for everyone, but selective approaches or a combination of them might be appropriate. Various methods follow:

1. Adopt an attitude which sees yourself as responsible

for and in charge of your life and environment. Areas you have control over should be dealt with and those that can't be affected should be let go.

2. Develop self knowledge and self understanding through counseling or other effective methods that work for you.
3. If suffering from anxiety, depression headaches or other stress-related symptoms, consider getting outside help.
4. Put your money where your time is. If time spent on home repairs or cutting lawns is irritating and lengthy, consider hiring a handyman or gardener and spending your time in more fulfilling ways.
5. Pay attention to the small, ordinary things that lift your spirit, whether it be calling your kids or your parents, walking around the block, visiting a friend, etc.
6. If your schedule is always full, set aside some self-indulgence time every day, even if it's only fifteen minutes.
7. Try to listen to what your body is telling you when struggling with a problem.
8. If a particular worry keeps nagging you, find out, "What's the worst thing that can happen?"
9. Set priorities, especially if there are dozens of juggled tasks each day.
10. After weathering a tense situation, analyze the way you coped.

Experts across the country are constantly seeking a recipe for health and happiness. A pair of insurance investigators followed nearly 7,000 adults for five and one half years. They found that people who lived longer did the following:

1. Ate breakfast.
2. Have no between-meal snacks.

3. Maintained their ideal weight.
4. Didn't smoke.
5. Had no more than two drinks a day.
6. Had a regular amount of sleep (7 hours).
7. Were active every day, whether gardening, walking or whatever.

Men who met 6 or 7 of these standards lived 11 years longer, on the average, than those who met 3 or less. For women there is a 7 year difference. Furthermore, there was a difference of 30 years expectancy between the absolute extremes: the person who broke all 7 rules consistently and the person who observed all 7.

How we choose to use our time and energy will determine the type of lives we lead. If we are workaholics, we will have limited time for our families or social lives. If we devote most of ourselves to raising children, there will be little left for spouses or friends. Most of us try to find a balance between these elements. When things get out of balance we try to redirect our energy and adjust to the change. We can look at how we distribute our energy in Figure 6. If married, it is interesting to compare our perceptions to those of our spouses.

For many of us, the pace of modern life is so fast that we have a tendency to lose track of ourselves. Taking stock of the stress in our lives can cause us to look at ourselves and make some decisions about how we want to be in the future.

MODEL PLAN TO REDUCE STRESS

1. State the basic question: "What do I want to do about this stress situation?"
2. List the alternatives open to you: "How can I deal with this situation? What options do I have?"
3. Note the results you think will occur if you carry out each option: "What would happen if...?"

4. Choose the alternative that has the best results for you in all dimensions.
5. Develop a plan to carry it out.
6. Carry out your plan.
7. Evaluate your results: "Has my plan solved the problem of the stressor?"
8. Make any change or modification that will give you improved success in carrying out your plan.

Figure 6

HOW ARE YOU USING YOUR LIFE ENERGY?

Rate yourself on a continuum of 1 to 10 with 1 indicating a very low level of energy expenditure and 10 a very high level of energy expenditure.

	1	2	3	4	5	6	7	8	9	10
CAREER										
MARRIAGE										
SOCIAL										
SPOUSE										
CHILDREN										
SPORTS										
HOBBIES										
SELF-DEVELOPMENT										
COMMUNITY										
POLITICS										
SEXUAL										
WASTED										
WORRY										

Then examine if you are comfortable with the distribution of your energy output and if not, determine which areas you want to change, including what you would have to do to redirect your energy.

The following list provides a variety of ways which have enabled people to take charge of the pace and direction of their lives while handling stress effectively.

1. Engaging in physical exercise.
2. Talking to someone.
3. Developing healthy attitudes.
4. Escaping for a while.
5. Taking one thing at a time.
6. Mastering and directing anger.
7. Giving up the superman complex.
8. Improving one's mind.
9. Doing something for someone else.
10. Controlling one's job pressures.
11. Avoiding negative stressors if possible.
12. Choosing when to fight and when to submit.
13. Living a healthy life style.
14. Knowing one's comfort zone—and how flexible/inflexible it is.
15. Getting involved with other people, other causes or improving personal relationships.
16. Trying to schedule one's stressors.
17. Appreciate one's self as an individual and learning to appreciate others.
18. Establishing a strong, stable support group of family and friends.
19. Thinking through to a sound, workable philosophical/religious view of life and the cosmos.
20. Improving one's environment.
21. Building some on-going relaxers into one's life.
22. Avoiding medication.
23. Examining one's total life stance.
24. Learning passive-relaxation exercises.
25. Being good to one's self.
26. Lifting one's spirits.
27. Having fun and adventure.

Most forward-looking corporations are taking a positive view toward their employees. They are concerned about the employees' physical and emotional health. They believe healthy employees add to the welfare and well being of the company.

During the past decade, law enforcement agencies in ever increasing numbers have developed a variety of programs to assist their employees in reducing stress and performing more effectively. The most important ingredient to any of these programs is the administration's attitude and approach toward the employee. Successful organizations see employees as important and allow them to participate and contribute to the agencies' goals.

A recognition of employee issues and concerns by an administration clearly acknowledges management's interest in the officer. Administration must at times be vocal advocates for their personnel. In law enforcement, encouragement of the superman or superwoman image leads to a denial of problems and a false expectation of officers' abilities and skills. Instead, it is more realistic to treat policemen as human beings, with a normal amount of problems.

If this is done, a variety of employee assistance programs could be devised. These programs are cost-effective, increase productivity and morale and they include any or all of the following:

1. Confidential counseling. The officer is provided the opportunity to discuss personal problems with someone who is an "expert" in the area of emotions and people. Whether this "expert" be a psychologist or a peer counselor, he or she will know how other people have successfully handled similar situations. Confidentiality is essential for the open communication that is necessary during these times. The problem is the concern of the individual officer; his work performance is the concern of the organization.

2. Alcoholism programs.
3. Management consultations regarding employee problems, beneficial programs, and appropriate interventions.
4. Spouse programs which demonstrate management's believe in the importance and value of the marriage partner.
5. Emergency services. A police officer's hesitancy to ask for help makes it a necessity that someone be on call to help at any time of the day or night.
6. Training. Knowledge about law-enforcement marriages, alcohol, and stress should include methods and solutions to diminish or avoid unsatisfactory consequences for all officers—cadets to executives.

All new assignments and duties an employee will be expected to perform should be provided for in training. Any new experience in police work can be potentially dangerous or threatening to an officer. Training should include all levels of supervisory and management from sergeant to chief, internal affairs investigators, detectives, etc. Too often, it is assumed if someone has been a good cop for a number of years, he will also be a good supervisor or detective. While past performance is a good predictor of future success, training makes the chances better.

Officer Scott M. is a good officer, respected by all. Scott throughout his career has never had to handle a family disturbance call. Although he is an excellent officer, he would perform more effectively with prior training in family disturbances. This is true for all new assignments that officers receive.

Officer Dick C. is promoted to sergeant. This has been a promotion he has been anticipating with both pride and excitement. He has passed the exam and the interview with high scores and feels he can do the job well.

Dick takes all the ribbing from his fellow officers good-naturedly and vows that he'll always be a part of them regardless of his rank. But no one explains the sergeant's job to Dick, as they are sure he automatically understands it. The first few weeks on the job are tiring but full of the action Dick had anticipated. About the third month things begin to change. Dick realizes he isn't invited out for a drink after work with the boys as much as he used to be. He resents this, although he convinces himself he understands. Then he has to discipline a past partner. This really upsets him, particularly because his wife and ex-partner's wife are best friends. He begins to notice that the support from the administration is not always there. In fact, he wonders if they even read his memos. He feels like the man in the middle—the fall guy—catching it from both ends and having nowhere to turn. He wonders if the extra money is worth all the hassles. But he can't turn back.

The department is each and every member of it. However, most line officers view the department as the top administrators. How officers are treated by these managers reflects in their eyes how they are being treated by the department. Therefore, it is essential that administrators be aware of their own and their officers' stress levels and find ways to keep them manageable. Supervisors need to:

1. Remember what it felt like to be on the streets—the fears, anxieties, stress, etc.
2. Talk with younger officers so they can learn from them and, even more important, so they can share their knowledge and experience.
3. Understand that riding patrol demonstrates a personal interest in their jobs and what they do.
4. Take the time to discuss with officers things other than their jobs, i.e., spouses, families, what they did over the weekend, etc.

5. Be eager to give encouragement at necessary times.
6. Stay in good condition, so that stress doesn't effect how you deal with others.
7. Exercise.

The high correlation between effective exercise and one's health is clearly evident, and has caused agencies to develop physical fitness programs for their employees. The Dallas Police Department conducted a study which showed that officers who practiced aerobic exercise used less sick days and fewer were off duty as a result of disability. The Kansas City Police Department has implemented semi-annual physical fitness tests resulting in one to three paid days off for officers who perform at pre-established performance levels. The San Diego Police Department provides up to $1,000 a year for members with certain levels of physical fitness. The Los Angeles County Sheriff's Department has established a physical agility test which it requires officers to pass on regularly scheduled intervals, dependent on age. They have also established Universal Gyms at all work locations.

All the methods and suggestions mentioned to reduce stress are worthless if we don't listen to one another. Although some still hold fast to the belief that stress is unmanly, this is changing. The recognition of stress and finding ways to eliminate it are essential to a healthy officer, family and organization.

REFERENCES

Benson, H. *The Relaxation Response.* New York: Morrow, 1975.

Brown, B. *Stress and the Art of Biofeedback.* New York: Bantam Books, 1977.

Clary, T., and Clary, E. *How to Live with Stress.* Washington: National Training and Development Service Press, 1977.

Cooper, K. *Aerobics.* New York: Bantam Books Inc., 1968.

Cooper, K. H. *The New Aerobics.* Des Plaines, Illinois: Bantam Books, 1970.

Dyer, W. *Pulling Your Own Strings.* New York: Funk and Wagnalls Book, 1978.

Fixx, J. *The Complete Book of Running.* New York: Random House, 1977.

Friedman, Meyer and Rosenman, R. *Type A Behavior and Your Heart.* Greenwich, Connecticut: Fawcett Crest Books, 1974.

Gherman, E. M. *Stress and the Bottom Line: A Guide to Personal Well-being and Corporate Health.* News York: AMACOM, 1981.

Goldberg, P. *Executive Health: How to Recognize Health Danger Signals and Manage Stress Successfully.* New York: McGraw-Hill, 1978.

Hassett, J. "Teaching Yourself to Relax." *Psychology Today,* 12(8) 1978.

Holmes, T., and Rahe, R. H. "Social Readjustment Rating Scale." *Journal of Psychosomatic Research,* XI, 1967.

Lecker, S. *The Natural Way to Stress Control.* New York: Grosset and Dunlap, 1978.

Levinson, H. *Executive Stress.* New York: Mentor Books, 1975.

Menninger, K. *The Vital Balance.* New York: The Viking Press, 1963.

Pelletier, K. R. *Mind As Slayer, Mind As Healer.* New York: Dell Publishing Company, Inc., 1977.

U.S. Department of Health, Education and Welfare. National Institute of Education. *Coping With Stress.* Arlington, VA.: February, 1980.

Veninga, R. L. and Spradley, J. P. *The Work/Stress Connection: How To Cope With Job Burn-out.* Boston: Little, Brown and Company, 1981.

13

POLICE WIDOWS— THE FORGOTTEN ONES

On May 29th, Pat C. went to her doctor to get the results of her pregnancy test. She was almost positive that she was indeed carrying her and James' second her child, but she hadn't told her husband yet, because they had been trying for a long time and she didn't want to get his hopes up only to have them dashed. However, the doctor confirmed her suspicions—she was pregnant— and Pat was overjoyed. She went home and began preparing for a special evening when James got home from his patrol shift at 11 that night. Pat put out candles, chilled a bottle of champagne, and fixed James's favorite dinner. All the while, she prayed that the baby would be a boy, because their first child had been a girl and James had always wanted a son.

However, 11 o'clock came and went that night, and James didn't pull into the driveway. Pat figured that he had to work late because of an arrest, and her excitement began to dwindle as the clock passed midnight.

Finally, at 1 a.m., there was a knock at the door. Pat, startled, peeked out the window and saw two deputies in uniform. Immediately, she was afraid—even more afraid when she opened the door and saw the expressions on the men's faces. "I'm sorry, Pat," said one of them. "There was nothing we could do. He's dead and I'm terribly, terribly sorry."

Shocked and in a daze, Pat called her mother and asked her to come over. Then she notified the others who needed to know. She couldn't sleep that night, but by 8 in the morning Pat started to make the dreaded funeral arrangements.

As with all police funerals for an officer who has been killed in the line of duty, there were many hundreds of mourners. Later, Pat couldn't remember much of this day, but she did recall the 21-gun salute, the sheriff handing her the American flag, and the playing of Taps at the end of the service.

Pat had been contacted by the department's psychologist and by another police widow but she saw no need for their assistance in the immediate aftermath. She was an independent woman, and she threw herself into her assistant bank manager's job. Soon, Pat moved out of her and James' house and into another one closer to her mother.

In September, four months after the tragedy, the department psychologist called Pat to tell her that several police widows were meeting at his house and to ask her to attend. She did this, and although it was a difficult evening she enjoyed the other women's support and was glad for the chance to talk about her feelings with people who truly understood her anguish. Another widows' meeting was held a month later, and Pat attended that one, too. She also saw the psychologist privately from time to time.

By now, Pat was two months away from delivering the child that was to be James' second. The women in the support group, sensing the pain that would accompany such a birth, wanted to do something special for Pat, and so they planned a surprise shower. It came off just as they'd hoped it would, and Pat was overcome with gratitude. Tears of both joy and sorrow streamed down her cheeks as she saw the caring faces around her and opened the thoughtful gifts—hand-sewn outfits for the baby, quilts, comforters, furniture. It turned out to be a moving experience for everyone.

About a month later, Pat gave birth to a beautiful baby. It was not the boy that James had wanted, but a girl. Yet Pat wasn't disappointed in the least. She was thankful for this final blessing from her husband, and her dreams now turned to how these three ladies—she and her two daughters—would make a future together.

Officers and their families deal constantly with the spectre of violence, and the possibility of injury and death. But death is a subject that is difficult to discuss. Officers tend to gloss over and depersonalize the death of a criminal suspect, because that's the easiest way to handle it. But when death comes to a fellow officer—whether it be by shooting, accident, or heart attack—it is impossible not to identify with the deceased and the struggles of his family.

Cathy F., a young wife, was deeply affected by the violent death of an officer in her husband's department. Each day as her husband dressed for work she started crying and was anxious most of the time he was on duty. She was so overwhelmed with fear that she had him call her several times a shift. About a week later, a veteran officer's wife called her to make plans for a party. The other wife realized that Cathy had been crying when she answered the phone. When questioned about her crying, Cathy explained it was because of the officer's death and her fears that the same thing would happen to her husband. Fortunately, the veteran wife was able to share her experiences and some facts which helped to alleviate some of Cathy's fears.

The death of an officer is like losing a family member and brings closer the realities of one's own mortality. Although there is no adequate way to prepare an officer and his family for the possibility of death, there are some ways to make the consequences of death less severe.

Living with their husbands' lives in constant jeopardy is something that police officers' wives manage to handle in many subtle ways. As one wife put it, "It's in the back of our minds, but we don't want to be reminded of it. We don't want to talk about it. If we let ourselves think about it every time our husbands come home late, we would go nuts." Another wife added, "Wives who get nervous about their husbands' jobs don't last. You don't worry about it. If you brought it out and looked at it, you'd go crazy!"

A guide for police officers' wives address this same problem:

> Wives can overwhelm themselves with fear. Their husbands are in a dangerous occupation, every assignment can be life threatening, but probably is not. The wife who becomes overly fearful and constantly expresses her fears shows little faith in her husband and his abilities. A husband, who is constantly being told by his wife that she is afraid he is going to have an accident, probably has a greater chance of having an accident. If they have faith that their husband is a good peace officer, and has received good training, they should try to accept the possibility of an accident without living in constant fear.

Fear, at some level, is with officers' wives no matter how it is denied. "The only time your heart stops is when you're driving in your car and the radio announcer says something about the death of a policeman," said one wife. Another wife said, "The only time I got scared was when Mike worked undercover and the van he was staked out in was blown up by a grenade. Mike was out of the van at the time. But that really scared me when I heard about it.

There's no way to fight a bomb. And I didn't find out about it until three days later. Mike didn't talk about it."

An unexpected phone call is received with caution. Instinctively the wife becomes apprehensive and dreads that this communication might involve her husband. When officers show up at the house, she knows something has gone wrong.

Widows generally have two possible reactions. The shock of the event usually provokes an outburst of emotion or a controlled, dazed reaction with little expression of emotion.

The controlled reaction by widows is similar to that of officers who have been exposed to a tragic incident. The officer can go into shock to filter what is seen or heard, yet continue to perform his duties in the midst of tragedy. It is only after the assignment or task has been completed that the officer begins to experience emotional reactions. The wife similarly can go into shock and not experience any emotional reaction until after the informing officers have left, or later. A numbness may appear, with the widow showing little signs of sorrow for days, weeks or even months.

The officers who inform the wife should know her personally and be prepared for these initial reactions. The informing officers must be able to control their emotions and be supportive of the widow. As one widow stated, "The officer who told me had such a hard time, I tried to console him rather than the reverse. There was no way he could assist me."

It is valuable for the sheriff or chief of police to contact the wife, as well, to express concern and offer assistance for family needs.

After the initial reaction, events rush at the new widow. She finds herself in a public event involving, among others, high police officials and the media. Funeral arrangements must be made, and a quiet private ceremony is not one of the options. The funeral is a form of public expression at which brother officers can express their concern for each other, their grief, and their solidarity.

The widow is often the focus of attention. Even though she is concerned with her personal loss and her children, she is also aware of the attention directed toward her. The concern she may feel about others can make it even more difficult for her to go through her own grieving process and emotional release.

When the funeral is over and the crowds are gone, the widow becomes profoundly aware of her husband's absence. She heard it, she saw it, but only now, alone and finished with the services, does the reality sink in. Her husband is no longer alive, no longer available, but she wants his children to be proud of him, to know him, and remember him. She believes it is important for the children to retain an image to be proud of and to cherish. She must decide what to do with her husband's badges, name tags, uniforms, various pictures, awards and mementos, all of which are constant reminders of the good times that won't return. One widow commented, "I have no desire to move his things. The mementos in the den are important to the kids. I'm not going to change it. How can you erase 18 years of life?"

Police officers' wives, by necessity, get caught up in the police life style. They often are immersed in their husband's jobs, but they have also altered their own lives to accommodate the police world. They have struggled with their husbands through the academy, suffered through shift changes, and answered hundreds of questions about what it's like to be a cop's wife. After death, not only have they lost their men, they have also lost their way of being, their security, and perhaps their identities. "To me," said one widow, "he was the John Wayne of the department. I always felt that no matter what happened, he could handle it."

Other difficult times are anniversaries of the officer's death and holidays. The date the officer died is never forgotten, and yearly the widow is reminded of her loss. Holidays, wedding anniversaries and other important dates are also difficult, although the loss appears to get easier with each passing year. As one friend of a widow explained it, "December was a particularly trying time for her. During Christmas she was very bitter and didn't even want to see me. It was a difficult month for her. Their wedding anniversary is then, their two birthdays, Christmas and New Year's. She got really down. Personally, I don't know how she could do as well as she did." An officer's widow also is reminded of her loss by posthumous awards and by annual memorial services that honor those officers who have died in the line of duty. The presentation of portraits and bronze badges all bring back the realization that he is dead. She knows she must let go, but he and the police environment were a large part of her life. Fellow officers stop by to see how she is doing or offer assistance to help the family adjust. While this is truly valuable for her morale and very helpful, it, too, serves as a constant reminder that her husband is gone.

The decision about when to start seeing other men is complicated by these connections. Should she go out two months after the death of her husband, six months, a year? What will her children think? What would their friends say? Fellow officers? Other people? Who can help her answer these questions?

The widow also has to deal with her reactions to society. There can be feelings about the person who killed her husband. Or if he died from a heart attack, say, there may be strong feelings about a career and a department that pushed him to that end. A car accident may provoke feelings of "why him?" or "why me?" There might be emotions about a husband who was so dedicated to his job that at times, his family suffered. He cared about serving society, and it cost him his life. How does she feel now toward strangers? How many times does she go by the scene of the incident? How often does she rehear the call as it came over the radio? How does she let go? How does she cope with the feeling of unfairness? Was it really worth it? Should he have been such a dedicated cop? And, now that she has lost him, is the $50,000 she is awarded going to pay for it? If he were alive he would have earned that money in two or three years. Must she change her life style? What are her options?

Men in law enforcement tend to be strong, dominant marriage partners, good providers, very protective, courtly, and the primary decision makers in their partnership. The women they choose are correspondingly often content and proud to be "the woman behind the man," preferring a sheltered existence. Some police officers have a tendency to be overprotective of women as a result of their street experiences. They may caution their wives a great deal and make them hesitant about getting too involved in society, traveling at night, or going through certain parts of the city.

Unlike the woman who has voluntarily ended her marriage, the police widow is forced against her will and by circumstances beyond her control to find new ways to get around in the world and to establish her own identity. She must handle finances and take over in many areas she may have never considered before. Unlike a divorcee who chooses to live without her mate and often has made some move on her own into society, professionally or otherwise, the widow faces society alone, and, perhaps with resentment. She takes comfort in the memories she cannot escape, and she has a tendency to idealize the relationship, making it difficult for anybody to even approach the greatness of her departed husband. As one young widow explained, "Your automatic reaction to any death is to recall only the good qualities, perhaps to even exaggerate them a bit. And, too, you want your children to remember their father as a noble, kind and generous person, so naturally you help to create this picture. Everybody you know, all your friends and realtives, add to it. Before long you have forgotten almost everything else about your husband."

This tendency to idealize the lost partner and the marriage is often quite strong. Perhaps, in part, such idealizing helps to keep buried the resentment that the surviving partner has not yet been able to air, even to herself. "It took me three years to realize that I was really mad at my husband for having 'left me.'" said one widow. "How can you be mad at someone who dies? Without even realizing it you cover up by emphasizing how good he was."

Perhaps idealization brings the widow closer to the lost spouse. "We look at pictures of my husband; we talk about him; I don't want the children to forget him." When remembering him, she feels temporarily less alone. "It's only human to romanticize your memories of marriage when you compare them with your present loneliness."

Those who have been through years of widowhood believe it is wise to retain a balanced perspective. "Let's be honest with ourselves," one of them said. "Was there ever a husband who was *always* patient and good and kind? Was there ever a marriage made up of *just* happy times? Isn't it true that small irritations and petty quarrels are bound to crop up in even the most harmonious of family realtionships? And aren't the most harmonious of relationships pretty rare?"

Often wives are more concerned over the health of their husbands than of themselves. They are not so much imperiled by ill health as by widowhood. Still, a wife needs to find a sense of importance and a means of independent survival before the death of her husband. Otherwise, she may let her fears dictate the very future she most dreads— becoming helplessly dependent on other people.

Some widows who had depended on their husbands for both financial and emotional support transfer their dependency to the the department, which in general does a lot for the widow. But, as time goes on, the department must turn its attention to other matters. It must break the widow's dependence. When this happens, the widow may feel abandoned and disillusioned, resenting the department and the whole concept of law enforcement.

What makes a "successful" widow—one who eventually picks up the pieces of her life and makes it whole and good again? The answer is complex, perhaps not even fully known. But, fortunately, a few of the well-understood points are as simple as they are important.

The outstanding prerequisite for good recovery after the death of a spouse is a strong ego structure and a sense of respect for one's own identity. The woman who has never thought of herself as anything but a wife is almost assured of trouble, for, when she isn't a wife anymore, she has, by her own standard, ceased to exist. On the other hand, the wife who also sees herself as a career woman, a board member of a club, a force in the community, a significant person to a large circle of friends, a reader, a concert-goer, an art lover, a gardener, a choir singer, a horsewoman, a cellist, a swimmer, a pot-maker, a rug-weaver, a conservationist, a political worker—anything at all—will continue to be these things after her mate's death. Women who function on a variety of levels, if widowed, have an immense advantage over those who do not. Extra hours spent with the garden club or on the tennis-tournament committee cannot make up for the absence of a mate, but they are a big improvement over hours spent alone with nothing to do.

The first step for a widow in creating an independent identity is to realize that she can deal with the physical necessities of daily life even though the emotional problems may be overwhelming. For the police officer's wife who has not learned to drive, handle a checking account, change a fuse, etc., the death of a husband will not only be an emotional crisis but a physical one as well. She may feel that she is unable to function alone in this world, and so she needs to discover that, indeed, she can handle most of these chores.

Financial problems are also a cause of continuing depression. There is nothing neurotic about being depressed if you can't pay the rent. But it might be neurotic, or just poor judgment, to wait until rent day comes to find out about your financial situation. Every police officer's wife, or any woman, should know her assets, income and financial situation.

How can the present living arrangement be maintained on one income or less? Is there any insurance money? If so, how much? Is the widow entitled to any portion of her husband's retirement or pension fund? What about Social Security—is the widow eligible? Where are the bank books? The key to the safety deposit box? Is there a list of all insurance policies, and does the widow know where they are? What about securities, real estate deeds and debts payable? These are the types of questions that all families in and out of law enforcement should be able to answer.

"People always think that police widows get a lot of pension money from the city," said one widow, "but it's not true. They have a choice between $50,000 in a lump sum or monthly payments. I chose the payments, because $50,000 sounds like a lot, but I could go through that too easily. I took the payments thinking that's what my husband would want me to do."

The widow's life changes abruptly. While considering the reactions of others, she must come to her own decision regarding dating, children's school, how to define herself in the world, etc. A psychologist or helping professional may be of assistance in exploring her alternatives. Other widows can help by sharing their grieving processes and experiences. It's often a great comfort for a new widow to talk with someone who has been through it and is now leading a happy life. One widow called her best friend, a woman who also had recently lost her husband, and asked: "Is something wrong with me?" She told me that it was a stage I would go through, that all widows go through. "Having her to talk to, to relate to, has helped me."

Despite differences in women's age and temperament, the loss of a husband is always traumatic, with people tending to undergo similar experiences. The trials of bereavement and overcoming can be fully understood only by someone who has been through them herself. So it is beneficial for widows to be able to talk to other widows or to be involved with a group, whether it be law-enforcement widows or others. In Los Angeles County there is a group of police widows who meet with new widows when they lose their husbands. This approach has proven to be effective and helpful. Viewing documentaries of various widows sharing their experiences has made it easier for others. Counselors and chaplains are also made available, and at times they provide the only setting in which the new widow can comfortably release her anxieties.

Some departments provide widows with the opportunity to receive financial advice and investment counseling. Police officers and their spouses should be cognizant of the necessity of keeping their wills and insurance policies up-to-date. In instances where this has not been done, many legal problems have arisen, especially if there had been a prior marriage or if there were children involved. Many departments are beginning to provide periodic reminders to their employees to keep important documents updated.

It would also seem appropriate for someone in the department to check back with the widow every few months, just to see how things are going. It is true that she must break away and start a new life based on decisions only she can make, but she will benefit greatly from support and encouragement. This could be done on a very personal level, with former widows or officers volunteering, or it could be set up systematically to ensure that the widow doesn't feel totally abandoned after only a few months.

The Israeli nation, because of its frequent involvement in war, has been forced to find ways to deal with death and the people death leaves behind. This nation takes the position that any society owes its members both respect and honesty, and should value all that life offers while dealing directly with the ramifications of death. The government feels a responsibility for providing more than adequate means of supporting those left behind. Services provided include informational, monetary and psychological support. Detailed information is given to the widow concerning the exact situation of her husband's death. Although this may be viewed by some as a cruel step into a cold reality, and probably not totally necessary, the Israelis have found that this is the most humane way to deal with the widow. It allows her no illusions and persuades her to deal with the realities that death brings. The widow is viewed as an important member of society. The Israeli government encourages her to take her role in a society that needs her. Her integration back into life is supported by professional staff who help her deal with aspects of finding a job which suits her needs and abilities, or who encourage her to get training through various vocational and educational institutions. The government pays for babysitting for her children while this training is going on and offers counseling to both the widow and her children. The counseling encourages the widow to be honest with her children and to also lead them back into the mainstream of society after their father's death. This government has given the widow a priority within the "war system" and has found that with support, encouragement and caring she may once again live a meaningful life.

Israel provides these many services for widows of war veterans because their soldiers are viewed as working for the welfare of their society. Their widows and orphans are entitled to services from a society for whom these soldiers gave their lives. It follows, then, that those who believe our own society should support dependents of war veterans should also advocate the same support for the spouses and dependents of our nation's police officers killed in the line of duty.

A newly bereaved spouse feels that her life has ended. Progress is made a step at a time. As the work of mourning is done, re-entry into the everyday world becomes possible, and when mourning comes to an end, re-entry is complete. For one who is in the time of deepest despair, it is impossible to believe that life can ever be good again. But it can!

REFERENCES

Caine, L. *Widow*. William Morrow and Co., N.Y., 1974.

Colgrove, M. Bloomfield, H.H., and McWilliams, P. *How to Survive the Loss of a Love*. New York: Bantam Books, Inc., 1980.

Conroy, R. C., M.D. *Widows and Widowhood*. New York State Journal of Medicine, 77 (3) 1977.

de Luna, P. *Police Widows—Never Prepared*. Long Beach: Independent Press-Telegram 1/25/76.

Glick, I.; Weiss, R., & Parkes, C.M. *The First Year of Bereavement*. J. Wiley and Sons, N.Y.: 1974.

Grollman, E. A. (ed.) *Concerning Death: A Practical Guide for the Living*. Boston, Massachusetts: Beacon Press, 1974.

Kenny, K. *Young Widowhood: Picking Up the Pieces*. Los Angeles Daily News, 1/9/84.

Kubler-Ross, E. *On Death & Dying*. MacMillan, 1969

Kubler-Ross, E. *Questions on Death & Dying*. MacMillan, New York, 1974.

Kubler-Ross, E. *Death: The Final Stage of Growth*. Englewood Cliffs, N.J. Prentice Hall, 1975.

Peterson, J. A. *On Being Alone*. Washington, D.C.: NRTA-AARP, 1974.

Peterson, J.A. and Briley, M.L. *Widows and Widowhood: A Creative Approach to Being Alone*. New York: Association Press, 1977.

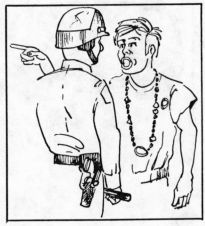

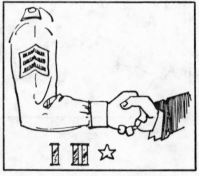

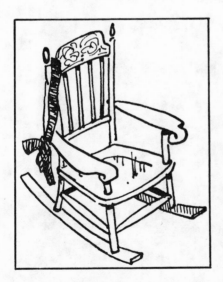

ROY

One of the most important people in my life died not long ago. Her name was Royanna, but friends called her Roy. She was married to Earl—also important in my life—and in their 35 years together they had developed an enviable outlook on human existence.

Earl remains my closest friend. Like him, I still feel the influence of Roy in many things I do, though surely not to the same degree that he must.

Two days after her death, when I desperately needed to understand my sorrow and adjust to my loss, I took a walk on the Venice beach. I walked and walked, with anger burning inside me that such a special friend should have been taken so abruptly. Tears streamed down my cheeks. As I stepped onto the Venice pier, I noticed a young man with a Bible talking to passersby.

My distress must have been obvious, for he quickly turned his attention to me. "Do you know Jesus?" the young man asked, as he began walking along with me. "He can help you in your time of need."

"I know," I said, "I want to be alone."

"If you turn to Jesus, he'll help you. If you accept him, your life will be richer."

"I know," I told him again, "and I want to be left alone."

Then he said something about helping me accept Jesus.

"*Leave me alone.*" I accelerated my pace and left him behind. At the end of the pier, I stopped and thought for a moment about the young man's behavior, and how it was in direct opposition to everything I'd ever learned about Christianity. Then I lost myself in thinking about Roy's death. Before long, however, he approached me again.

"I want to apologize for my previous behavior," he said.

"Thank you, I accept your apology. Now *please* leave me alone."

"We're having a church service at 7:30 tonight," he said, "and I'd like to take you."

"I told you I want to be left alone."

"Here's a card with the address of the church. Jesus can redeem you."

"Please," I said "*please* leave me alone!" The young man stepped back at last and began walking away.

Now, however, I was so upset that I could not concentrate on Roy. I had an urge to confront the Bible-bearer and explain his effect on me. Calling, "Hey, man!", I ran until I caught up with him, about midway along the pier.

Taking my return as a hopeful sign, he put an arm around me. "Yes, brother," he said. Then he paused, as if waiting to be asked to show the way to Christ or, at least, to that evening's church service.

"I have to tell you something," I said. "It's important to me that you understand what I have to say. I've repeatedly asked you to leave me alone, but you've insisted—even demanded—to know if I know Jesus. So I'll tell you what I know about Jesus.

"I know he prayed wherever he needed to pray—on the mountains, at the ocean, in the desert. He also knew the necessity of being alone, and he asked others to leave him alone when he had to pray. He even went into solitude in the desert for 40 days to pray.

"Jesus respected and accepted people for what they were. But you couldn't do that with me today. You interfered with my need for solitude—my need to pray.

"I hope you've been able to understand what I said. And now, I'd appreciate it if you'd leave me alone."

Having said my piece, I resumed walking back toward the shore.

He followed me, saying, "I can help you find your redemption in Jesus. I was redeemed eight months ago myself."

"I'm glad for you," I said. "Now leave me alone."

When I reached the end of the pier and stepped onto the sand, he was still beside me. But he stopped as I began walking along the beach. Within a few moments he shouted to me, "I will still help you find redemption in Jesus."

"To hell with you and *your* damned Jesus!" I yelled.

I took a few more steps, stopped, turned and went back. "I have one more thing I want to tell you about Jesus.

"The only time He became angry was when He went into the temple and found the moneychangers not doing what they were supposed to do. You haven't done what *you're* supposed to do, either, and I think you're a failure as a Christian." With that I walked away—not waiting for his answer.

They say death is hardest on the survivors, and there I was, trying to get my bearings after losing a friend, thrown entirely off course by this tempest. I found a quiet spot to sit on a nearby jetty.

What did Roy mean to me? Why am I so angry? I forced myself to think, and the answers started to come: Roy had accepted me. She had accepted my sadness and my pain. My childish moments. My crazy moments. She accepted *me*. She didn't ask that I change to fit into her scheme of things. I am who I am—that's how she found me, and that's how she left me.

Roy's love was so different from what the "Christian" offered me. When I wanted solitude, he gave me a sermon; he said he had my answers for me. But Roy knew I should—and would—find my own.

—John